Helping Children with ADHD and Oppositional Defiant Disorder

Easy CBT Therapy Workbook for Emotional Regulation to Transform Behaviors, Develop Social Skills, and Sharpen Focus

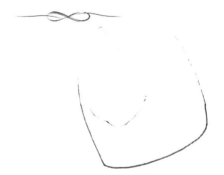

By Spreadlife Publishing

a result of the use of the information contained within this document, including, but not limited to, errors, omissions, or inaccuracies.

Contents

Introduction 2

Part 1: Understanding ODD 7

Chapter 1: Understanding ODD 9

ODD and Its Influence on Family Dynamics 9

The Prevalence of ODD in Children and Adolescents 19

Possible Root Causes.. 20

Recognizing Early Warning Signs 24

ODD Across Different Age Groups 26

Differentiating ODD from Other Behavioral Disorders............. 30

The Impact of ODD on Family Dynamics 40

Myths and Misconceptions about ODD 41

Workbook 1 46

Key Takeaways... 47

Chapter 2: Early Intervention and Diagnosis 49

The Importance of Early Detection: Don't Just Guess; Know...... 50

Seeking Professional Help: Who to Consult............................. 57

Diagnstic Assessment and Tools... 58

Building a Support Network 63

Parental Self-Care Amidst the Diagnostic Process 65

ODD Comorbidities.. 66

Workbook 2 67

Key Takeaways... 68

Part 2: Strategies for Empowerment 69

Chapter 3: Communicating to Overcome 72

The Power of Positive Communication 72

Fostering Empathy in Parent-Child Interactions.......................82

Intentional Parenting...87

Active Listening Techniques 95

Encouraging Open Dialogues 98

Perfecting Non-Verbal Communication 102

Setting Realistic Expectations for Communication.................107

Workbook 3 109

Key Takeaways...109

Chapter 4: Reshaping Behavioral Patterns with CBT 111

Understanding the Cycle: Thoughts, Emotions, and Behaviors..114

Helping Your Child Reframe Their Thinking..........................115

Taking Action for Change 116

CBT Techniques and Applications 119

Identifying Triggers and Early Warning Signs...........................120

Developing Positive Coping Mechanisms 122

Sustaining Motivation...124

Workbook 4 125

Key Takeaways...128

Chapter 5: The Emotional Rollercoaster.........................129

The Role of Emotions in ODD 130

Emotional Regulation in Children with ODD..........................131

Teaching Emotional Intelligence.........................132

Empathy Development 140

Cognitive Behavioral Strategies for Kids.........................148

Art and Play Therapy 151

Building Emotional Toolkits...154

Practical Techniques for Anger Management 158

Workbook 5 163

Key Takeaways..163

Chapter 6: ADHD + CBT: A Combination for Better Days 166

Addressing the Eleph-ANT in the Room: The Importance of Talk Therapy 167

Community and Teamwork...169

Teaching Emotional Regulation to ADHD Kids 171

ADHD and Social Skills 173

Focus, Attention, and CBT..178

Building Positive Self-Esteem..180

Workbook 6 183

Key Takeaways..184

Chapter 7: Building Cooperation and Compliance....................186

Establishing Routines and Structure...............................187

The Power of Positive Reinforcement 191

Implementing Effective Rewards and Consequences 196

Collaborative Problem-Solving.......................................204

Parenting Styles That Promote Cooperation 206

Setting Age-Appropriate Boundaries and Consequences...........209

Handling Public Outbursts and Meltdowns....................215

Dealing with Resistance and Defiance.............................217

Workbook 7 219

Key Takeaways..219

Part 3: Thriving Together..221

Chapter 8: The Family Environment and ODD 225

Creating a Nurturing Home Environment............................226

Sibling Rivalry and ODD 229

Consistency in Parenting Styles..................................233

Handling Challenging Situations: Homework, Mealtime, and
Bedtime 236

Addressing Sibling Dynamics......................................240

Balancing Attention Between Siblings.............................244

Workbook 8 249

Key Takeaways..249

Chapter 9: Self-Care for Parents 251

The Parental Stress and Emotional Exhaustion Cycle 252

Balancing Your Needs with Your Child's Needs 261

Letting Go of Guilt: No Such Thing as Perfect Parenting..........264

Self-Care Techniques 266

Finding Support and Community Resources 271

Maintaining a Positive Outlook on Your Parenting Journey 274

Workbook 9 276

Key Takeaways..277

Chapter 10: Long-Term Success.....................................278

Workbook 10 302

Key Takeaways..302

Your Review Can Inspire Change! 304

Conclusion 306

References 309

Your Free Gifts
Breathtaking BONUS #1

BONUS WORKSHEETS

- Reduce stress and anxiety, and find inner peace.
- Boost your mood and emotional well-being for a happier life.
- Build stronger relationships and communicate effectively.
- Cultivate resilience and bounce back from setbacks.
- Develop healthy coping mechanisms for life's challenges.

Click here to get this BONUS.

Introduction

"You can learn many things from children. How much patience you have, for instance."

—Franklin P. Adams

Colleen's expectations about motherhood before and after she had her four children are quite different. Granted, she wasn't so overly optimistic that she expected having children who never misbehaved or were always docile, obedient, and *Shepford-bound*.

But she certainly never expected a child with oppositional defiant disorder either.

When Tim was nearly seven years old, Colleen and her husband discovered there was something different about their second son. He had an anger and defiance that Colleen recognized weren't typical of a child his age. His formerly cheerful and sweet demeanor had made way for something rather unpleasant—to put it mildly.

His behavioral change began with sudden outbursts of rage several times a day. Outbursts morphed into arguments and hurtful tantrums as his cognitive and intellectual abilities developed. It wasn't long enough before Colleen admitted that her son's behavior was far beyond her pay grade.

Registering her despair, Colleen confessed in her diary that she thought the "latest child from hell" in her neighborhood had chosen her family as a landing pad. "Today has been horrible," she scribbled in the tear-stained diary. "Tim has pushed me to my absolute wits' end."

Describing her woes, she cheerlessly penned, "When he isn't knocking down another child's block tower or tearing papers all over the floor—for no reason other than that he has the strength to—he is throwing tantrums that could last for several hours."

Concluding her entry, Colleen resolved, "I definitely need God's help now—and *possibly* the help of a professional."

After consulting with her family doctor, Colleen discovered her son was exhibiting behaviors of oppositional defiant disorder (ODD).

It was her first time hearing of such a behavioral disorder.

Colleen was immediately concerned, like any loving mother who has great plans and dreams for the future of her kids and family. Questions ran in all directions through her mind.

What challenges are ahead for my son, and the rest of the family? What's the way out of this?' What are the unavoidable or potential long-term effects?

Is this terminal? No. Life altering? Definitely.

The world of oppositional defiant disorder and parenting a child with this disorder—the subject of this book—can be complicated.

Sadly, many people don't feel this is a real diagnosis, erroneously thinking a child is just not being raised well. Perhaps the parents or school teachers aren't handling enough of the rod. Or the parents aren't insisting on enough respect from the child, leaving the child to be *in charge*.

But as this self-help and easy-to-read parenting guide will show you, all that may hold some water until you speak with any mom (or dad) of an ODD kid. They could fight you all day on the fact that not only is this a real diagnosis, but they're probably drowning in the situation.

ODD tries the limits of their wherewithal and patience, and they're possibly fighting feelings of being a failure daily. They can remember the sweet baby they cuddled and cared for. Their adorable kid lavished the family with sweet giggles and growth spurts.

Suddenly, as quickly as a zap, everything about their adorable prince or princess changed.

Without using the words of real-world parents with children who have ODD as our sole reference, this book will show you what psychologists and other medical researchers say about ODD ADHD and their symptoms.

Do you have to raise a child with ODD or ADHD? Perhaps there's no better way to begin than by telling you that you're not alone in this.

About 10.2% of all children will have ODD, and 11.3% will have ADHD. These figures, among many other implications, predict that there are pretty substantial chances you know a child with ODD or ADHD.

Thankfully, you don't have to grapple with the emotional stress or guilt of raising a defiant child forever. As various unconnected studies show, oppositional defiant disorder improves with time—IF (note that "if") the parent or caregiver manages the condition appropriately.

Now, I hate to share bad news with my audience—at least while I'm still introducing my subject. But knowing that your child's ODD could develop into a more lasting personality disorder, like anti-social personality disorder, might be all the encouragement you need to apply the principles in this book as you fight for (and expect) the best in your child's future.

However, overcoming ODD or ADHD, like any other recalcitrant habit, begins when parents relieve themselves of the guilt and emotional stress that comes with having an ODD child while seeking to understand their condition.

That's probably why you headed online to find this book: to leverage the perspectives of parenting experts like me and the various real-world success stories and strategies I'll share in this manual of families who overcame the difficulty of parenting ODD.

After going through this manual, you can rest assured you'll have a deeper understanding of ODD and ADHD, their symptoms, and how they affect families and individuals.

By applying the emotional regulation skills this book offers to both parents and children, you can become more effective at detecting ODD early, managing children with ODD, and permanently bringing them out of unpleasantness or irritation.

You most likely love your kid so much and want them to love you in return. No doubt, they like you back, but sometimes you wonder if they like you or dislike you at the moment. Do they remember the good times you shared before they became defiant?

You may still have choice memories of good days that didn't have any arguments or tantrums. Let these memories inspire you towards the hope of brighter days ahead as you follow the invaluable principles of parenting ODD and ADHD I'll share with you in this guide.

Are you still here with me? I invite you to say the following with me.

"ODD won't rule my life—or my child's life. It might cause me some heartache and problems from time to time today, but I won't let it change the way I feel about my baby. I won't give it the power to diminish my love for them.

Instead, I am going to work on the plan and provide my child with what they need: understanding and discipline. Most of all, I'll give them love. Because soon enough, I'll look back and be glad I've become a better parent because of ODD, and my child will eventually grow to become the polished, well-cultured, and successful adult I've always dreamt of them being."

A thorough self-help parenting guide, this book is ideal for parents and caregivers who don't mind putting in the effort and intentionality that successfully parenting ODD requires.

It doesn't promise quick-fix solutions. But its recommendations WILL benefit parents, caregivers, and children in the short- and long-term toward fulfillment and eventual success for the entire home.

With the art and care of a Lego builder, I'll walk with you through every stage of your child's—and your—journey to recovery and wholeness.

Your journey into successfully parenting ODD and ADHD has begun already! Come along and get ready for a rewarding experience!

PART 1

Understanding ODD

One of the greatest privileges of living as a human is the opportunity to build relationships with others. Regardless of how great and highly placed in society you become, you'll always need that peaceful connection with others.

A happy adult and their significant other at the park. Or a socially conscious leader whose empathetic and compassionate approach to work makes everyone on board eager to resume duty at work.

Or, let's go a little lower in the age bracket. Tweens who cherish their dogs and always want to play with them.

These, at the very least, are a glimpse of what parents expect their toddlers to grow into: sociable, helpful, and cooperative adults.

Unfortunately, these hopes, which often brighten your day and lessen the burden of caring for your ward, can suddenly turn sour when the child goes beyond being *just difficult* and starts developing behavioral disorders like oppositional defiant disorder.

You know already that relationships are only successful when each party contributes positively to them. It's almost impossible to imagine your child growing into a parent who wants things so badly that they want to control everyone except themselves. Feel free to *attempt* to imagine other more dreary possibilities of people you don't want your baby to turn into.

Now, this isn't about you drawing up or holding any negative expectations or projections for your child's future. It's no threat; the self-affirmative words I led you to say with me in this book's introduction already contradict that idea. You'll need to keep high hopes and be optimistic.

Sometimes, the best way to seed your mind towards envisioning the best from the presently tiring situation you find yourself in is to think *away* from the worst possible scenarios.

Instead of thinking your child could grow to hate you and not appreciate you for doing your best to be a great mom or dad, why not go to the extent of imagining your kid as a great mom or dad themselves who always tells your grandkids how helpful you were to their development? Imagine you're sitting on the beach hearing your child reel off all these niceties and appreciation of you to your beloved grandchildren.

Beautiful contrast. Right?

I bet you're itching to get into the first chapter already! You're in good company; I can't wait either.

In this book's first part, which includes two chapters, you'll find fundamental information about parenting ODD—its implications for everyone in the family, as well as its early diagnosis and intervention.

Of course, there's even more to discover in this resourceful, practical, and hands-on parenting guide to help you and your child overcome the challenges of living with ODD.

Here we go!

CHAPTER 1

Understanding ODD

"Trust in the Lord with all your heart, And lean not on your own understanding; In all your ways acknowledge Him, And He shall direct your paths."

—Proverbs 3:5- 6 (NKJV)

"Understanding why a kid is challenging is the first and most important part of helping them."

—Dr. Ross W. Greene

"I think I know who's been hiding your keys."

ODD and Its Influence on Family Dynamics

M*y boy, TJ, and I went through a rough patch when he was a pre-teen and teenager. Middle school turned things up a notch. Most mornings, getting him to school felt like pulling teeth. He would stay in his* *room till I came to drag him into the car, pajamas and all. Then I'd plead and beg that he change out of pajamas into something more presentable, all to no avail.*

TJ had these… ways. Taking his brother's things, scattering his dad's tools until they wouldn't work again. Getting him to do his homework was also a never-ending war. I came to dread the homework more than the student. But eighth grade took the cake. For weeks on end, he'd walk around like a walking laundry basket reject, choosing to wear the dirtiest and ugliest clothes. Our fights grew loud and ugly. One night, my voice choked with tears, I begged him, "TJ, why are you doing this?" It was one of the lowest points I can remember.

To the outside world, TJ was just my "tough kid." The one who flitted from hobby to hobby, losing interest as fast as you could say "commitment." But beneath it all, I saw a different story. He was a kid who tested every limit we set. By 14, "grounded" became a mere suggestion, met with a nonchalant walk out the door. That's when I knew we were in deep water.

A doctor's visit led to the diagnosis: ODD. ADHD was suspected, too, but dismissed because TJ wasn't hyperactive. Honestly, at that point, the specific label didn't matter much to me. TJ's defiance was suffocating me, stealing my power as a parent and replacing it with a simmering, ever-present rage.

ODD: You Didn't Get a Bad Child

Yes, you heard that right.

The fact that your beloved child tests your limits and those of other authority figures is not the end of the world. It doesn't even mean you got a bad child that landed from the worst part of hell with one of the seven deadly sins either.

Neither does it mean you're a bad parent.

No. None of it.

If your child shows symptoms of ODD, you probably already know some of the common signs of this behavioral disorder. We'll delve fully into the possible root causes, early warning signs, and unique symptoms of ODD compared to other behavioral disorders later in this chapter.

What you may have less information on is just *how unique* your situation is, or *exactly* how to think about your child's situation.

Take it from me: even if your child is in the most *unique* of situations or is in a "one-in-a-million" class of their own, the way you think about their behavior affects how you feel and act toward them.

Perpetuating negative thoughts will impair the way you interact and respond to their behavior—and to them as an individual.

That's why your first port of call when you want to change your child's (and family's) experience is to replace negative thoughts with more positive musings.

1 in 6 U.S. Children Are in Similar (If Not Worse) Situations

Mind you, 1 in 6 U.S. children aged 2–8, according to the Centers for Disease Control and Prevention, has a diagnosed behavioral, developmental, or mental disorder. If your child has ODD, then their condition might be less challenging than it appears along a spectrum of other *exclusively* difficult children across America.

Meanwhile, other research shows that ODD is most prevalent or chronic in children between ages 6–8. The good news, however, is that over 65% of children with ODD overcome the symptoms in 3 years or less.

Back to straightening your thoughts out.

Sticking to a blame game (either inwards or toward someone else) won't do it. And playing tug-of-war can give you a rope burn that complicates your emotional and physical exhaustion. Sometimes you don't even need to answer your child! Otherwise, you might be further drawn into their power struggle.

Accept Your Child

Everyone has their unique temperament or disposition—and children aren't any different. While some children tend to be cooperative, others seem to argue about virtually everything.

Some are easygoing while others have a low frustration tolerance and are quick to anger. Some kids are quiet and shy, and then there are those who want others to hear them…well, every moment of the day!

With an oppositional defiant child, it can be challenging to accept the child's fundamental personality. You could spend years trying to convert your baby into someone else, but the bottom line is: this is your child at this moment.

Of course, accepting your child doesn't mean you're embracing their behavior or agreeing with all their decisions. It does, however, mean you accept them at a basic level of being human—with their emotions, flaws, and struggles.

On a brighter note, rather than concentrate on their explosive feelings and flaws, how about diverting your thoughts to a silver lining in the cloud?

"Is there possibly a silver lining in this cloud?" you're probably asking.

Yes. There's a silver lining to your child's extreme behavior. And that includes some common strengths of children with ODD you don't want to ignore.

While you'll discover some of them on your own after reading through this chapter, I'll be more than glad to let you in on some of them now.

The Unavoidable Strengths of the Oppositional Defiant Kid

Understandably, it's hard to see social media updates about your friends' kids getting straight A's when your son throws a cuss word at you every night over his homework. But, believe it or not, some definite strengths go hand-in-hand with challenging behavior like ODD.

1. ODD Kids Are Creative

Children with ODD can be extremely creative when it comes to getting something they like. The same young child who can't overcome the challenge of dealing with their friends can get out of a locked house when grounded in a manner that would impress Michael Scofield.

Who knows? Your child who seems to *destroy* every object they find might never need a mechanic to fix their vehicles—or they may even become a successful engineer themselves.

If you still doubt this, consider Richard Branson's idea of the impact of dyslexia on his entrepreneurial success.

Branson, the British billionaire brain behind Virgin Airlines and several other mega products, had dyslexia as a child—a reading difficulty that made him perform poorly in class as a kid and is still with him today.

Calling dyslexia his "superpower," Branson says he's convinced that his childhood disorder "made him a better businessman because he has an original perspective, is more innovative and willing to take risks" (Sylvester, 2022).

Now, of course, I'll show you how to work your way out of coping with your child's ODD. But you want to appreciate your child's potential strengths as I show you more upsides and strengths of ODD kids.

2. ODD Children Are Trailblazers

ODD kids would rather travel on roads less traveled. Without some amount of defiance, think of what we'd miss in the grown-up worlds of business and entertainment.

It might sound cruel to say this (or not), but many actors, musicians, and business leaders are oppositional defiant and had childhoods that featured skipping or dropping out of school, stubbornness, or arguments with authority figures. Despite their explosive tendencies, defiant kids can grow into successful trailblazers the world wants to see.

Without reiterating all you may have already heard about Robert Downey Jr., Steve Jobs, or Erin Brockovich, suffice it to say that successful industry leaders who dropped out of school had their personalities as their biggest strengths in the absence of a degree.

Meanwhile, just because your child isn't well known or famous today, doesn't mean they aren't a trailblazer. Their willingness to go against societal norms and take less traveled paths might just be the impetus they'll need to have the world hear their name someday.

3. ODD Kids Are Determined

Children with oppositional and defiant personalities are some of the most determined individuals you'll ever meet. Some nice kids would rather follow than lead, quickly following rules and traditions. Others don't mind "going with the flow," hardly making any positive or negative waves because they're scared they might fail.

But you'd never find ODD kids in this pack. While everyone else is paddling downstream, the ODD kid screams, "I'd rather go upstream because it's more interesting and challenging!" and "The more you oppose me, the more determined I'll be to stream upstream."

4. And Many Other Strengths

Irrespective of their explosive behavior, here are other strengths your child might have up their sleeve:

- A passion for fairness and justice
- Potential for strong feelings, including feelings of love and empathy for others
- Being perceptive and knowledgeable
- Taking in so much information at once
- Strong self-advocate
- Defending peers who are marginalized or bullied

Three ODD Kids with Amazing (and Encouraging) Eventual Display of Strengths Despite Defiance

I share three encouraging real-world stories of ODD children whose strengths shone through their flaws and defiance into something their parents could be proud of. My rationale for sharing these stories with you? It's to get you motivated about your child's inherent potential, get your mind reoriented about your child's situation, and, of course, give you enough hope and courage to apply the principles I'm sharing in this book.

However, for professional and ethical reasons, I'll stick to the initials of these children to keep us focused on their stories and how they can help other ODD kids.

C Doesn't Care What Others Think of Her Clothes—And Doesn't Want You To, Either

12-year-old C's mom was a teacher in an American school district, and in a school that C also attended. She was terrified when C started wearing clothes to school she practically picked from the dirty laundry pile.

Perhaps one of the most horrific memories C's mom has about her child's misbehavior was the day she wore a pair of jeans their dog had slept on the night before. Disregarding any neat pile of clean clothes her mom may have placed on the bed, C would still wear the clothes she'd worn the day before—stains and all.

C's mom even tried bribing her with expensive name-brand clothes. She begged her daughter, "Please wear clean clothes… People will think I'm a terrible mother."

All pleas fell on deaf ears, as C even ignored the final reason: that her mom was also a teacher at her school. After months of daily arguing and having to avoid the teachers' lounge, C's mom eventually gave up, concluding that there was nothing she could do about C's choices. "I can only dress myself in the morning," C's mom said, resigning herself to her fate.

Miraculously, the following week, C began wearing clean clothes! But perhaps more stunning was her reason. Here's what C said to her mom:

"You always told me it doesn't matter what people think of you and that your true friends will love you for who you are. You are always saying that I shouldn't judge others. I wanted to show you what a hypocrite you are."

Well, what did C's mom do in response?

Years later, C's mom would recall how her daughter's actions during this period led to her personal growth. She admitted, "(C) was right. I cared a lot—too much—about what others thought of us, and I did judge others. It's a lesson I never forgot."

Profound, if you ask me.

J's story

Thirteen-year-old J was mechanically gifted. He fought his dad and mom about everything from who he hung out with to attending school; however, he could fix the toughest of problems if a car was placed before him.

Sensitive to his strengths, J's parents decided to build on his strengths and purchase the old, rundown car he'd been pleading for. "He'll never get it running," his dad said. But only six months later, J was tooling around in his newfound toy.

Ensuring their son stuck to the rules, his parents told J he mustn't drive the car until he got a license. You can probably guess that J drove it anyway. To keep J in check, his mom and dad took to locking the vehicle with an anti-theft club on the steering wheel and were quite proud of their creativity.

But their satisfaction would last only a few months, as they soon found the car parked just a little bit off-center in the driveway. J had cleverly bought a separate steering wheel, which he kept in the woods. Whenever his parents left, he'd simply remove the original steering wheel—club and all—and replace it with his spare, and he was ready to hit the road.

No doubt, this was dangerous and defiant behavior. And his parents were certainly frustrated at his level of obstinacy. However, they soon learned to appreciate their son's resourcefulness: 10 years later, J never needs to pay a mechanic to fix his cars.

L Would Rather School Herself about Raising Animals Than Attend School

Fifteen-year old L would argue daily with her parents, skip school, and stay outside past curfew hours. L also had an undying love for animals. Soon, it became her mission to save as many lost, abused, and abandoned animals as she could.

Her mother's fear was that she could get hurt in some way by picking up strays she knew nothing about. Friends and family joined L's mom in criticizing L's efforts as being reckless.

L realized that her mother's rules and the large number of animals she could rescue were real threats to her mission. Consequently, L schooled herself on how to safely rescue local animals while minimizing the risks she faced.

She became connected to local animal rescues that would care for the animals she found. When she couldn't link with these resources immediately, she broke her mother's rules and kept an animal in the garage for a couple of days.

Needless to say, L's determination was frustrating to her mom. However, it led to hundreds of animals finding a safe haven over the years. Today, L is a noted animal advocate who has earned the admiration of people around her, including her mom.

Many people are determined. But not everyone has the strength and courage many ODD kids like L have to pursue their goals in the face of opposition from others.

The Prevalence of ODD in Children and Adolescents

Why learn about the prevalence of ODD in children and adolescents?

First, there's the self-empathy a child gains by understanding how many other young people have ODD. But beyond that, understanding all relevant facts around your child's ODD arms you with enough information to guide your actions going forward.

As I already shared in the introduction, about 10% of children will develop ODD, research says.

It was once popularly thought that the disorder affects mainly boys, but it's now widely known that girls also display ODD, even though through a different pattern.

Boys are slightly more likely to display ODD behavior than girls, with males having an 11% higher occurrence than females (9%).

The thin line between prevalence levels of ODD between boys and girls might well not exist, as some experts think that girls and boys are equally affected. That's because evidence supporting its prevalence in boys appears somewhat inconsistent. In a 2011 study, some professionals suggested using different criteria to diagnose ODD in girls, who might display these symptoms differently than boys.

Consequently, reports denote that ODD affects between 2 and 16% of children and adolescents. The range is wide because some kids may be misdiagnosed as having conduct disorder.

Additionally, other research has proven that teenagers as a whole are often under-diagnosed. Of course, that suggests your child might not have ODD, so you might want to recheck your diagnosis with a professional.

However, you still want to monitor your kid's recalcitrant behavior and keep them compliant enough to give you, the family, and themselves the peace everyone deserves.

ODD prevalence declines with increasing age, potentially peaking between ages 6 and 8.

Turning to related behavioral disorders in children, studies show that at least 40% of children with attention deficit hyperactivity disorder (ADHD) have coexisting oppositional defiant disorder.

That might suggest that you might want to confirm you don't have more than one disorder to treat your baby for.

Possible Root Causes

Generally, there's no clear cause of oppositional defiant disorder. However, experts suggest it may be caused by a combination of genetic and environmental factors. Temperamental and personality factors are other potential causes of ODD.

Researchers, in a bid to unravel the potential root causes of ODD, have created two main theories for why the disorder develops. These theories capture every other root cause or sign we'll later explore in this sub-section.

Developmental Theory

This theory suggests that ODD begins in children when they're toddlers. Children and teens may have developed challenges from being forced to become independent from a parent or some other person they were emotionally attached to. Their behavior might begin from normal developmental issues that spiral beyond their toddler years.

Learning Theory

The learning theory proposes that the negative symptoms of ODD are learned. They reflect the effects of negative reinforcement methods or actions used by parents and other authority figures. This theory suggests that the use of negative reinforcement increases a child's ODD behavior. That's because these behaviors let the children get what they want, such as reactions and attention from parents or others.

Let's dig a little deeper into what these possible root causes mean in deciding a child's behavior, and possibly your child's defiance.

Genetic and Biological Factors

Research suggests genes are responsible for about 50% of a child's risk for the condition. Similarly, children with a family history of depression or ADHD have a higher chance of developing ODD.

Other neurological research shows via brain imaging that differences in some parts of the brain can also induce ODD in children. These brain parts are responsible for regulating, controlling impulses, solving problems, social behavior, and empathy.

These irregularities may develop into ODD, especially when you combine them with other factors.

Environment and Upbringing

Many environmental factors at home may contribute to ODD, and they may include:

- Inconsistent or neglectful parenting
- Harsh or permissive parenting
- Negative reinforcement for disruptive behavior, which can promote future explosive actions
- Rejection from peers
- Violence and abuse in the home or neighborhood
- A stressful or unpredictable home life
- Living in a low-income household or disadvantaged community
- Inconsistent or neglectful parenting
- Having multiple caregivers, especially those who offer inconsistent or detached care

Personality and Temperament

Similar to their genetic heritage and environment, your child's personality and temperament could potentially cause ODD. Underlying personality traits and temperaments linked to the disorder include:

- Callous-unemotional traits, such as emotional insensitivity and lower empathy
- Low tolerance levels to frustration
- Impulsivity
- Irritability
- High emotional reactivity
- Difficulty with emotional regulation

Of course, not every child with these traits will go on to develop ODD. However, they might contribute to their frequent misbehavior.

Summarizing ODD Risk Factors

Having seen the potential root causes of ODD, how about we highlight the leading risk factors of the disorder to better put things in perspective?

- Parenting issues: children who suffer from abuse or neglect, harsh or inconsistent discipline, or a lack of proper supervision
- Temperament: children who have a temperament that includes difficulty managing emotions, including reacting with strong emotions or having trouble coping with frustration
- Environment: challenging behaviors are reinforced through attention from peers and inconsistent discipline from authority figures like teachers
- Other family issues: children who live with parents or family relationships that are unstable or a parent who has a mental or emotional health condition or substance abuse disorder

- Other behavioral disorders: children with other behavioral disorders like ADHD, conduct disorders, or mood or anxiety disorders

Both nature (biological factors) and nurture (environment and upbringing) contribute to your child's personality, not to mention their overall mental and emotional health, alongside other risk and protective factors.

Recognizing Early Warning Signs

It can sometimes be challenging to recognize the difference between a strong-willed or emotional child and one with oppositional defiant disorder. As I've discussed earlier, it's common for children to develop oppositional behavior in different aspects of their development.

Children with ODD usually start showing these symptoms around ages 6 to 8. However, this disorder can emerge at younger ages too. The symptoms can last throughout their teen years.

Oppositional and defiant behaviors are frequent and ongoing. They lead to severe problems with relationships, social activities, school, and work for both the child and their parents.

ODD behavioral symptoms generally last at least six months, and could include a range from an angry and irritable mood to argumentative behavior and hurtful or revengeful disposition.

Here are some early warning signs of ODD to look out for in your child.

- Frequent temper tantrums

- Often touchy and easily annoyed by others

- Often angry and resentful

- Engaging in excessive arguments with adults

- Refusing to comply with requests from authority figures or other adults

- Always questioning rules

- Refusing to follow rules

- Acting deliberately to annoy or upset others

- Blaming others for their misbehavior or mistakes

- Speaking harshly or unkindly to others

- Has shown vindictive behavior at least twice in the last six months

- Tries to hurt others' feelings and seek revenge (i.e., is being vindictive)

Severity

ODD can be mild, moderate, or severe in children.

Mild ODD symptoms occur only in one setting, like home, school, or with friends. In moderate situations, some signs are shown in at least two settings, while severe ODD might be responsible if your child displays ODD symptoms in at least three settings.

Some children may display oppositional behavior only at home. However, with time, their challenging behavior may also happen in other situations, such as with friends, in school, or during other social activities.

ODD Across Different Age Groups

ODD is considered one of the most common behavioral disorders in children and adolescents. However, considerable data shows that ODD behaviors can remain in teens beyond adolescence and develop into more lasting behavioral disorders in adulthood.

A 2000 study on ODD children by UN-backed researchers in the University of Northern Iowa estimates that about 6.5 million American children suffer from ODD. Without a doubt, the number of children with ODD in this country today is far more than 6.5 million.

According to the report's authors, the prevalence of ODD is between 2 and 16% of the country's child and adolescent population. In a related study, researchers found that 4.9% of 6- to 10-year-olds, 5.7% of 11-year-olds, and 1.7 to 2.5% of adolescents were diagnosed with ODD.

Now, don't let these datapoints scare you away from this book.

You can just take away the fact that researchers discovered that ODD prevalence decreases with age. Fair enough. But you're probably asking, "What exactly does ODD look like in children, teens, and adults?"

Here's an explainer to help you differentiate ODD symptoms across the different age groups.

Children with ODD

Most of the symptoms I've described so far in this book reflect the challenges parents of children with ODD will often find in their kids.

Without boring you with unnecessary details, a child with ODD will almost always stick to their guns and be unwilling to negotiate or compromise. They'll speak harshly or unkindly to others, defy authority, seek revenge, and, of course, throw temper tantrums repeatedly.

In addition to these behavioral symptoms, a child with ODD may show one or more of these symptoms:

- Low self-esteem
- Persistent negativity
- Difficulty concentrating
- Difficulty making friends

These symptoms may interfere with a child's learning, making school difficult. School challenges may further frustrate the child, leading to a cycle that could lead to more symptoms or outbursts.

ODD in Adolescents

Teens can be naturally difficult and rebellious—thanks to their hormone production and a natural desire to assert their independence. However, children who don't outgrow the symptoms of ODD might develop more disruptive behaviors during adolescence.

First, teens with ODD may be able to hold in their feelings more than younger children. Instead of lashing out or throwing tantrums, they may stay annoyed or angry all the time. And that could lead to antisocial behaviors and depression.

ODD in teens can have serious consequences, like:

- truancy;
- trouble with the law;
- a decline in academic performance; or

- dropping out of school.

A teenager with ODD might have their interpersonal relationships suffer, as their peer group finds it difficult to maintain a friendship with someone with ODD traits.

Meanwhile, remember that ODD in teens may occur alongside other disorders, such as ADHD, a learning disability, or a mood disorder. These other conditions may fuel the ODD, making them act out even more when they feel frustrated or misunderstood.

This is why it's always worth the effort to seek out a comprehensive evaluation of your teen's mental health when you suspect they're experiencing ODD. Where a coexisting issue is present, your mental health professional can treat and address all conditions or disorders.

ODD in Adults

Adults with ODD display a string of negative, hostile, and defiant behavior that could last for six months or more. Some of the symptoms of ODD in adults include:

- Deliberately annoying others
- Blaming others for their misbehavior or mistakes
- Often losing their temper
- Getting easily annoyed by others
- Being angry or resentful
- Being spiteful or vindictive
- Often arguing with family and coworkers

Adults with ODD go beyond just feelings of aggression and irritation. They act like they're mad at the world every day, and may lose their temper often. This may manifest as road rage or verbal abuse.

Adults who defend themselves relentlessly when someone tells them something they did wrong likely also have this condition. These adults often feel disliked, hemmed in, misunderstood, or bossed around.

Constant defiance to authority figures makes it difficult for adults with ODD to maintain relationships and keep jobs. They're particularly quick to anger, impatient, and have a low tolerance for frustration. They tend to think that others mistreat, misunderstand, or underappreciate them, seeing themselves as victims rather than being the cause of pain in the family system.

Let's take the discussion a bit further now by addressing symptoms of ODD in adults at home or work.

At home, a spouse with ODD will be overly argumentative. They're unnecessarily hostile and may show any of the following manifestations:

- Always feel they should win an argument with their spouse
- Keep fighting against "the man" (i.e., authority figures in society)
- Leave socks on the floor, for example, just because they know it annoys their partner
- Has been arrested for disorderly behavior by the police
- Has a hair-trigger temper
- Involved in physical altercations in public or bar brawls

At work, the following manifestations of ODD or similar ones may be apparent:

- Almost constant arguments with their bosses or coworkers
- Commonly feeling oppressed by office rules
- Purposely engaging in behaviors that irritate coworkers
- Sanctioned by human resources for violating company policies time and again
- Fired for being physically aggressive with coworkers during heated moments
- Experiences mental meltdowns during meetings or annual reviews after receiving constructive criticism

Differentiating ODD from Other Behavioral Disorders

Conduct disorders (CDs) and ODD are some of the most prevalent behavioral disorders in children. Like I've highlighted earlier, 4 in every 10 children with ADHD have also been diagnosed with ODD.

This subsection shows you the differences (and similarities) between ODD and other behavioral disorders like conduct disorders and ADHD.

Conduct Disorder

Both conduct disorder and ODD are types of disruptive behavior disorders in children. Disruptive behavior disorders often involve children or adults acting out against others through defiant and disrespectful behavior.

A conduct disorder is an intentional rule-breaking attitude alongside a continual pattern of aggression toward others. According to the *Diagnostic and Statistical Manual of Mental Disorders, Fifth Edition* (DSM-5), a conduct disorder is a condition where a child intentionally violates rules and others' rights.

Conduct disorder begins around age 11. However, it can still develop in early adolescence. Common symptoms of conduct disorder include aggressive displays toward other children, adults, and animals, and stealing, lying, or destroying other people's property.

Some common signs and symptoms of conduct disorder are:

- Running away from home many times overnight
- Staying out later than they should for their age (before age 13)
- Truancy from school without a reason (before age 13)
- Breaking into another person's private property
- Lying to avoid duties or obligations
- Finding multiple ways to destroy someone else's property
- Displaying aggressive behaviors, such as bullying or intimidation tactics
- Initiating fights
- Using weapons to hurt people or animals
- Previous instances of physical cruelty to people and animals
- Directly stealing property from victims
- Forcing someone to execute an activity (e.g., sexual activity)
- Intentionally causing major havoc, like setting a fire

Similarities Between Conduct Disorder and ODD

The severity of each disorder in a child or how many they exhibit is unique to them and their specific environment. However, the two disorders have similar signs and symptoms. Here are some of them:

- In both cases, children may be defiant and won't obey rules imposed on them by society or those closest to them.

- Both disorders may co-occur with other behavioral conditions, like ADHD, mood disorders, anxiety, or depression.

- Both disorders can be successfully treated by medical professionals.

- Both conditions are likely caused by a mixture of genetic, environmental, and psychological factors.

Differences Between Conduct Disorder and ODD

1. Diagnosis

CD is diagnosed using criteria such as aggression, destruction, deceitfulness, theft, and serious violations. On the contrary, ODD's diagnostic criteria include anger, irritable mood, argumentativeness or defiance, and vindictiveness.

2. Physical Violence

Comparing the diagnostic criteria of both disorders, it's evident CD is more characterized by physical violence than ODD. Conduct disorder includes physical fights, rape, mugging, and arson, while the latter generally relates to mood upheavals, nonconformity, and spitefulness.

3. Duration of Symptoms

ODD symptoms must last for at least six months before they may qualify for diagnosis, while symptoms of CD must last for at least twelve months with at least one criterion being met in the past six months. Generally, CD observation and diagnosis will take a longer time compared to ODD to finalize.

4. Severity

ODD symptoms are said to be mild if the symptoms are merely restricted to a specific setting; moderate if they occur in two settings; and severe if they occur in at least three settings.

On the other hand, the severity of CD is marked based on the frequency and extent of actions. CD is said to be mild if there are few conduct issues which cause only minor harm; severe if there are many conduct problems with considerable harm unleashed; and intermediate if the conduct issues have a severity between the two extremes.

5. Temperament Risk Factors

The temperament risk factors for ODD are high emotional reactivity levels, low frustration tolerance levels, and other emotional regulation dimensions. With CD, leading temperament risk factors include difficult and uncontrollable infant temperament alongside a below average IQ (especially verbal intelligence).

While CD's temperament risk factors are a combination of affective and cognitive factors, ODD's temperament risk factors are more affective-oriented.

6. Subtypes

Oppositional defiant disorder has no specific subtypes. However, conduct disorder has three subtypes: childhood-onset, adolescent-onset, and unspecified-onset.

7. Limited Prosocial Emotions

According to the DSM-5, diagnosis of CD must include limited prosocial emotions like:

- Guilt

- Lack of remorse

- Absence of concern for performance

- Shallow affect

- Callousness

On the other hand, ODD doesn't have similar qualifiers.

Here's a table that sums up the differences between oppositional defiant disorder and conduct disorder.

Oppositional Defiant Disorder	Conduct Disorder
Displays an angry or irritable mood, is argumentative or defiant and vindictive	Displays aggression, destruction, deceitfulness, theft, and other serious violations
Less violent symptoms	More violent symptoms
Symptoms should last for at least six months	Symptoms should last for at least twelve months

Severity is based on the number of settings where the behavior manifests	Severity is based on the frequency and extent of misconduct
No specified subtypes	Includes three subtypes
No specific requirements on limited prosocial emotions	Has specific requirements on limited prosocial emotions
Affective-oriented risk factors	Both affective- and cognitive-oriented risk factors

Attention Deficit Hyperactivity Disorder (ADHD)

ODD is the most common comorbidity (illness occurring alongside another) with ADHD. It's not unusual for a child to have both conditions at the same time.

We've already seen ODD traits and its definition to some extent as being uncooperative, defiant, and aggressive. But what exactly is ADHD?

ADHD is a type of brain disorder that affects millions of American children and often lasts well into adulthood. If your child has ADHD, they might experience a combination of major problems like:

- Hyperactivity
- Lack of attention
- Impulsive behavior

Now, both conditions might appear similar from a distance (as some of their symptoms can overlap). However, a closer look at their leading causes and detailed symptoms will prove helpful in separating these two types of disruptive behavior.

For instance, while both ADHD and ODD can originate from genetic and environmental factors, ODD is largely caused by learned behaviors that stem from developmental or environmental issues; meanwhile, ADHD is mostly a genetic condition that's often passed down from family members.

While ODD is more linked to antisocial behavior that makes a child purposely hurt others, get unreasonably annoyed, or disobey authority, kids with ADHD find it difficult to control their behavior.

Let's see other leading differences between these conditions.

ODD vs. ADHD

A major difference between ADHD and ODD is that with ADHD, kids are often hyperactive and have trouble paying attention, while ODD makes a child cranky, angry, and defiant.

ADHD symptoms would likely show up when your child is 12 years old or younger, sometimes as early as 3 years old. However, ODD symptoms can show up much earlier, often before the child is 8, and as early as when they're toddlers (though ODD symptoms may also start to show in a child's teenage years).

Being largely genetic, ADHD symptoms in a child serve as an indicator that a close relative has it. With that said, it's also important to note that poor parenting or too much screen time can also contribute to ADHD in children.

While ODD can also occur due to genetic factors, experts believe a child is more likely to develop the condition by mirroring negative behaviors like inconsistent or harsh discipline from authority figures like parents and teachers.

Another category of differences between ADHD and ODD is the way doctors treat each disorder.

When treating ADHD, doctors often seek to reduce symptoms while improving daily function. ADHD treatment plans could include:

- Prescribing a stimulant drug: These medications work to increase a child's dopamine and norepinephrine, which may help improve attention.

- Prescribing a nonstimulant drug: These drugs may take longer to begin working, but they can help many find improved focus and concentration.

- Therapy: Therapy concentrates on altering a child's behaviors and helps them become more self-aware rather than being reactive.

ODD treatment, on the other hand, covers all environments in the child's life to help ensure their successful development. These treatment conditions may include:

- Treating at home: Uses techniques like parent management training, which teaches parents to use positive reinforcement to help kids reduce unwanted behaviors.

- Treating at school: Provides support to schools to improve students' performance, peer relationships, and problem-solving skills.

- Treating everywhere else: Medication isn't the first choice for treatment here. However, when other treatments fail, prescription drugs might help. Stimulants and psychotic medications may prove effective. Additionally, behavioral therapy for anger management may help children reduce the severity of their symptoms.

Lastly, we consider age factors in the differences between the diagnosis of ODD and ADHD.

For minors with an ADHD diagnosis, doctors often look for at least six symptoms of inattention and hyperactivity-impulsivity. However, in people aged 17 and older, they only need to present five signs.

ODD, on the other hand, is largely a childhood mental health condition prevalent in the preschool years and can remain present until the child is about 10 years old. After that age, ODD symptoms tend to decline. Otherwise, the child might develop other conditions like conduct disorder or antisocial personality disorder.

Similarities Between ODD and ADHD

Both conditions display a change in brain chemistry that leads to uncontrolled, impulsive, or aggressive behavior, and both conditions are more common in boys than in girls.

It can be easy (and, of course, misleading) to consider ADHD and ODD displays in kids as being normal behaviors of young children. However, children with these conditions don't outgrow these phases as easily as their peers.

While some of these symptoms might ease with age, especially if the condition was initially mild, severe forms of ADHD and ODD may never go away (except after exposure to professional help).

Now, again, let's list out some ADHD symptoms alongside those of ODD to see the common ground:

ADHD symptoms may include:

- A short attention span
- Being easily distracted
- Making careless mistakes
- Being forgetful
- Having difficulty concentrating on time-consuming or demanding tasks
- Having a hard time organizing themselves
- Having a tough time sitting still
- Constantly fidgeting
- Talking a lot or interrupting conversations
- Having little to no sense of danger
- Acting without thinking

And we already know the traits a child with ODD might display: vengeance, vindictiveness, and rage.

Both sets of symptoms may lead to low self-esteem and make it harder for your child to make and keep friends. Your child may also perform poorly at school if they suffer from either or both conditions.

It'll help to observe the differences between these disorders and see which traits or combination of traits you might find in your child. That way, you're better informed to seek professional help towards building a safe, satisfactory, and danger-free experience for your child and family.

The Impact of ODD on Family Dynamics

Parenting a child with ODD can be an overwhelming challenge – not only because they appear so unwilling to obey adult authority, but because many intervention actions that work with most kids, like removing privileges or grounding, wouldn't budge a child with ODD.

Various studies show that children with ODD may not respond well to punishments. And others have found that adolescents and kids with severe ODD symptoms may feel threatened by situations where there are unclear messages and expectations, triggering further hostile reactions.

Not to mention the fact that children with ODD often have poor frustration tolerance, adding to the difficulty in soothing or calming them when they get annoyed.

Often, such patterns of behavior can leave many families feeling helpless. They're likely to begin walking on eggshells to avoid triggering an unending tantrum by making the slightest wrong move.

On the other end of the spectrum, ODD can trigger harsh behavior from parents and others around children with ODD. And it's understandable. It can be tough to be calm or apply mild rebukes when your child is always running away, rejecting mild corrections, or throwing things.

However, harsh parenting might just complicate things.

Many times, parenting children with ODD causes parents to develop struggles with their own emotions or mental health. These emotional issues could then spiral to affect other relationships within the home or affect other things like the health or finances of either parent.

However, the disorder also affects the child's experience in the home.

The reaction of other family members to their ceaseless demand for attention can make them feel isolated or anxious. They're also likely to be unsure of themselves as others anticipate their irritability and explosive actions even before they occur.

What's more, your child will likely know their family members are disappointed in them, or even resent them. However, while that might badly affect their self-esteem, it's often not enough to change their behavior.

Bottom line? ODD impacts everyone in the family—including parents, caregivers, siblings, and the child themselves.

Myths and Misconceptions about ODD

As you may have guessed, some children with ODD might only show symptoms at home or with family. Others display their defiance without being irritable or angry. However, children with mood-related symptoms display argumentative and defiant behavior.

Sadly, people often judge children with ODD symptoms or view them negatively due to their behavior. And in a society where labeling is rife, the child may soon be described with the label "ODD."

But stigma goes beyond just being tagged with a name you don't like. It can negatively impact your child's development and growth, especially when it springs from a false belief that ODD can't be treated.

When parents or teachers conclude a child is problematic or one who will always misbehave, it might dampen their efforts to help the child.

Consequently, the child may continue to act abnormally, and their behavior might worsen.

Grades may keep falling, and their relationships might never leave the trouble zone. Worse still, they may also frequently have to survive severe conflict with authority figures throughout their lives.

Children with ODD may be partially stigmatized due to a fear of outbursts, violence, or aggressive behavior. Although ODD isn't as violent as other behavioral disorders, children may throw frequent tantrums in an attempt to annoy others and provoke reactions.

Without throwing all the blame on parents, teachers, siblings, or peers for being afraid of a child's next outburst, thinking too negatively or badly of any child is harmful to their mental health. The stigma and the isolation that results from such external reactions can lead to other serious developments like substance abuse, depression, and suicidal ideation in the child.

Notably, stigma and isolation often occur because people around children with ODD hold one or more misconceptions about the condition.

With that said, here are some common myths about ODD—and corresponding facts to dispel them AND help you show your child some more love!

1. ODD IS ALWAYS A RESULT OF BAD PARENTING

While ODD is truly associated with absent or neglectful parenting, it's not always the cause of every case. Even children with the most loving and present parents or caregivers can develop the condition.

Psychologists and medical practitioners haven't determined a clear cause for ODD. However, various studies show that other causes apart from just parenting style may also be complicit.

For instance, some children may be genetically more likely to develop ODD. Other mental health and developmental issues can also cause the condition. Lastly, the way parents, siblings, and peers respond to the first symptoms of ODD can affect whether these actions will get better or worse.

2. ODD AND CONDUCT DISORDER ARE THE SAME THING

Studies from the American Academy of Child & Adolescent Psychiatry have shown that 3 in 10 American children with ODD also develop CD. Alongside ADHD, CD is one of the two most common illnesses that are comorbid with ODD.

Many people erroneously attach symptoms of ODD with CD or consider them to be the same thing. When severe, ODD increases the risk of the child developing conduct disorder. But the disorders clearly vary in their propensity for violence.

Just a recap of what we've clarified earlier on the differences between ODD and CD:

ODD usually involves irritable, argumentative, or defiant behavior. Children with ODD may ignore rules or demands from authority figures. But violent or outright illegal actions aren't something you'll often find with ODD.

On the other hand, those with CD often display repeated violence, illegal activity, and/or disregard for other people's rights or property.

3. ODD OCCURS ONLY IN CHILDREN

Children and teens are the most likely to be diagnosed with ODD, and the likelihood of someone getting diagnosed with ODD reduces with age. However, adults can also have ODD.

More often than not, these adults developed ODD during childhood. The condition probably persisted into adulthood because they weren't diagnosed or treated appropriately.

Adults with ODD show similar behaviors of anger and irritability. They might also find it difficult to concentrate or forgive others for their wrongdoings, and often pursue revenge when they feel cheated. These traits are typical of people who try to control or disobey others.

Adults with ODD are also likely to struggle in relationships and experience conflict with people in authority. These conflicts may often land them in unemployment, legal disputes, or even behind bars.

4. ODD IS ALWAYS CAUSED BY TRAUMA

It's not completely clear what leads to ODD. However, psychologists believe a combination of various factors leads to the condition. Undoubtedly, one such possible cause is trauma, but not every child with ODD is traumatized.

Potential biological risk factors for ODD include a family history of ODD, mood issues, brain impairment, malnourishment, or exposure to some toxins like cigarette smoke.

Potential social risk factors include poverty, unstable home experience, absence of parents or caregivers, or a lack of supervision and involvement from parents.

Potential psychological risk factors could include difficulty understanding social cues or developing relationships with peers.

5. PUNISHMENT IS THE BEST WAY TO CORRECT ODD

Various studies have shown that punishing actions related to ODD doesn't help. Often, harsh discipline may induce or worsen ODD behavior.

According to research by psychologist Lin et al. (2019), harsh parenting practices place children at high risk for emotional deregulation, depression, and aggressive behavior.

And psychologists don't think that sending your kids to camps or retreats for "difficult children" will do much, either.

While finding the best way to discipline your child can be challenging, it's worth it. Fortunately, the latter sections in this book address instilling discipline the right way and locating the best approaches for your child.

One of the most recommended strategies for parents of children with ODD is parent management training. The training shows parents various ways to positively discipline disruptive behavior and introduce consequences for them.

6. IT'S IMPOSSIBLE TO TREAT ODD AND EXPECTING ANY IMPROVEMENT IS FRUITLESS

Here's perhaps the most dangerous misconception about ODD. It couldn't be further from the truth; ODD is very treatable. Over 65% of children with ODD see their symptoms stop in 36 months or less.

Treating kids like they'll never improve could morph into a self-fulfilling prophecy. Kids can often sense when you write them off or have little to no hope in them. If they think no one ever cares about them, they may be unmotivated to improve their behavior or could even develop worse conditions.

When working with a child or adolescent with ODD, it's recommended that parents and teachers be compassionate and patient. Regardless of how badly your child is acting, it's important to show them that you love and accept them.

Lastly, instead of simply punishing or ignoring children when they throw tantrums or disobey rules, consider the underlying conditions for their acting out and seek to address them.

Workbook 1
Finding Their Strengths

Do you have a child you suspect might have ODD? I sympathize with you and understand how challenging the situation can be for you and the entire family.

However, can you take a couple of weeks to spot **at least** two strengths your child displays that you won't find in most other children?

Do this for your child, for your emotional and mental health, and to gain perspective about your baby (and do it for me! I'm happy to work you through every step of the recovery process for you and your child).

Have you written down these strengths? Were you able to find at least two?

How do they change your perspective about your child's potential situation? Does this encourage you to read the rest of this book and apply the expert principles for leading your child away from a permanently disruptive disposition?

Key Takeaways

Oppositional defiant disorder (ODD), a common mental disorder in school-aged children, is characterized by defiant behavior toward authority figures and others. It often affects a child's social or academic performance.

Early warning signs of ODD include fits of rage, vengeance, vindictiveness, and disobedience to authority figures or older persons, at higher rates than children of comparable age or circumstances.

It'll help to understand that kids with ODD don't often view their behavior as being defiant or oppositional. Instead, they may simply believe they're reacting to unfair circumstances or unfair demands from parents and other authority figures.

ODD affects not just the child's behavior, but also other members of the family. Parents' emotions, health, and finances might be at stake. The family's happiness might spiral. Furthermore, the child might grow to loathe themselves or condemn themselves to more severe behaviors.

However, showing a child with ODD that you love and accept them can go a long way in encouraging them to improve. So does showing them you *believe* they can (and will) improve. Fortunately, children with ODD also have some exciting strengths that may be hidden treasures waiting for a loving parent and family to unearth as you walk them out of disruptive behaviors.

CHAPTER 2

Early Intervention and Diagnosis

"Can a woman forget her nursing child, And not have compassion on the son of her womb? Surely they may forget, Yet I will not forget you. See, I have inscribed you on the palms of My hands; Your walls are continually before Me."

—Isaiah 49:15-16a (NKJV)

"Having a child is like getting a tattoo…on your face. You better be committed."

—Elizabeth Gilbert

"Hmmm. They all look so similar. Maybe number 4?

The Need for Early Detection
The Importance of Early Detection: Don't Just Guess; Know

"Being correctly diagnosed can be life-saving," says 52-year-old J.W., in an interview with a leading health website.

But her assertion isn't based on the experiences of others or because she's a professional psychologist. J.W. suffered with a mental disorder for 15 years while being misdiagnosed by different medical practitioners and receiving the wrong therapy and medication all the while.

I've culled J.W.'s story here to help you realize how important it is to detect behavioral disorders, including ODD, early and accurately. Her story and subsequent facts will provide enough basis to help you verify your child's condition—if they have any.

Yes, you heard that right—your baby might not have a disorder after all. They may be a victim of misdiagnosis or something else that's external to their psychology.

Can we hear about J.W.'s story already?

Sure!

In retrospect, J.W. has so many regrets about her parenting skills; not because her children behaved out-of-the-ordinary, but because *she* behaved a little differently than she normally would.

"My kids were raised in a disordered home," J.W. recounts. "I was off the handle with the oldest [and] had a sharp temper with her."

J.W. says although she was in her best psychological state when her second oldest daughter was growing up, she soon became overwhelmed when a third daughter joined the scene. Raising three girls under age 10 became too burdensome for her emotions as she battled with constant crying spells in the home.

Soon, she developed difficulty concentrating on anything and started underperforming. The psychological burden became too much for J.W. just after her youngest daughter's first birthday. She'd crawl out of bed at night, leaving her husband and the girls to travel far from home.

"I was going to kill myself," she explained.

Fortunately, police officers around the city to which she escaped rescued her and brought her to a hospital. Her husband soon learned of J.W.'s ordeal and would bring her to a psychiatric hospital close to the family.

But J.W.'s woes would have been less complicated if the doctors accurately diagnosed her mental condition. For 15 years, J.W. went from wrong diagnosis to wrong diagnosis (and, of course, the wrong therapy).

While some specialists diagnosed obsessive-compulsive disorder, others blamed postpartum depression or post-traumatic stress disorder (PTSD) because she'd lived through a hurricane.

Eventually, she was diagnosed with bipolar disorder, a mental health condition where a person has unpredictable mood swings that could range from extreme happiness to sadness.

When she was extremely happy, J.W. wouldn't seek any medical help. "No one goes to the doctor for being too happy," she explained. It never occurred to her that something more was deeply wrong with her.

Other Bewildering Statistics on Misdiagnosis of Behavioral Disorders and Other Mental Health Issues

J.W. isn't alone in the dilemma of suffering from a serious mental health condition misdiagnosis. Millions of American children and adults are potentially misdiagnosed with various behavioral disorders or mental health issues.

According to a study, over 33% of patients with a severe psychiatric disorder were misdiagnosed. The study also discovered that patients with bipolar disorder were 60% more likely to be misdiagnosed with schizophrenia. And those with schizophrenia are 56.25% more likely to be misdiagnosed with bipolar disorder.

According to another report from Michigan State University researchers, nearly one million children are potentially misdiagnosed with attention deficit hyperactivity disorder (ADHD). This threat, the report explains, occurs because these children are the youngest (and most immature) children in their kindergarten class. For instance, if a child is four years old, they may misbehave, be inattentive, or be unable to sit simply because they are younger than the other kids, who are five years old.

The report concluded that about 900,000 children (or about 20% of the 4.5 million children diagnosed with ADHD) may have been misdiagnosed.

How (Not) to Verify ODD Behavior—in Numbers

Nearly every child in the U.S., the UK, or any part of the world at that would admit to arguing with their parents and throwing tantrums occasionally when things don't go their way.

However, a growing number of children are now being diagnosed with ODD for just being naughty. Now, that might not sound treacherous, until you hear what the UK's NHS has to say about ODD.

According to the NHS guidelines, about 50% of children with (*actual*) ODD not only miss out on parts of their childhood but go on to develop severe mental health problems like antisocial personality disorders.

Generally, experts say only children who display ODD-related behavior more often than children of their age range should be tagged with the condition.

Here's what they mean. For children younger than five years old, the behavior must occur on most days, for at least six months. And when the child is five years old and above, the behavior must occur at least once a week for at least six months.

What Could Cause Mental Health Misdiagnosis?

Misdiagnoses are incredibly common for many different health conditions, according to Itai Danovitch, a professor and Chair of Psychiatry and Behavioral Neurosciences at a Los Angeles-based specialist hospital.

Explaining the occurrences, Prof. Danovitch says, "Identifying symptoms is one thing. Figuring out what is causing it in another thing... [that needs] a thoughtful and comprehensive assessment."

Another reason why behavioral conditions like ODD and ADHD may be misdiagnosed is that many of their symptoms often overlap with those of other conditions.

For instance, symptoms of ODD, such as having difficulty concentrating, restlessness, or disobedience to instructions, are linked to a large range of causes.

Let's examine some other conditions and factors that can lead to a misdiagnosis of ADHD.

1. Mood Disorders

Examples of mood disorders are depression and bipolar disorder. Experts say that mood disorders in children (and adults) could occur due to an imbalance of chemicals in the brain, stressful life events, or as a response to major illness or medication.

Some symptoms of mood disorders similar to those of ODD include irritability and difficulty concentrating on anything.

2. Sex

Various earlier research on behavioral disorders like ODD has shown that boys are more likely to receive a diagnosis of the condition than girls. These studies claim that this disparity occurs because boys tend to display more symptoms of *overt* defiance than girls.

This is why many subsequent studies have advocated a different way of diagnosing ODD in girls. With that said, it's still possible that your child's behavior is less due to a disorder than their high alpha male potential.

3. Anxiety Disorders

Anxiety disorders make people constantly anxious, have panic attacks, or experience various phobias. Some of these disorders often bear similar symptoms to ODD, like:

- Irritability
- Restlessness
- Difficulty concentrating
- Difficulty with social skills due to social anxiety

Anxiety disorders can also cause people to act uncontrollably, quickly become tired, or have excessive fear about a situation or object.

4. Sleeping Difficulties

When people experience sleeping difficulties like insomnia or obstructive sleep apnea (OSA), it can lead to similar symptoms to ODD, including:

- Difficulty concentrating
- Restlessness
- Decrease in performance at work or school

Insomnia makes it challenging to fall or stay asleep. OSA is a condition that gets the upper airways blocked during sleep, restricting airflow. People with OSA may frequently wake at night to urinate, gasp for air in their sleep, or snore loudly.

5. Auditory Processing Disorder

Auditory processing disorder (APD) is a condition that makes it difficult for people to correctly understand the sounds of words. It affects the way someone's central nervous system interprets verbal messages.

People with ODD can correctly process auditory information through their central nervous system. However, their inability to comply with information or rules mirrors the obvious effects of APD.

Common symptoms of APD include:

- Difficulty listening, especially in noisy settings
- Difficulty following spoken instructions
- Problems with receiving verbal information
- Asking for people to repeat speech (could appear similar to people who just have difficulty hearing)

Doctors can't diagnose APD by only considering the symptoms, as there could be several other causes for difficulty in communication, language, or learning. Audiologists diagnose APD by conducting a variety of tests that verify a patient's response to sounds.

6. Symptoms Evolve Over Time

Another leading reason for misdiagnoses isn't because an assessor did something wrong, but because symptoms sometimes evolve. For instance, a child who begins by displaying scattered "naughty" behavior (as evaluated by medical assessment) may only be showing very mild ODD symptoms.

7. Other Conditions

Other conditions can present similar symptoms to ODD in children, including:

- Attention deficit hyperactivity disorder
- Visual problems

- Learning disorders
- Obsessive-compulsive disorder
- High or low blood pressure

Sadly, if ODD isn't the cause of the symptoms, it can worsen with the wrong treatment. There's no overstating the importance of pursuing an early and accurate diagnosis when you find ODD behavior in a child.

Seeking Professional Help: Who to Consult

J.W. thinks her illness started in her teenage years. However, in the early '80s, her community wasn't ready for a mental health disorder like hers. As she got older, her insurance didn't cover mental health visits, and so she never saw a psychiatrist. Instead, she kept relying on her obstetrician and internist for assistance.

While it can be sometimes helpful for someone with a potential behavioral disorder to start with a consultation with an internist, this approach has its downsides. Meanwhile, a primary care provider may only spend up to 15 minutes with the patient, without giving adequate time to fully assess someone with a mental health disorder.

However, primary healthcare providers can help with eliminating underlying medical problems, such as thyroid disease, that could cause mental health symptoms.

Many people shy away from seeing a professional early enough, as they feel others might look down on them.

While the next subsection shares further details on how to get professional help, suffice it to say that you don't need to entertain any stigma or shame that your child is experiencing a behavioral disorder.

Diagnstic Assessment and Tools

How do psychiatrists diagnose ODD in people, especially school-aged children? What tools or screening measures do they use before concluding that a child has ODD?

We'll not only consider the general indicators psychiatrists use in diagnosing ODD, but also how they differentiate it from other disorders. I'll also show you some of the popular assessment tools medical practitioners use in evaluating a child for the presence or absence of ODD behavior.

To begin with, all characteristics I shared in the section on early warning signs of ODD in the last chapter are in tandem with the criteria provided in the *Diagnostic and Statistical Manual of Mental Disorders* (DSM-IV, 2000).

The frequency of these symptoms must also surpass those often observed in individuals of comparable age and developmental levels.

Besides the indicators we've already seen, here are three other fundamental indicators of ODD in children:

- The behavioral disturbance causes clinically significant impairment in social, academic, or occupational functioning.

- The condition doesn't meet the criteria for conduct disorder; if the individual is age 18 or older, it doesn't meet the condition for antisocial personality disorder.

- The behaviors don't occur exclusively during a psychotic episode or mood disorder.

Other Linked Indicators

The DSM-IV-TR (2000) also correlates ODD with the following indicators:

- Emotional reactivity
- Hyperactivity
- Difficulty in soothing before starting school
- Very high or low self-esteem
- Emotional reactivity
- Conflict with others
- Learning disorders during school years
- ADHD
- Conflict with others
- Disrupted attachment
- Authoritarian parenting
- Parental neglect
- Maternal depression
- Parental discord

Differentially Diagnosing ODD

DSM-IV-TR (2000) recommends differentiating ODD from at least seven other behavioral challenges: conduct disorder, antisocial personality disorder, mood and psychotic disorders, attention deficit disorders, developmentally appropriate defiance, mental retardation, and language comprehension.

In a little more detail, here's how each of these conditions that can occur comorbidly with ODD are differentiated according to DSM-IV-TR (2000) recommendations:

1. Conduct Disorder: CD can be ruled out if the child doesn't display cruelty, violence, stealing, or lying.

2. Antisocial Personality Disorder: ASPD is primarily ruled out in children since they're under 18.

3. Mood and Psychotic Disorders: These disorders need to be ruled out using the DSM-IV-TR criteria for the various disorders in this category. For instance, ODD is ruled out if the behaviors occur only during periods of abnormally high or low mood, such as after someone sharply rebukes them or they perform poorly at something they love.

4. ADHD: This disorder can occur comorbidly with ODD. The DSM-IV-TR recommends that the professional diagnose both disorders. (Refer to the last chapter for more on differentiating ADHD from ODD.)

5. Mental Retardation: Mental retardation can also be diagnosed comorbidly, but only if a child's defiance is "more intense than average" for their level of mental impairment. In these cases, the diagnostician has the prerogative to determine what is "intense," "average," or "appropriate."

6. Developmentally Appropriate Defiance: The DSM-IV-TR also suggests ruling out developmentally appropriate defiance.

However, it leaves the definition of such behavior to the diagnostician. That said, it infers that the term "developmentally appropriate" should consider children of comparable ages or circumstances (for instance, children from separated parents, or those suffering abuse, etc.), as applicable.

7. Language Comprehension: Problems with language comprehension, like hearing loss, should also be ruled out, as they can produce defiant-seeming actions.

Family-Centered Approaches

Compared to other treatments like drugs, behavior modification, punishment, or removal from the home, researchers agree that a family-centered approach (or family therapy) is one of the most effective ODD treatment courses. That's because the affected child or individual may not benefit in the long-term from ODD treatments if they keep returning to a family system that hasn't changed.

At its foundation, a family-centered approach (or therapy) to treating ODD involves the entire family when working with children and adolescents with ODD. By involving the family, the therapist works towards ultimately changing or adapting the family system to reduce or completely halt disruptive behavior.

Here are more details on what this approach means.

Specialists believe that disruptive behavior is partially caused by the family system. For instance, families with interaction systems that are difficult for children with ODD to adapt to may reinforce coercive behaviors. And this doesn't just include homes with separated parents;

it also includes homes with both parents present but with defective family communication patterns.

Using family therapy with ODD children and adolescents will help therapists (and parents) understand the patterns by which a family self-organizes and determine how the family copes with changes.

Often, intervention programs to cure children with ODD under this light will then focus on training and educating parents towards transforming events or mindsets that trigger or encourage disruptive behavior in a child.

How Family-Based Approaches Work

Examples of effective family therapy intervention for ODD include parent training programs like Helping the Non-Compliant Child and Parent-Child Interaction Therapy. You may not have access to these programs; however, you should be able to locate a similar training program in your city if you live in the U.S.

These programs help to facilitate parent training through managing their children's noncompliant behaviors in a structured yet flexible way. Again, these methods ensure all curative provisions concentrate on building stronger relationships between parent and child.

Additionally, rather than focusing on your child's disruptive behaviors, these techniques teach parents to divert their attention to the child's prosocial behavior.

It's like focusing on improving your child's positive qualities rather than fighting to quench their disruptive tendencies.

Specialists recommend the use of positive reinforcement procedures like:

- attaching tokens to good behaviors
- rewarding positive wins
- providing time-outs
- and other contingency management techniques

Other helpful strategies include positive communication, skill building, and implementing family-based problem-solving rather than individual-based solutions.

While family-based therapy may be more challenging logistically, its long-term effects are often worth the hassle, especially when you consider the effect that this approach will have on your child's overall social well-being.

Building a Support Network

Parenting is a journey filled with highs and lows, joys and challenges, both for parent and child. If your child was diagnosed with ODD, you (and, of course, the child) are likely facing unique hurdles.

However, you first need to remember that you're not alone in this. It's also important to not fight this condition all by yourself.

One way to ease your—and your child's—journey is to build a support network. The network, a chain of "actors" encouraging and supporting one another, includes support offers that link:

- you to your child
- other family members to you and your child
- external parties (to the home) to you and your child

At home, you can work on creating a support network that includes all three links through:

- Recognizing and praising your child's positive behaviors.

- Ensuring that family members model the behavior they want the child to show. Watching you interact well with one another can help boost or improve your child's social skills.

- Building time together by planning a weekly schedule that includes you and your child doing stuff together.

Creating a support network also involves establishing a nurturing and supportive environment at home that's helpful for children with ODD.

The next part, beginning from Chapter 3, provides practical strategies to create a nurturing environment that helps the child in question as well as the entire family. In the meantime, here are some tips about how to create this kind of environment:

- Set clear expectations.

- Implement consistent routines (preferably "approved" or "created" by your child) that can help them stick more to rules.

- Provide a safe space for emotional expression. This could mean making your child feel comfortable enough to express their deepest concerns or logic with you.

- One way to help your child open up is by providing them with a private notebook or journal that lets them draw or write how they honestly feel without the fear of being judged.

The goal here in supporting your child through their healing process is to create a structure of consistency and a calm atmosphere.

Parental Self-Care Amidst the Diagnostic Process

Caring for yourself as a parent while raising a child with ODD is part of creating a support network to make the process easier.

Remember J.W.'s story that I shared with you at the beginning of this chapter? While J.W. was battling her psychological disorder and running away from home before being in and out of the hospital, her youngest daughter could have also developed some psychological disorders due to her mother's absence.

My point here? People raising a child with ODD may be at risk of mental health distress, which can make it increasingly challenging to apply positive parenting tips.

Your emotional health as a parent or caregiver is equally important to your child's emotional state as you walk them toward recovery and behavioral stability.

You will also do well to self-regulate your behavior as a means of modeling and being in a place where you can support your child.

A mom or dad who destroys things or throws things at the kids after a drinking bout won't be of much help to a child with ODD. The list of unhelpful emotional behavior from parents is possibly endless. But I believe you understand the point here.

This is why you may want to seek out psychotherapy or counseling for yourself.

What if you've had past traumas to deal with? You almost definitely need to see a psychologist. Parents who find it hard to self-regulate around their child might also need to consult a counselor.

Practical ways to get help include:

- Parent support groups
- Positive parenting classes for parents of children with ODD or related issues
- A behavior analyst
- Counselors
- Psychologists

ODD Comorbidities

As I've highlighted earlier, a disease's comorbidities are illnesses that can co-occur with the illness. We've also seen in detail how psychologists differentiate two of the common conditions that researchers have concluded co-occur with ODD:

- Attention deficit hyperactivity disorder (ADHD); and
- Conduct disorder (CD)

Other disorders that could co-occur with ODD include:

- Anxiety disorder
- Emotional disorders
- Mood disorders

Mood disorders may also be linked to major depression or bipolar disorder. Other indirect consequences of ODD may include a later mental disorder.

Again, researchers have found a strong comorbidity between ODD and conduct disorder: 3 in 10 children with ODD will likely develop CD.

ADHD also has a strong relationship to ODD. Experts believe that about 4 out of 10 kids with ADHD also have ODD. Children who fall into this category (by having both ODD and ADHD) will usually be more aggressive and have more of the negative behavioral symptoms of ODD, which can lead to poor academic performance.

Other conditions you could predict to co-occur in children or adults with ODD are language disorders (which can significantly affect a person's academic performance) and learning disorders (which can affect their language production and/or comprehension).

Workbook 2
Getting Them to Open Up

There are various ways to get your child to open up to you and feel comfortable explaining their truest feelings, without the fear of being judged, criticized, or punished for doing so.

One might be to buy a private notebook or journal for your child, asking them to write how they honestly feel.

If your kid doesn't like writing or isn't old enough to put down coherent details about their feelings, you may want to consider other ways to make them open up to you.

You could still buy the journal for them; wait until they're calm and happy, and then interview them, asking them sincere questions about what they think of you, your partner, their siblings, teachers, or how you treat them.

It could help to keep a weekly review of these facts. Soon enough, you can get crucial information about underlying factors that are encouraging your child's defiance at school, home, or elsewhere.

Key Takeaways

Misdiagnosis can occur because many ODD symptoms overlap with those of many other conditions. Families responsible for parenting children with ODD will do well to properly diagnose not just the presence or absence of ODD, but also other possible disorders responsible for the symptoms they observe.

Family-based solutions are among the best techniques to approach treating ODD in children and adolescents. These family therapies help the entire family understand the involved child's situation and learn how to work together.

PART 2

Strategies for Empowerment

A.D. (let's call him that) was introduced to an ODD therapist at age 12. His school contacted the therapist because A.D. was always complaining about being bullied to cover up for his wrongdoings.

Even though A.D. had significant behavior that showed a behavioral defect, he had good to average grades in school. There were no school records of any earlier diagnosis of behavioral problems like ODD or being on the autism spectrum.

However, his school knew that referring him to a therapist was the best way to help him overcome his bad behavior.

Here's what a typical day in A.D.'s school life looked like.

A.D. was apparently working diligently on his paper as the entire class worked to complete a task. The instruction was to submit their responses as they walked out the door for lunch.

On his way out, A.D. tore his paper, crumpled it, and told the teacher he couldn't do his work because another student next to him wrote on his paper. Unknown to A.D., the teacher, and the therapist who had come to observe him, saw him rip the paper.

The teacher started to straighten out the paper. However, A.D. snatched the paper from his teacher and started to eat it.

Even though the rest of the class was dismissed, A.D. stood his ground, explaining over and over how the other student had ruined his work while he chewed his paper.

Resigning to his defiance, the teacher dismissed him for lunch while the therapist looked on in utter amazement.

This behavior was common for A.D. As A.D. left for lunch, the therapist took pieces of the torn work only to find that it included a quite detailed architectural drawing.

Besides failing to "take responsibility" and wrongly accusing others, A.D. also displayed a significant level of shyness and avoided eye contact when speaking with the therapist.

The therapist's work began, and in four years, 16-year-old A.D. had become an object of pride to his family. He graduated from high school with good grades and began pursuing what he loved doing best. He now helped his grandparents co-manage their construction firm by creating architectural designs and supervising their execution.

How did the therapist take A.D. from point A to B? What strategies did she use in converting the excessively shy child into a responsible teen who could handle real-world building projects and become someone his family was proud of?

We'll consider some of these strategies in this part as I take you through the details of:

- Communicating effectively to overcome ODD

- Developing emotional intelligence

- Building cooperation and compliance

I'm sure you can't wait to hear the rest of A.D.'s story and get armed with these excellent tips to help your child survive oppositional defiant behavior.

I can't wait either.

CHAPTER 3

Communicating to Overcome

"And you, fathers, do not provoke your children to wrath, but bring them up in the training and admonition of the Lord."

—Ephesians 6:4 (NKJV)

"The way we talk to our children becomes their inner voice."

—Peggy O'Mara

"HEY! I'm glad you're getting along so well but can someone get me some chips?!"

Improving Family Communication
The Power of Positive Communication

Soon after beginning therapy, A.D. had to visit the therapist's home, not too far from his, to continue his sessions. In a bid to encourage A.D. and get him talking, the therapist (let's call her Miss T) incorporated architecture into the therapy. She also ensured that his reading and grammar work were all related to architecture.

A.D. never liked math, and he often told Miss T that he was going to be an architect, build her a house, and that he didn't need math. Miss T then asked him how he would figure out how many materials he needed to build her house.

You probably can't guess his response, right?

A.D. deleted the computer file containing all his work, tore up the drawings he had done in his sketchbook, and ran out the door. He threw himself into the swimming pool and intentionally hit his head against the side of the pool until Miss T jumped in and held him as tightly as she could.

A.D. calmed down as he sat on the side of the pool with Miss T quietly for a while. He wouldn't make any eye contact and never said a word. Miss T told him to head along to his home and she'd meet him there after changing her clothes to continue their work.

The only thing he said in response to this directive was that he would still make Miss T a house.

About 30 minutes later, Miss T went to A.D.'s house to find him informing his mother that she'd thrown him in the pool and made him hit his head and that his brother had deleted all his work.

Miss T wasn't surprised. And neither was his mother.

However, his mother's reaction surprised Miss T, as she excused A.D. to the kitchen for some ice cream and sent his younger brother to his room for touching his brother's computer—even though she *knew* A.D. was lying.

She then turned to Miss T and apologized for her child's behavior. Miss T took a deep breath as she turned to the kitchen, only to find A.D. laughing and pointing at her.

His mother went into the bedroom to admonish A.D.'s younger brother (apparently another apology session for not being able to confront her child).

A.D.'s laughter became louder.

Instead of reprimanding A.D. for his wrong behavior, Miss T walked up to him and planted a kiss on his cheek.

Now, this wasn't because she approved of his mom's seemingly helpless disposition, but it was her way of positively communicating love to a child who would have expected a rebuke or beating for lying to an adult's face.

We'll get to other details of how Miss T helped A.D. recover from ODD. However, let's take a break from A.D.'s story to emphasize what I mean by positive communication—and how it can help fast-track a child's recovery process from disruptive behaviors.

Understanding Positive Communication with Children

Do you remember that I recommended in Workbook 2 (in Chapter 2) that you purchase a personal journal for your child to encourage them to open up?

It's one of the helpful tools Miss T used to help A.D. open up about his true feelings, and eventually break through to his inner self—and this can help your child open up to you, too.

Again, the bottom line here is to communicate to your little one in a way that makes them feel respected and loved, regardless of their apparent disruptive tendencies, and ultimately open them up to constructive and compliant behavior.

But what does positive communication mean, anyway?

At its simplest level, positive communication with children means paying attention to a child and respecting the child's feelings, while watching your tone of voice.

It also involves using language that's understandable and appropriate for their age. You want to communicate, and specifically, without using any derogatory words.

Additionally, positive communication involves using kind language (rather than abusive or hurtful words). Using kind language also helps to set a positive example for your kids. They learn from your choice of communication instruments that they shouldn't bully or hurt others with their words or actions. It slowly but surely teaches them kindness, and to communicate positively with others in the home and at school.

But positive communication surely begins with you, the parent, before it spirals down to them, doesn't it?

I've put together five powerful tips to help you communicate positively with your children as you walk them (and the entire family) through this challenging period.

1. Listen to Understand

A child will either share details of what they know when retelling a story or they may only give basic information about the event. It all depends on how they perceive the environment or situation.

One way to keep communication lines open between you and your child is to listen, rather than respond to them. Listen to understand.

Your child wants to know that you understand him or her, regardless of how significant or insignificant the occasion might seem to you or other grown-ups around.

Ensure your little one feels free to speak, as this can build their confidence and esteem when communicating with you. Notably, this can also be foundational to subsequent conversations with them in the future as the child ages.

2. Bend to Their Level

Here's another important way to maintain positive communication between you and your child: make them feel comfortable by bending, so to speak, to their eye level.

Yes, there will be times to address negative behavior from a child. But it's important to communicate negative feedback in a way that leaves the child with a positive outlook.

Bending down and speaking calmly to a child about their behavior can help them feel less intimidated so they can comprehend what is being said to them. It'll help to give them some gentle guidance about how they could make a better choice next time, which helps them feel positive about the interaction.

Speaking to their level can also prepare them for how they manage negative conversations in the future.

3. Acknowledge Their Feelings

You can develop communication with your child by helping them express how they feel. When a child opens up about their feelings (even when it seems they aren't truthful), they want to be acknowledged.

Don't dismiss what your children share with you by saying, "Stop whining," or "You're being silly."

These statements can make a child feel invalidated and are a definite reason for your child to hide their feelings in the future. Keep communication lines open and offer empathy instead.

Respond with lines like, "I understand how you feel" or "I can relate to your feelings right now," and possibly share a real-life story about yourself that helps to corroborate your point. Like, "I'm sorry someone disturbed your peaceful game time. I never like someone disrupting my work either."

When you do this, you encourage them to share how they feel freely with you without the fear of being judged or misunderstood. They're also better positioned to feel heard and understood.

4. Control Your Responses

Children can inadvertently say or do things that can provoke an emotional response from you. At other times, children *deliberately* provoke your emotions.

However, positive communication with your child relies a lot on how well you control your emotions. Avoid saying words in the heat of the moment that you may later regret. Control strong outbursts and try to remain calm—especially when very bad behavior occurs.

A helpful tip to get through this might be to count from 1 to 10 before responding to a child displaying disruptive behavior. That way, you're better prepared to diffuse your emotions before speaking them out.

5. Communicate Clearly

Ensure you're clear about each instruction when speaking with your kids. Being clear also involves being confident. You're probably already aware of this; children can sense a lack of confidence or assurance in grown-ups when speaking with them.

And when a child (especially one used to non-compliance) senses a lack of confidence, they'll likely do the opposite of what you asked them to do. The way you deliver your intentions is important to create an atmosphere of mutual respect.

Additionally, the way you speak to your children reflects your character, which can ultimately create an example for them. Children, as we already know, learn by imitating others more than by heeding instructions. Your kids will likely imitate any behavior they see.

It also helps to be assertive when communicating with your child. That way, your child can learn to be assertive when communicating with their peers, siblings, and other adults.

Here are some additional tips for communicating with your child:

Use Positive Language

Positive communication involves speaking diplomatically and using a positive tone when addressing your child's behavior.

To do this effectively, take a moment to think about what you would have said if you were to respond spontaneously. Then, you might want to imagine how you would feel or respond if you were on the receiving end of such a statement from someone you hold in high esteem.

Here are helpful examples of how to get this done with children and adolescents with ODD.

Example 1: Telling your child that something cannot be done. (Let's call the child in this example Sara.)

"I'm sorry, Sara, but it's not possible for me (and Dad or Mom, where applicable) to do THIS…"

Instead, how about highlighting what can be done?

"I (and your dad or mom, where applicable) would be more than happy to help you with this. However, we'll be even happier to help you do this on your own when you grow older by helping you do THAT"—diverting their attention.

Example 2: Using negative words.

"Unfortunately, Sara, that particular option is unavailable."

How about suggesting helpful alternatives?

"Sara, I have many options available apart from this. Let me show you…"

Example 3: Communicating blame in an accusatory manner.

"You (falsely) claimed or stated that…"

Instead of introducing an accusatory tone, consider taking a helpful or encouraging approach.

"Might I suggest you…"

The essence of speaking in a positive tone is to reduce, as much as possible, the chances of emotions rising on the side of both parent and child. It helps to provide a suitable atmosphere that fosters character development.

Communicate Bad News Effectively

No one always gets what they want in life. If everyone got what they wanted in life, then there might as well be no single life on this planet— and your child needs to start learning that as soon as possible.

Bad news is sometimes avoidable, but how you convey it to your child can go a long way in influencing their reaction or understanding things from *your* point of view.

Whether it involves making a cancellation or it's that a promise you made to your child now has to face some cutbacks, it's often difficult to communicate something negative.

However, your method of delivery can soften the blow on children and adolescents with ODD. Let's see some helpful examples, like we used with using positive language, on how to do this.

This time around, we're dealing with a tween named Bob.

Example 1: Choosing positive over negative phrasing.

Rather than say,

"Bob, this damage can't be fixed for a week…"

How about:

"Bob, you can have this fixed next week?"

Example 2: Using questions to make suggestions that improve the situation.

Rather than say,

"Bob, you really ought to…!"

How about:

"Wouldn't it be better to…?" or "Bob, couldn't you…?"

Presenting suggestions as questions like this helps to convey your idea diplomatically and ask for their response. It certainly beats making a direct statement, which can detonate a trigger-happy tween into explosive behavior from feeling bullied.

Remember, the right methods to help your child recover from disruptive behavior are those that'll help your child become (or feel) vulnerable enough to open up to you or trust your judgment rather than defy your orders (or those of other authorities).

Example 3: Avoiding negative words entirely.

People, and of course, children, react better to positive-sounding words.

Here's what I mean. Rather than tell Bob,

"I think that's such a bad idea."

How about telling him,

"I don't think that's such a good idea."

Example 4: Using modifiers to make things seem less of an issue.

Instead of saying,

"Doing this will create problems for your future and the future of all of us, Bob!"

How about saying,

"This might cause a little problem for you and all of us later."

Using the word "little" helps the statement come across as softer. You can also use other modifying phrases like "sort of," "kind of," "a bit," or "slight."

In all, remember that every child, regardless of their ODD behavior, deserves to be treated specially and appreciated for their unique traits. One way to do that, and possibly get more compliance or cooperation from your child, is by always using positive communication when speaking with them.

Fostering Empathy in Parent-Child Interactions

Emotional intelligence, or the proper understanding of emotions and how to respond to them, is one of the core aspects of family-based therapy for treating ODD.

And that's logical, since the bulk of ODD behaviors express themselves through a child's emotions.

Positive communication is one way to connect with your child emotionally (and rightly). And if you ask me, positive communication belongs to a larger world of empathetic parenting.

"What does empathetic parenting mean?" you're probably asking.

Empathetic parenting, sometimes called empathic parenting, is a parenting approach that concentrates on understanding and responding to a child's emotional needs.

This parenting style nurtures a strong emotional parent-child bond that helps children grow into emotionally intelligent, compassionate, and empathetic individuals.

In contrast to punitive parenting, empathetic parenting connects to the underlying feelings and motivations behind a child's behavior instead of simply concentrating on eliminating unwanted behaviors. It's how you guide a child into becoming emotionally aware of their own emotions and those of others.

Why Empathy in Parenting?

Empathy is the ability to understand and share others' feelings. It involves sensing what others think and feel while gaining insight into their underlying needs. Empathic people can relate well to others, foster deeper connections, and provide support and understanding. Additionally, empathic people are more likely to be compassionate, kind, and emotionally intelligent.

So in terms of parent-child interaction, empathy helps parents build a strong emotional connection with their children. This connection is vital to help your child develop emotionally as they grow into a healthy and happy adult.

Empathetic parenting has several benefits for a parent-child relationship, especially when the child involved shows symptoms of oppositional defiant disorder.

Let's examine some of them.

1. Stronger Parent-Child Bond

Empathetic parenting helps to facilitate a deep emotional connection between parents and their kids. This strong bond provides a secure foundation for the child's emotional development. It's what tells your child you love them despite their sometimes irrational behavior and makes them feel safe and supported by you.

2. Enhanced Communication

Empathetic parenting also encourages open and honest communication between children and their parents. This can lead to a deeper understanding of others' feelings and needs towards a more supportive and harmonious family environment.

3. Greater Resilience

Children raised with empathetic parenting are more likely to develop strong emotional resilience. It prepares them to navigate and cope with their emotions in a healthy and supportive environment.

4. Improved Emotional Intelligence

By guiding children with ODD into emotional awareness and helping them understand their emotions, empathetic parenting sets them up to become more emotionally intelligent individuals. This can in turn help them better regulate their emotions, relate better with their peers and siblings, and ultimately enjoy greater success in life.

5. Happier and Healthier Children

Do you want a child with ODD to be happier, healthier, and more balanced? Research has shown that empathetic parenting can go a long way. That's likely because it nurtures a strong emotional connection with and support for your child.

A.D. (remember him?) began to recover and grow from being a defiant tween into a socially responsible teen as he learned to open up about his real emotions to Miss T.

Without a doubt, one of the verified causes of ODD in children is an abusive home environment. As Miss T would find, it was one of the leading causes of A.D.'s defiance and shyness.

A.D.'s father (who was diagnosed with autism in his younger years) emotionally abused everyone under his care—his wife and kids—keeping everyone quiet when he was around except when he asked them to speak.

His father's behavior was what made A.D. shy and, of course, defiant and seemingly irresponsible. He ought to, since his father wouldn't let him even express happiness when he was around.

Now, that's not putting all the blame on A.D.'s dad for his child's defiance.

However, the absence of empathetic parenting only helps to encourage a defiant child's disruptive ways. It discourages them from making efforts to truly improve and unveil their deepest emotions (which isn't always wrong!).

Practical Ways to Foster Empathy in a Parent-Child Relationship

Let's look at some practical tips and strategies to help you implement empathetic parenting in your family.

1. Label Your Child's Emotional State Before Any Response

Before responding to your child's explosive behavior, it helps to take a moment to label their emotional state.

For instance, "You're angry with me because you can't have ice cream before dinner, right?"

Labeling your child's emotional state (and, I should add, *accurately* labeling it) helps you automatically empathize with their feelings. It also increases your chances of responding with understanding and compassion rather than frustration and anger.

2. Be Mindful of Your Own Emotional Needs and Practice Self-Compassion

Empathic parents need to be mindful of their own emotional needs and take steps to address them.

This could involve creating time for self-care, getting support from friends, support groups, or a therapist, or engaging in activities that help you recharge and maintain an emotional balance.

Additionally, you want to show self-compassion by admitting that it's fine for both you and your child to have big feelings. It helps to recognize you can't possibly make everything better all the time.

Spare yourself; give yourself some love and understanding for supporting your child without everything having to be perfect.

3. Model Empathy in Your Family Culture and Your Interactions with Others

Your child is likely to learn more about empathy and emotional intelligence by observing your family culture and how you interact with others.

Make emotional connection and empathy a priority in your family culture. That may mean everyone in the family creates time for family discussions, engaging in regular activities that facilitate bonding, and fostering open and honest communication about everyone's feelings.

You also want to model empathy to your child in interactions with friends, family, and strangers. That will (slowly perhaps, but surely) help your child understand the importance of empathy and compassion in their relationships.

4. Encourage Your Child to Express Their Truest Emotions

Support your child in becoming more emotionally aware and expressive by encouraging them to speak about their feelings and emotions, especially as they learn to express themselves clearly.

You could do this by asking open-ended questions, providing a safe space for them to air their emotions, or validating their feelings.

5. Be Patient and Persistent

Empathetic parenting is a journey that demands patience and persistence. You want to recognize that you and your child are constantly learning and growing and that building emotional connections and intelligence takes time and effort.

Intentional Parenting

Intentional parenting is having a game plan instead of relying on chance. It involves you making conscious choices in how you raise your kids rather than flying on autopilot. The opposite approach to intentional parenting is reactive or autopilot parenting. This is when you're kind of just going with the flow, handling situations as they come without a specific strategy. It's like trying to steer a boat without a paddle—you might get where you're going, but with a couple of mishaps.

So, why bother with intentional parenting? The benefits extend to both parents and kids. For parents, it means less stress and more confidence in handling challenges. For kids, it translates to a more stable and supportive environment. It is a win-win situation for both you and your kid.

Core Principles of Intentional Parenting

These core principles aren't just theoretical concepts; they form the practical foundation of intentional parenting. Identifying values and goals is your first step to intentional parenting. Think of it as setting the coordinates for your parenting GPS. Identify your core values and set specific goals for your child's upbringing. Define the kind of person you want them to become and create a plan that will get you there.

Next up is empathy. Empathy isn't just a feel-good concept; it's a cornerstone of intentional parenting. As we've covered in the previous section, it involves putting yourself in your child's shoes, understanding their emotional journey, and acknowledging their struggles. It's like developing a radar for your child's feelings, making your connection more profound and supportive.

Communication is the lifeline of any relationship, and parenting is no exception. Intentional parenting emphasizes effective communication: being clear, honest, and open with your child. Active listening skills are crucial here. It's not just hearing; it's understanding. Think of it as tuning in to the same frequency, ensuring you and your child are on the same wavelength.

Setting Clear, Consistent, and Age-Appropriate Expectations and Boundaries

Boundaries are important in human relationships, and intentional parenting is about setting them clearly, consistently, and in a way that matches your child's age and developmental stage. You don't have to be a strict referee to achieve this; rather, make use of a framework that helps your child understand what's expected of them. This consistency brings a sense of stability and predictability to their world.

Practice positive reinforcement and rewards for desired behaviors. In intentional parenting, positive reinforcement is your go-to strategy. It involves acknowledging and rewarding desired behaviors, creating a positive cycle of encouragement. You can see it as planting seeds of positive actions that, with nurturing, will grow into lifelong habits.

Let's go on to how intentional parenting affects discipline. Discipline is not punishment; rather, it is a way to teach responsibility to your kids. Intentional parenting incorporates the use of both natural and logical consequences. Natural consequences result from the child's actions, allowing them to learn from the cause-and-effect relationship. For example, running on wet floors may earn your child a few bruises if they fall. On the other hand, you create logical consequences to teach a specific lesson. It's like a tailored learning experience for growth. For example, you may take away certain privileges whenever your kids misbehave just to drive home your point.

Also, try to consistently model desired behaviors and emotional regulation. Modeling involves you embodying the behaviors and emotional regulation you want your child to develop. You become their primary role model, showing them how to go through life, express emotions, and interact positively with others.

Applying Intentional Parenting Strategies

Intentional parenting involves having to deal with negative emotions without triggering a full-scale meltdown. You need to be calm in the storm, acknowledge emotions, and find constructive solutions. See it as sidestepping power struggles and steering towards resolutions that benefit both you and your child. This helps you and your child understand and manage thoughts and emotions, turning potential conflicts into opportunities for growth. Trust me, it is not as complicated as it sounds.

You also need to create a structured and predictable environment for your child. Have a routine that provides stability and a sense of order. See your home as a mini kingdom with its own set of rules. Intentional parenting involves developing routines that help positive communication. You might not necessarily need tight schedules; simply create habits that encourage open dialogue. These practices build a foundation for healthy communication, making it easier for your child to express themselves and for you to understand their world.

Furthermore, encouraging positive coping mechanisms and emotional expression is like giving them a backpack filled with strategies to deal with challenges. Encourage emotional expression—let them know it's okay to feel and express their emotions in a healthy way.

Parenting isn't a solo gig; it's a team effort. Intentional parenting involves collaborating with teachers and professionals. You don't have to face it alone; it's okay to leverage the expertise of others. See it as you building a support squad, working together to provide the best possible environment for your child's growth and development.

Specific Challenges and Adaptations

ODD and ADHD come with their unique set of challenges, requiring tailored strategies. Intentional parenting involves adapting techniques to suit these behaviors. You need to customize your approach to fit your child's needs and find what works best for them in managing their impulses and behaviors.

Defiance, arguing, and negativity can turn a peaceful home into a battlefield. Intentional parenting tackles these challenges head-on, focusing on constructive communication and problem-solving. You must set clear expectations and boundaries while assuring your kid of your love and care. Think of it as diffusing conflicts with empathy and finding resolutions that promote positive growth.

Impulsivity and hyperactivity can feel like trying to tame a wild horse. An intentional parent recognizes these traits and works within the framework to manage them effectively. It involves providing structure and routine while also teaching self-regulation techniques.

Maintaining Self-Care and Managing Parental Stress Alongside Intentional Parenting

It's easy to lose yourself in the chaos of raising kids, but then, you cannot afford to lose yourself. Intentional parenting also emphasizes the importance of parental well-being. You need to create time for yourself, practice self-compassion, and seek support when needed. Go on a vacation if you need to. You can make plans for something within your budget. Go alone, or go with your friends and/or spouse; it's all up to you. Think of it as putting on your oxygen mask first so you can better care for your child.

These specific challenges require a nuanced approach, and intentional parenting allows one to address them effectively. You need to be proactive, flexible, and compassionate in dealing with all that comes with raising children with ODD or ADHD.

The Intentional Parent and Social Media

Getting your kids off their phones is a modern parenting challenge. To deal with social media addiction and obsession, you can set clear boundaries for social media use from the get-go. Discuss appropriate screen time, the types of platforms allowed, and the importance of balance between online and offline activities. Children often mirror their parents' behavior. So, you have to demonstrate a healthy relationship with social media by balancing their usage and prioritizing face-to-face interactions. Lead by example and show that there's more to life than the digital world.

Promote a diverse range of activities offline. This could include sports, arts, or simply spending quality time with family and friends. It's like offering a buffet of experiences, ensuring your child has a well-rounded life beyond the screen. Teach your kids responsible online behavior, including the importance of respectful communication and being cautious with personal information. You can also leverage parental control features on devices to manage and monitor your child's online activities. This is like having a security system in place, ensuring a safe online environment.

While social media has its pitfalls, intentional parents can harness its potential for positive influence. For example, you can introduce educational apps and content that align with your child's interests. Social media can serve as a gateway to learning when used intentionally. Check out online communities that align with your family's values and interests. You can create a virtual support system, connecting with other parents or families who share similar parenting goals. Social media platforms can be avenues for creative expression. Encourage your child to post their talents or interests in a positive and constructive manner. Teach your child about discernment and critical thinking online. You need to teach them how to navigate the digital world responsibly, distinguishing between reliable and unreliable information.

Help your child cultivate positive online relationships. Whether it's connecting with relatives or making friends who share common interests, intentional parents guide their children in fostering healthy digital connections. You can instill the values of friendship and community even in virtual spheres.

Being an Intentional Parent in a Large Family

Being an intentional parent in a large family demands a strategic and adaptable approach. Establish a rotating schedule for one-on-one time with each child. This could be as simple as a shared hobby, a bedtime story, or a weekend outing. Acknowledge each child's strengths and achievements in a personalized manner, reinforcing their individual worth within the family. Conduct regular family meetings to encourage open communication. Allow each child to express their thoughts, feelings, and concerns in a safe and supportive environment.

Practice active listening during daily interactions, validating each child's perspective. This helps build trust and lets your child know they are heard. Engage the entire family in discussions about core values.

Allow everyone to contribute their ideas, fostering a sense of ownership and unity. Create a visual representation of family values, perhaps as a poster or a shared document, as a constant reminder of the collective principles guiding the household.

You can also organize team-building activities that promote cooperation and mutual understanding among siblings. Teach effective conflict resolution skills, emphasizing compromise and empathy. Maintain a family calendar that tracks everyone's commitments, allowing for effective time management and coordination. Conduct regular check-ins to assess the needs and interests of each child. Flexibility in routines helps accommodate evolving schedules and individual preferences.

Prioritize quality time over quantity. Be fully present during shared moments, minimizing distractions and focusing on meaningful interactions. Establish unique family traditions that every one of your children can relate to. This creates memorable and cherished experiences. Assign age-appropriate chores to instill a sense of responsibility and contribution. Rotate responsibilities regularly to prevent monotony.

Provide opportunities for decision-making, allowing each child to exercise independence within a structured framework. Develop specific rituals for celebrating individual achievements, such as a "Star of the Week" or a special family dinner after a notable accomplishment. Ensure that each one of your children's achievements is acknowledged during family discussions, reinforcing the value of their unique contributions.

Active Listening Techniques

Experts agree that active listening is an essential part of compassionate parenting. But actively listening, reflecting, responding, and giving feedback aren't always easy even for regular communication.

It can be much more challenging when dealing with a child who seems to be bent on defying orders from authority and lacks a sense of reason and compliance.

Here are some helpful tips to help you show your child or adolescent that you care about their feelings by practicing active listening.

1. Pay Attention

Active listening aims to set a comfortable ambiance that gives your child a chance to think and speak freely around you. One way to do this is by paying attention.

Allow "wait time" before responding. Don't cut your child off when they're forming a sentence. Avoid paying attention to your body language and your mental frame when engaging in active listening. It also helps to maintain eye contact as much as possible.

2. Avoid Judging Abruptly

Active listening requires an open mind. Avoid judging your child when speaking with them. Admit that you might not perfectly understand your child's rationale for behaving the way they do—other than their ODD.

It's a good listening practice to suspend your final judgments, hold back any criticisms, and avoid unnecessary interruptions such as arguing or faulting their point almost immediately.

3. Reflect

When you're listening, don't assume you understand your child correctly—or that they think you heard them correctly.

One way to reflect accurately is by mirroring your child's information and emotions by periodically paraphrasing their key points. Reflecting helps to confirm that you and the speaker are on the same page during a conversation.

For instance, your child might say something like,

"I like my school, but everyone in my class hates me."

To show you empathize with them and understand them, how about saying,

"So your school is great, but you wish your classmates could better get along with you?"

4. Clarify

Don't be afraid to ask questions that can help clarify any ambiguous issues around things your child tells you.

After hearing their account of an incident of misbehavior or any other event, it could help to say,

"Wait a minute. Let me see if I quite understood you. You mean…"

OR,

"Let me see if I'm clear. Are you saying…"

Open-ended and probing questions are helpful active listening tools that encourage children to self-reflect and work towards possibly solving the problem in the future, rather than just defending their actions or guessing at an answer.

Again, in active listening, the emphasis is on asking, rather than telling. It ultimately invites a thoughtful response and enshrines a spirit of collaboration.

5. Summarize

Where necessary, restating key themes as your conversation proceeds helps to confirm and solidify your grasp of your child's view.

It also helps you and your child to be clear on mutual responsibilities and follow-up actions that are necessary. It can help to briefly summarize what you understand about their grievances or requests. In turn, ask your child or adolescent to do the same while listening actively to them.

6. Share Your Point of View

Remember, active listening is first about understanding the other person, *and then* getting the other person to understand you.

As you better understand how your child feels or what they think, you can start introducing your ideas, feelings, and suggestions to them.

Again, your goal is to help your child develop emotional intelligence, be compassionate and cooperative, and eventually comply with rules virtually everyone else follows.

One way to introduce your point of view is to speak to them about a similar experience you had in childhood or share an idea that was triggered by a comment they made earlier.

After you introduce your point of view to him or her, your child will likely have a good picture of where things stand, and the conversation can shift into finding a way out or trying out new approaches.

Why Actively Listening to Children with ODD Matters

Actively listening helps to establish trust between you and your child with ODD. Showing empathy to them can help you foster an ambiance of psychological safety.

Moreover, listening thoughtfully to them, asking clarifying questions, and encouraging them to share their perspective will reinforce your role as a parent.

Now, unlike the famed caveat in WWE ads, *DO try this at home*.

Active listening ultimately makes you a better parent, as you show your child in one more way that you truly care about them.

Encouraging Open Dialogues

Before, during, and after you break bad news to your child, it helps to keep communication lines open between you and them.

Encouraging open dialogues in the home helps each member of the family feel loved and respected, whether or not their behavior is often undesirable. Also, a home that encourages open dialogue makes it easier to handle conflicts when they arise.

Here are some helpful ways to do that.

Make Conversations with Your Kids a Priority

Developing open and comfortable communication with your kids helps them to develop confidence, self-esteem, and cooperation, and also builds healthy and warm relationships.

It helps to take the time and effort to build effective relationships and communication skills by speaking with your kids as often as you can. Remember, each conversation is a two-way street where you listen as well as talk to them.

Create Opportunities for One-on-One Conversations

This tip is helpful especially if there's an age gap between your children. Some kids may feel more comfortable talking about their concerns in the absence of their siblings or any other third party.

Sometimes, your younger children may talk over the older ones; other times, the younger siblings give in and let the older ones do the talking.

Meanwhile, your conversations with your older children can sometimes supersede the younger children's level of comprehension. Your older children may also require stimulating conversations where they can learn to their level and ask questions accordingly for more information.

Try to get some one-on-one time with your kids so you can speak with them at their level and use the right vocabulary. Hold meetings regularly to give your child a chance to say what's on their mind.

You could also consider talking in the car while driving somewhere with him or her alone.

Encourage Conversations

As much as you can, keep dialogues open between you and your children. One of the best ways to do this is to ensure you hold conversations with your children about almost everything.

Don't make every conversation about how they're complicating issues in the home, or how they need to improve their grades or respect you and their siblings more. They may soon start to avoid your conversations altogether.

Also, consider using phrases or questions that require more than one-word or yes/no responses to encourage a conversation with your child. Think phrases like, "Let's talk about what we want to do during our next outing," or "What did you do in school today?"

What if they don't seem to want to talk? Don't force the discussion, especially if it triggers some negative emotions in them. It helps to consider their mood and timeframe, too.

If they're having a bad day (children have bad days too!), or are already too tired during a discussion, appreciate their space by discontinuing the conversation till a later time. Also, reassure your children that they can speak with you about anything they're worried or concerned about.

Listen to What they Have to Say by Practicing Active Listening

Here's where to practice all the active listening tips I shared with you earlier in this chapter. Give your child your full attention when they ask questions or are speaking with you.

Treat their questions or comments seriously, even if they're touching on matters that are sensitive to you or the family.

Encourage Their Questions

Tell your child that it's fine to ask you sensitive questions about your feelings, theirs, or even your instructions. Even if they think a question might upset you, reassure them that you'll answer as truthfully and as best as possible.

However, remind them that you may not have the answers to all their questions.

Answer Their Questions

Children and adolescents sometimes ask difficult questions. Don't avoid their question or give them a misleading answer when they do this.

Children battling with dysfunctional behavioral disorders like ODD should be encouraged to speak up and speak to their parents about their feelings, ask relevant questions, and let their parents know when something concerns them.

If they're courageous enough to ask, try to find the courage to answer. If they ask questions you can't answer, don't be afraid to tell them you don't know or haven't decided on the matter.

Should you notice that your child has become increasingly withdrawn and won't communicate with you, consider speaking with your family doctor or a psychologist.

Perfecting Non-Verbal Communication

What you don't say is often as crucial as what you say. Experts say that nonverbal communication plays as high as a 93% role in communication.

Nonverbal communication refers to the use of facial expressions, body language, gestures, and other nonverbal cues to convey messages.

While verbal communication concentrates on the words we use, nonverbal communication plays a significant role in expressing emotions, intentions, and attitudes.

It helps to understand and master nonverbal communication—not just how to use it, but how your child uses nonverbal behavior—and guide your child to master nonverbal cues.

A Caveat

Before we delve into the why's, what's, and how's of nonverbal communication, here's a caveat to note: Nonverbal communication is practically the same for all children, whether or not they have special needs. Therefore, the tips I'll share here can help any child, including (but not limited to) especially "difficult" ones, become better at mastering nonverbal cues.

Why Master Nonverbal Communication with Children and Adolescents?

Parents of toddlers are often told to keep speaking to their kids to boost their language readiness. While that's an important part of their development, it also helps to consider how you demonstrate nonverbal communication to your kids.

Helping your kids master (your) nonverbal cues can help them refine their social skills and build their overall emotional intelligence, enhance their listening skills, and increase their chances of building stronger relationships.

Let's see why your inability to understand your adolescent or child's nonverbal communication might be an additional reason why helping them become more compliant or cooperative seems extremely complex.

During adolescence, middle schoolers often rely on nonverbal communication as they navigate their way through a maze of social dynamics, made more difficult by peer pressure. Their need for acceptance and to fit in can also influence how they express themselves nonverbally.

However, research shows that middle schoolers sometimes face challenges in expressing themselves nonverbally, as they're still developing their social skills. Therefore, it's vital to master your teenage child's nonverbal communication while equipping them with strategies to help them master nonverbal communication as well.

A General Guide to Understanding Your Child's Nonverbal Cues

All children have various ways of expressing themselves through body language. Here's a guide to common nonverbal cues that can help you understand your child's gestures.

1. Body Language

Positive cues: nodding head, sitting up straight, facing the same direction, opening arms, etc.

Negative cues: fidgeting, shaking head, slouching, facing another direction, crossing arms, etc.

Facing someone or leaning towards them can suggest an "open" position. However, "closed" positions like crossing arms may demonstrate that your child is unreceptive or might be frustrated.

2. Hand Gestures and Touch

Positive cues: hand on shoulder, high-fiving, fist-bumping, thumbs-up, hugging, etc.

Negative cues: wringing hands, holding palm out in "stop" sign, shaking finger, wild gesturing, etc.

Every child is unique in the way they respond to touch. Some love hugs and cuddling and others may feel more at ease with a high-five or a thumbs-up. Some kids may also fidget or wring their hands when feeling nervous or uncertain.

3. Facial Expressions

Positive cues: smiling, widening eyes, winking, etc.

Negative cues: frowning, raising eyebrows, rolling eyes, pursing lips, etc.

If your child notices you raising your eyebrows or pursing your lips, they may think you're angry or being dismissive.

4. Eye Contact

Eye contact is a critical element of facial expressions. Making eye contact while communicating with others is a way to show them attention and interest. However, note that some kids with behavioral challenges are shy or easily distracted.

5. Tone of Voice

Positive cues: pleasant tone, easy speaking speed, right volume, use of "mm-hmm" or "uh-huh," etc.

Negative cues: raised voice, sarcastic tone, distracted speech, etc.

You want to keep your ears attuned to the tone, speed, and volume of your child's voice. Kids may also speak with annoyance or sarcasm when trying to communicate their frustration or use rapid speech when they're over-excited.

6. Space and Physical Boundaries

Finally, respecting others' physical boundaries is vital. If your child stays too close or too far away from a speaker, they may accidentally convey the wrong message.

It's vital to teach your child the right distance when speaking with others so they don't invade their personal space.

How to Help Your Child Improve Their Nonverbal Communication Skills

A great way to help your child improve their nonverbal communication skills is to help them focus on activities that inspire emotional awareness and let them practice appropriate cues.

1. Modeling Nonverbal Cues

It's common for you to use a flat monotone or be distracted by your phone after a long day at work; however, take the time and effort to model the positive nonverbal cues you want your child to copy.

2. Leveraging Joint Attention

Another way to help your child improve their nonverbal communication skills is to create a task you have to do together. As you both concentrate on the task, your kid will get an up-close look at how you pay attention and collaborate with other people through joint attention tasks. Good examples of joint attention tasks include building a tower, baking cookies, shopping, etc.

3. Playing Nonverbal Games

Many enriching games can help your children boost their nonverbal skills. Examples of these games include "social spy" and charades (the internet is filled with tons of other ideas).

You can also practice using appropriate nonverbal communication through acting games. Try out various voice tones with the same sentence, or draw pictures of different emotions for your child to act out.

These types of practices can help your child become aware of others' body language.

4. Turning the Sounds Off

Let your child watch a TV show without the sound. Or allow them to page through a picture book without reading the words. Ask them to guess what's happening in the story via nonverbal cues.

Another way to "turn the sound off" and help your child master nonverbal cues is to introduce "silent snack time." During silent snack time, kids tell stories without speaking, leaving the audience to figure out the plot.

Setting Realistic Expectations for Communication

Remember the quote I shared with you at the beginning of this chapter? Unrealistic expectations are one of the two main things that can hinder or even destroy your relationship with your child.

Granted, a child's defiance can get them in real trouble. Your expectations for them often arise because you love them and desire the best for them and their future.

However, setting unrealistic expectations can severely damage the bond between you and your child. Sadly, even the most aware parents sometimes fall into this trap unknowingly.

Expecting a child to become a great artist by age 13, get brilliant grades in their academics, and win the next public speaking event at school can pressure them to the point of burnout.

But what can parents of children with ODD do in this case?

Set realistic expectations for your child, including whether they heed or reject your instructions and how they communicate with you and others.

You have to get this right from the onset. Is it wrong to push your child to become their best possible self? No.

If you don't give your children wings to become self-confident, cooperative, compliant, and productive members of society, who will?

However, it's important to differentiate between when you are gently nudging your kids to be cooperative or become better at their schoolwork or something they enjoy doing and when you're passing the buck too much.

Putting unpleasant pressure on kids can bog them down and may eventually affect their self-esteem.

On the other hand, you still can't have zero expectations for your child. Here's a short guide to help you set realistic expectations for your child—including the actions you anticipate from them.

1. Understand your child's strengths: Children have various strengths, whether it's in how they communicate, experience or share happiness, or their favorite school subjects. The trick is to concentrate your efforts on your child's strengths. Honing your child's strengths or academic interests can help them improve. It could be storytelling, math, a language, or something similar.

2. Set small incremental goals: If your child responds a little better than they did the last time you corrected them, celebrate their improvement and extend your expectations for a better response. Whether you're working with a therapist or a psychiatrist, inspire your child to grow slowly and consistently.

3. Avoid being too harsh: Asking your child to never watch TV, never play with a mobile phone, or never eat chocolate might seem like discipline to you. But look at the world we live in. It's quite unheard of and unreasonable to ask your kids to never watch TV or use a mobile phone at all. Extremes of any kind are bad. It'll help to find a balance for your children when setting boundaries around food, fun, school, and life.

Workbook 3
Practice Silent Snack Time

Look out for a time when your child is being warm and friendly and teach them about silent snack time. Give them some time to create their story plot and plan their gestures.

Then schedule an evening to have them act out their story over some snacks with you or other family members.

How does this help you bond with your child? To spice it up, how about getting your child a special costume for their next silent snack time?

Just ensure you avoid making things seem too serious so no one feels bad if they go against the game plan!

Key Takeaways

- Maintaining positive communication shows you're listening to what your child is saying. It also helps to build a long-lasting connection between parent and child.

- Be patient with yourself and your child as you encourage them to become more emotionally intelligent. And don't forget to celebrate your progress.

- Listening actively actually makes you a better parent, as you show your child in one more way that you truly care about them.

- Create time to speak with your child one-on-one while respecting their space and need to be alone.

- Lastly, your love for your child shouldn't push you into setting up unreasonably high expectations from them. Extremes are bad for anyone. It helps to find a balance between schoolwork and play.

CHAPTER 4

Reshaping Behavioral Patterns with CBT

"Train up a child in the way he should go, And when he is old he will not depart from it."

—Proverbs 22:6 (NKJV)

"The chains of habit are too weak to be felt until they are too strong to be broken."

— Samuel Johnson

ODD

"Wow. I don't know what to say!"

It's 7 a.m. on a regular school day, and the last thing I want to do is wake up my kid. But it's something that has to be done. So, I sneak into his room, sit on his bed, and take a moment before the day kicks in. In these quiet moments, he still looks like a little boy—rosy cheeks, messy hair, curled *up under his Lightning McQueen blanket, with a worn-out stuffed dog near his pillow.*

In my softest voice, I run my fingers through his hair and say, "Good morning, Johnny. Time to wake up." And as always, my nine-year-old rolls away, shuts his eyes tight, and says, "SHUT UP." And that's how our day starts.

Having a kid with oppositional defiant disorder (ODD) means every walk to school turns into a verbal battle. Every car ride ends with at least one kid crying. I try my best to be patient daily, but it's tough. How can you not lose it when your nine-year-old just told his little brother he wishes he wasn't born, all because he wouldn't share his yo-yo?

All the advice from well-meaning friends doesn't help when you've got a kid who thinks differently. I fail every day to make my kid happy. And it's hard to admit, but sometimes he's just hard to like.

For Johnny, it started early, like really early. I remember a 3D ultrasound when I was just 12 weeks pregnant. The kid hadn't even been born and was already trying to punch his way out. I thought it was cute back then. Awww, look! He's a fighter! But now, I wonder if he was just restless from the start.

He was colicky when he was born. He didn't like sleep, baths, or being held. He screamed during car rides and stroller trips. He nursed fitfully. Around five months old, the colic went away, and we had a year or so of things seeming normal. He smiled, stood up, and said "Mama" and "Dada."

We cheered for his firsts, enjoyed his giggles, and loved his spirit. But just before he started walking, he had these weird spasms where his whole body shook. I rushed him to a neurologist, fearing the worst. After a thorough check, the doctor said it was just Johnny's temper. "He just doesn't like being a baby." The spasms went away, but the temper stuck around.

We tried multiple therapists. Drew pictures of feelings and talked about what was happening at home. He loved one-on-one time, but it didn't change the fact that he argued through every moment of every day. The conflict was just his normal state.

We wondered if he was on the spectrum, anxious, or depressed. I even googled "sociopathic symptoms in children" because I thought something was wrong. Kids aren't supposed to be this hard. Eight-year-olds aren't supposed to wish their mommies were dead just because they can't have a Laffy Taffy before dinner.

When we finally got a diagnosis, I didn't know what to feel. I wanted an easy answer, a quick fix. Instead, I got a label saying, "Yep, your kid is mean, and I know you're tired, but now you're going to have to work hard to improve this."

If ODD isn't tackled when kids are young, it can turn into "conduct disorder," where things get really serious. These kids might do things like start fires or commit crimes. Thankfully, intense therapy, CBT, and coaching for parents can help before it gets that far.

It's going to be a long journey. But we're here for him every step of the way because we love him. And when it comes down to it, all we want is for him to be happy.

One of our therapists once told us that our kids choose us for a reason. I think about that a lot. Maybe Johnny chose us so he could teach us patience, understanding, and unconditional love. Somewhere inside all that defiance is a little boy who loves us and wants to be good. We just have to help him get there.

Understanding the Cycle: Thoughts, Emotions, and Behaviors

Our thoughts are like scripts running in the background of our minds, shaping how we perceive and interpret the world. When thoughts take a negative turn, they trigger a chain reaction affecting both our emotions and behaviors. For instance, constant pessimistic thoughts about an upcoming event can lead to feelings of anxiety or dread.

Emotions, on the other hand, send signals about what's happening around us and how we feel about it. You can think of emotions as traffic lights. Some lights are bright and happy, like yellow for joy or green for excitement. Others might be a bit darker, like red for anger or blue for sadness. Just like traffic lights, emotions can change quickly, depending on what's going on. For example, seeing a delicious cake might raise a yellow "joy" flag, but if someone else takes a bite, it could turn into a red "anger" flag.

Now, ODD kids sometimes have a lot of red "anger" lights, even when things seem calm. It's like their city has a lot of sirens and honking horns, making it hard to see the other lights. This can be confusing and frustrating for everyone, including the kid. Behaviors are the visible outcomes of these thoughts and emotions. They include our actions, reactions, and the way we interact with the world. Negative thoughts and emotions often manifest in behaviors that reflect this negativity. For example, a child with anxious thoughts might avoid social situations, while a child with optimistic thoughts will engage more openly with others.

To break the cycle, you have to identify and challenge negative thinking patterns, also known as cognitive distortions. Recognizing these patterns is the first step towards helping your child regain control over their mental well-being. One such pattern is catastrophizing, which involves magnifying the importance of negative events and expecting the worst possible outcomes (for instance, imagining a minor mistake on homework or a school project will lead to getting an F in the subject).

Another pattern you may notice is all-or-nothing thinking. In this case, your child tends to see situations in black-and-white terms without acknowledging gray areas. You might also notice overgeneralization, which involves sweeping conclusions based on limited evidence (for instance, assuming that one rejection in a social setting means they will never make friends).

Helping Your Child Reframe Their Thinking

CBT is a therapeutic approach that targets unhelpful thinking patterns and behaviors, equipping your child with all they need for emotional and behavioral regulation. It involves not only the child but also you, the parent, as active participants in the therapeutic journey. In therapy sessions, strategies are not only taught to the child but also shared with parents. This includes effective ways to manage your child's behavior, improve family communication, and establish clear and consistent boundaries. Your involvement enhances the likelihood of lasting improvements in your child's behavior and overall well-being.

Research has consistently shown the significant benefits of CBT for children with ODD (Conner *et al.*, 2013). Not only does it improve behavior, but it also positively influences academic performance and social functioning. Additionally, CBT contributes to a reduction in symptoms of co-occurring conditions such as depression and anxiety.

One important part of CBT is the process of cognitive restructuring and overcoming negative thoughts. Your child will learn to identify and replace negative thought patterns with positive and realistic alternatives. But you also have to be part of this, as active participation from both the child and the parent is needed. These interventions involve real-time identification and questioning of negative thoughts. Your presence is bound to be a good booster for the whole process.

CBT for ODD often incorporates relaxation techniques and mindfulness strategies. These tools help your child reduce anxiety, develop self-regulation skills, and become more aware of their thoughts and emotions. Techniques like deep breathing and guided imagery can be practiced at home, contributing to a more positive and constructive mindset. CBT treatment for ODD has yielded success stories, illustrating the transformative impact on children's lives. Common outcomes include improved academic and social functioning, enhanced problem-solving skills, and reduced defiant behaviors.

Taking Action for Change

Let's get to the real deal: How can you apply CBT principles with your child to enhance their well-being? You can start by being fully aware of what principles your child needs. Look for resources about anxiety and understand your child's specific triggers and fears. You don't have to read in order to become an expert—just to discover and gain insights that will help you build a bridge to understand your child.

Next up, set achievable goals together. Think of it as mapping a course together—not a rigid plan your child has to follow, but something you both agree on, something workable. Work side by side with your child to identify areas where they need to get better. These goals, small and attainable, will help you set milestones to monitor and celebrate progress your child has made.

You can also help your child to be more self-aware. This will help them become more aware of their thoughts, emotions, and behavior. Reflection and journaling can be really helpful for them, and for you also. Talk at length with them; go over their actions and why they did what they did. You can also encourage them to share their thoughts about certain situations. This way, you can know what's on their mind and how you can be of help in reframing those thoughts.

To do that, you can help them shift their thinking through cognitive restructuring. Instead of reeling out instructions on what to do and what not to do, you can make use of storytelling. Confront negative thoughts together, as if you are both co-authors reshaping a plot. For example, if your child is thinking of taking revenge by beating up someone who bullied them in school, you can reframe the thought by retelling the story. Encourage them to write out their emotions and report the bully to their teachers at school rather than take out their pain physically on someone else.

You both need coping skills. You can make use of positive affirmations and self-calming techniques. Practice together, not as a bossy figure but as a friend, a loving parent willing to help their child. Examples of these positive affirmations for you:

- I am strong and capable of supporting my child through this challenge.
- My love and patience make a difference in my child's life.
- We are a team, working together to overcome ODD.

- I accept my child for who they are, even when it's tough.

- I trust my own intuition and seek guidance when needed.

- I need to take care of myself so I can care for my child.

- Hope and progress are possible, even on difficult days.

- I celebrate my child's victories, big and small.

And for your child:

- I am learning to manage my emotions better.

- It's okay to feel angry sometimes, but I can choose how to react.

- I am braver than I think, and I can face my fears.

- I am capable of making good choices, even when it's hard.

- I can calm my body and mind when I feel overwhelmed.

- I am a kind and loving person.

- I can communicate my needs and feelings clearly.

- I am proud of myself for trying my best.

- I am worthy of love and happiness, no matter what.

For you both:

- We are in this together, and we will support each other.

- Our family is stronger in spite of what we go through.

- Every day is a new opportunity for progress and growth.

- We believe in each other and our ability to overcome anything.

- We have love and patience to build a brighter future together.

CBT Techniques and Applications

I'll go on to discuss some key CBT techniques and applications here that will be beneficial to you and your child. One of them is exposure and response prevention (ERP). ERP is a gradual training program that helps your child handle situations where they tend to be impulsive and hyperactive. To teach this skill, you have to start by identifying specific situations triggering impulsivity or hyperactivity. Once you have been able to pick out these triggers, work with your child's therapist to expose your child gradually to these triggers in a controlled manner. This will help your child practice coping strategies in a safe setting.

Another technique is behavioral experimentation. This involves testing out different ways of doing things to see what positively influences your child's behavior. For instance, you try different routines, use positive rewards, or establish consistent consequences to gauge their impact on your child's behavior. Keep a record to identify successful strategies.

Next up is problem-solving skills. This is for both you and your child, as it will empower you both to work together in identifying and solving issues associated with ODD. Some of these issues may include academic difficulties, emotional and social challenges, daily living challenges, and mental health concerns. You can have an open discussion with your child to pinpoint specific issues they may be dealing with. Work with them, as well as their therapist, to look for potential solutions and evaluate their effectiveness. Ensure that you provide an avenue where your child feels comfortable sharing their thoughts and feelings.

In addition, you can establish a system where your kid earns points or tokens for positive behaviors, cooperation, and following rules. These tokens can be redeemed for certain privileges like ice cream or 30 minutes of extra screen time, providing positive reinforcement for desired behaviors.

Then you can gradually increase the complexity of expected behaviors and adjust the reward system as needed to maintain their motivation.

In guided discovery, you work with your child to learn about their point of view concerning a situation. You can probe them with questions so they can challenge and extend their perspectives. You can even tell them to provide evidence to support and refute their point of view. For example, you can ask them what they feel should be the expected response for not getting their favorite cereal. Then probe and guide them gently until they arrive at the correct conclusions. During the process, they will learn to see things from other angles, particularly ones they may not have considered before.

You can also introduce them to journaling and thought records. Writing is a way of getting in touch with your own thoughts. We tend to think more clearly when we put our thoughts into words. You can ask your child to list negative thoughts they experienced during the day, as well as positive thoughts that they can choose instead. Another writing exercise can be to keep track of new thoughts and behaviors they practice. Putting these things down in writing will help them see how far they have come.

Identifying Triggers and Early Warning Signs

Understanding triggers allows you to anticipate potential challenges and intervene before the situation escalates into an outburst or negative reaction. This proactive approach can prevent tantrums, meltdowns, or harmful behaviors and create a more peaceful environment for everyone involved.

Early warning signs also give you a clue as to your child's emotional state. Recognizing physical sensations, emotional shifts, or negative thought patterns makes it easier to help them regulate their emotions before they become overwhelming. This is because knowing what triggers your child can help you develop specific de-escalation strategies tailored to address those triggers. This might involve removing them from the situation, providing calming tools like deep breathing exercises, or offering support and reassurance. A plan can prevent situations from spiraling out of control and promote effective conflict resolution.

By understanding and proactively addressing triggers, you're not just managing immediate situations but laying the foundation for long-term emotional well-being. As children learn to identify and manage their triggers, they develop healthy coping mechanisms, emotional regulation skills, and self-awareness that benefit them throughout their lives.

To identify these triggers, you can work with your child to identify specific situations, people, or even certain thoughts that seem to bring out the worst in them. Keep a "trigger log" to track patterns and identify common themes. Sometimes, underlying emotions like frustration, anxiety, or sadness can act as triggers. Observe your child's behavior and see what emotions might be bubbling beneath the surface. Teach your child to become aware of their inner dialogue. Help them identify negative thought patterns like "I can't do this" or "They're always picking on me" that can fuel their emotions and lead to challenging behaviors.

Before an outburst, your child might experience physical signs like increased heart rate, sweating, or clenched fists. Teach them to pick these as warning signs and take a moment to breathe or use a coping mechanism. Also, emotional changes like sudden irritation, frustration, or withdrawal can signal impending trouble. Encourage your child to communicate these shifts and talk to you or any other trusted adult around before things escalate.

Once you have mapped out some of these triggers, you can develop a "go-to" strategy for your child when they encounter a trigger. This could involve taking a break, removing themselves from the situation, or engaging in calming activities like deep breathing or mindfulness. You can also teach your child various coping mechanisms like journaling (I talked about that already), listening to music, or doing a physical workout to help them manage their emotions and avoid outbursts.

Communication is key. Encourage open communication and provide your child a safe space to express their feelings and concerns. This might mean more listening and hugging and less yelling and name-calling. This will help you to offer support and intervene before emotions escalate.

Developing Positive Coping Mechanisms

While CBT helps you manage challenging and difficult behaviors, it's equally important to cultivate positive coping mechanisms that act as life rafts, keeping your child afloat in rough waters. One coping mechanism I love is to encourage creative outlets like drawing, painting, or playing music to express emotions and channel stress.

Physical activities like dancing, swimming, or playing sports can also help to manage anxiety and release pent-up energy. Let your child find their groove, and you can join in the fun. Spending time outside, whether walking in the park, gardening, or simply sitting under a tree, can have a profound calming effect. So, you can imagine how effective outdoor physical activities can be.

Please help your child identify their individual strengths and interests. Whether it's building robots, playing chess, or writing stories, these passions can also help them develop a sense of purpose and accomplishment. Encourage positive social interactions with friends and family. Participating in group activities, clubs, or sports can provide a sense of belonging and support while teaching valuable social skills and conflict-resolution strategies. So, a good baseball game can help, whether it's your child playing or you both watching others play.

It's best to also prioritize healthy sleep. Sleeping well has been proven to help with emotional regulation and overall well-being. Establish consistent sleep routines, create a calming environment, and limit screen time before bed. Rather than letting them be on their phone till they fall asleep, you can encourage your child to write in their journal or read a book.

Aside from sleeping well, eating well also helps. Nourishing your child with balanced meals and healthy snacks provides the energy and nutrients needed to manage stress and regulate emotions. Also, as we've already noted, regular physical activity (e.g., a brisk walk or a quick dance break) can help your child's physical and mental health. You can encourage your child to find activities they enjoy and make movement a part of their daily routine.

I need to point out that your child's emotional well-being is intertwined with your own mental health. Prioritize your own well-being by asking for help from friends, family, or a therapist whenever you need to. You can also practice self-care activities like taking a long bath, watching your favorite movie, indulging in your favorite snack, or going for a pedicure. A healthy and supported parent is better equipped to provide the guidance and support their child needs.

Sustaining Motivation

First, it's important to acknowledge that setbacks and disappointments are inevitable. Instead of seeing them as failures, you can help children reframe them as learning opportunities. By openly discussing these challenges and highlighting how they can employ their coping skills, you can plant the seeds of resilience and teach them that growth often comes from facing obstacles head-on. Cultivating a growth mindset through affirmations like "I'm learning and growing every day" can help them view challenges as stepping stones rather than roadblocks.

But resilience alone isn't enough. Keeping the fire of motivation burning requires a clear vision of the future. Help your child visualize their long-term goals, the positive impact of managing their behaviors, and the fulfilling life that awaits them. Having a vision board or written aspirations to revisit can constantly remind them of their "why" and fuel their determination to keep moving forward.

Of course, celebrating progress along the way is key to sustaining motivation. Don't wait for monumental achievements to throw a party! Even small victories deserve recognition, whether mastering a new coping skill, handling a challenging situation with wisdom, or simply making consistent strides toward their goals. Regularly revisiting and acknowledging their progress is a powerful reinforcer, showcasing their efforts and inspiring them to keep climbing.

But extrinsic rewards like trophies or treats, while initially effective, can eventually become hollow motivators. Instead, focus on intrinsic rewards that come from within. Help children build pride in their self-improvement, the joy of mastering new skills, and the satisfaction of building stronger relationships. These internal rewards offer a more sustainable source of motivation that keeps them on track even when external incentives fade.

Self-compassion and self-celebration are just as important as external recognition. Encourage children to pat themselves on the back for their efforts and acknowledge their own growth. Building a foundation of internal validation empowers them to be their own cheerleaders, propelling them forward on their journey of positive change.

Workbook 4

1. Understanding the Cycle: Thoughts, Emotions, and Behaviors

In your own words, explain how thoughts, emotions, and behaviors are interconnected.

_____

_____

_____

_____

_____

Share a story or example of a time when your thoughts affected how you felt and acted.

_____

_____

_____

_____

_____

2. Helping Your Child Reframe Their Thinking

Name some negative thoughts your child might have, and let's brainstorm positive alternatives. I started with two already.

Negative Thought Patterns   Positive Alternatives

Catastrophizing   [ ] Challenge and reframe

All-or-nothing thinking   [ ] Find a middle ground

3. Taking Action for Change

What's one specific behavior you want to work with your child on?

[ ] Procrastination [ ] Impulsivity [ ] Other: _____

List three simple steps your child can take to start making a positive change.

1._____

2._____

3._____

4. CBT Techniques and Applications

Look up and write down the names of three CBT techniques.

1._____

2._____

3._____

Think about how these techniques can be used in real-life situations. Describe one situation for each technique.

1._____

2._____

3._____

5. Sustaining Motivation

What encourages your child to make positive changes? List at least two factors.

[ ] Recognition from family [ ] Personal achievements [ ]

1._____

2._____

Define achievable short-term and long-term goals related to the positive changes your child wants to make.

Short-term goal: _____

Long-term goal: _____

Key Takeaways

- As children learn to identify and manage their triggers, they develop healthy coping mechanisms, emotional regulation skills, and self-awareness that benefit them throughout their lives.

- Research has consistently shown the significant benefits of CBT for children with ODD (Conner et al., 2013). Not only does it improve behavior, but it also positively influences academic performance and social functioning.

- To break the cycle, you have to identify and challenge negative thinking patterns, also known as cognitive distortions. Recognizing these patterns is the first step towards helping your child regain control over their mental well-being.

- Our thoughts are like scripts running in the background of our minds, shaping how we perceive and interpret the world. When thoughts take a negative turn, they trigger a chain reaction affecting both our emotions and behaviors.

CHAPTER 5

The Emotional Rollercoaster

"Keep your heart with all diligence, For out of it spring the issues of life."

—Proverbs 4:23 (NKFV)

"If we can't laugh at ourselves, do we have the right to laugh at others?"

—C. H. Hamel

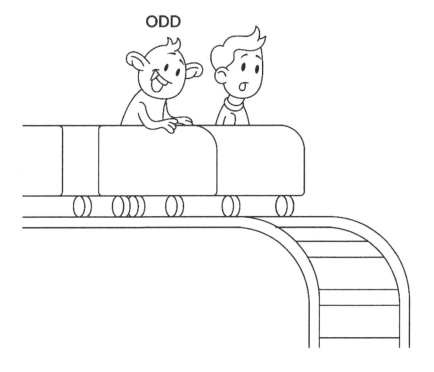

"Ooh, this is my favourite part: 'Tantrum Tumble'!"

Developing Emotional Intelligence

E very morning, before heading to the middle school where she teaches, Ms. Mitchell considers how her feelings will affect her students and her teaching.

When she feels frustrated or overwhelmed before arriving at school, she takes a few deep breaths and works towards managing her emotions so she can fully engage with her pupils and colleagues. As the kids arrive, you'll find her welcoming children as they walk through the door, asking each how they're feeling *today*.

Back in the classroom, Ms. Mitchell asks students to use a classroom mood meter to indicate their feelings all through the day. She uses this mood meter as a teaching aid to teach about feelings, the feelings of book characters, and how emotions change throughout a story.

These and more are many ways that Ms. Mitchell models emotional intelligence (otherwise known as emotional quotient or EQ) and supports its development in her students.

The Role of Emotions in ODD

I touched briefly on the need for emotional intelligence while describing the need for empathy in the last chapter. However, this chapter will take us on a deep dive as I show you how to cultivate emotional intelligence in children with ODD.

What roles do emotions play in ODD? How do parents help children with ODD improve their EQ and better regulate their emotions? Are there any practical ideas to help children improve their EQ without seeing a specialist?

Get ready for all-around answers to these questions and more as you walk your child through the emotional rollercoaster of nurturing children with ODD.

ODD symptoms include anger, tantrums, intense fear, vindictiveness, revenge, and other strong feelings; it's apparent why a child's emotional intelligence is critical in managing the behavioral disorder.

Now hold on to your hat—we're going to take a tour through various unconnected studies on the relationship between emotional regulation and ODD symptoms in children and adolescents, plus why emotional regulation might be the ultimate solution to helping kids improve their frequent disruptive behaviors.

Emotional Regulation in Children with ODD

Children and adolescents with ODD tend to think rigidly, simplistically, and reactively. For many of these children, emotions appear uncontrollable or entirely absent. Ultimately, their emotions peak in acts of aggression or defiance against people around them, particularly authority figures.

Researchers agree that ODD is common among children who have challenges regulating their emotions and that teaching a child to regulate their emotions can reduce symptoms of ODD in them.

Other studies show that children with ODD commonly experience unregulated emotions like temper tantrums, intense fear, inconsolable despair, low tolerance for frustration, and challenges with feeling and expressing their emotions.

But a child's ability to regulate their emotions also spans into many other domains of life. Various research has shown that a child's emotional regulation can affect their:

- mental health;

- physical health;

- social and interpersonal functioning;

- relationships with others; and

- overall well-being.

Emotional regulation may be the most important process in social interactions because it directly impacts how children interact socially and emotionally with others.

Other studies conclude that children with better emotion regulation skills tend to demonstrate higher social competence and peer status, more prosocial behavior, and better quality of relationships compared to others with lesser abilities.

The bottom line of all these for parents with children who display ODD behavior?

One of the best ways to help your child get out of disruptive behavior, no matter how young or old, is teaching them emotional intelligence.

Teaching Emotional Intelligence

Emotional intelligence is best developed during people's formative years at school and home. This is where we tend to build a solid foundation for future habits they're likely to take on later in life.

The term "emotional intelligence" was popularized by a journalist, Daniel Goleman, in the mid-1990s via his book *Emotional Intelligence: Why It Can Matter More Than IQ.*

The book's claim that emotional intelligence is more important than IQ remains a major debate topic among psychologists. What is clear, however, is that EQ can affect a child's social and emotional relationships—and possibly how well they perform at school.

On a broad scale, emotional intelligence is said to cover five main areas:

- Self-awareness
- Emotional control
- Self-motivation
- Empathy
- Relationship skills

But before I show you various tips on how to help your child become more self-aware, self-motivated, and relate empathically with others, let's see what emotional intelligence in children looks like.

A child's EQ is how they:

- Become aware, first of their feelings, and then of others' emotions.
- Recognize, identify, or perceive emotions. It includes what they perceive as a feeling, body language, facial expression, and tone of voice. They learn to attribute these signs to others, eventually labeling them as happy, angry, sad, excited, etc.
- Describe feelings, name their emotions, or learn to use emotional vocabulary to communicate how they feel.

- Empathize with how others feel, which eventually extends to feeling concerned or sympathetic for other people.

- Control and manage their emotions by learning and applying their knowledge of when it's suitable to act or react to events.

- Understand what causes feelings (both in themselves and others).

- Understand links between emotions and behaviors (for instance, Mom hit the steering wheel because she's very displeased).

How Teaching EQ to a Child Relates to Your Parenting Style

Here are a few things to note about how teaching EQ to your child can affect your parenting style.

- Your child can and will learn about EQ by observing you and other older people around them.

- Parenting practices and behaviors play a significant role in modeling behaviors and teaching them to children.

- Families create emotional climates for their children. This includes how (or if) they express their emotions. These emotional climates in the home can either be conducive or harmful to the child's emotional development.

Having seen how your home and parenting style could help your child become more emotionally intelligent, how about we look at some active ways to teach (and model) EQ to them?

1. Help Your Child Build an Emotional Vocabulary (Positive and Negative)

Kids throw tantrums because they have poor emotional self-regulation skills. They often don't have the right language to help them articulate their feelings in the heat of the moment.

However, being able to identify and articulate their feel-good and not-so-good feelings is important for at least two reasons:

- When things go south and they start behaving irrationally or in a way that's beyond your understanding, you won't be in the dark about what they're going through.

- The more robust a child's emotional vocabulary is, the more empowered they feel.

So whether your child is feeling excited, happy, curious, or furious, it won't be a mystery to you, as they'll be able to tell you exactly how they feel and what might be tinkering with their feelings.

2. Communicate the Difference between Emotion and Behavior

You can expect your child to, at one time or another, experience some extreme emotions. But the coach in you has to emerge when they're acting on these emotions.

Children who can work through their big feelings and solve challenges are less likely to suffer from anxiety, depression, and other mental health issues. Teaching your child to manage emotional conflicts will impart an emotional skill to them.

It's fine for Bob to feel angry that you didn't buy him the chocolate, but tearing up his school textbook is the wrong way to channel his anger.

Of course, this won't be an overnight process. And it'll cost you a truckload of patience. However, the reward is worth more than every tantrum or argument you might have with them along the way.

3. Reframe "Negative" Emotions into an Opportunity to Connect with Them

Parents have to do lots of "unlearning" on how they've managed their own emotions to help their kids better self-regulate their emotions.

For instance, adults have learned to either bury negative feelings, sweep them under the rug, or lash out in ways that hurt others.

But when kids display strong emotions, parents would do well to create time to address these emotions rather than blindly dismissing them. Listen actively to what your child is saying during those moments, and seek to validate their emotions (not their disruptive behaviors).

Remember to always create an atmosphere in the home where your child never feels they're putting you out by having big emotions or acting on them. Of course, they won't always be wrong.

4. Play Helpful EQ Games

This method might be unlike others in this list, but it's helped several children move up the EQ chart.

Games that help children boost their emotional intelligence include "Simon Says," self-awareness cards, and other EQ skills cards. These games are designed to help children train their brains to recognize their feelings.

5. Create and Model Healthy Coping Mechanisms

Your child will likely watch you go through various high and low moments, managing various moods as they arise daily.

How do you, for instance, cope with and manage your own emotions, particularly the negative ones? What do you do when you're stressed? How do you deal with anger, frustration, or pain?

Your kids will likely model similar behavior when handling their own emotions, especially as they watch you in their formative years. Parents have no better time than the present to start creating some healthy coping skills for their little ones.

Wondering how to go about this?

Take your child out to get some exercise. Moving your limbs helps to ramp up the endorphins. Additionally, being active with your child is an exciting chance for both of you to let off some steam.

Otherwise, consider taking your child out to see nature. Sightseeing in nature can help you and your child alleviate stress and redirect their negative emotions.

When you can, take them out to a place where your child will also feel safe (apart from home), take a few deep breaths, and process their emotions before they're ready to communicate their feelings with you.

6. Accept Mistakes and Evolve

The journey of raising an emotionally intelligent child is filled with various ups and downs. It won't be perfect, and the earlier you accept this, the easier your process will be.

Your child is likely to display some explosive behavior, and you'll sometimes lose your patience. It's perfectly fine. Parenting doesn't have to be perfect. Give yourself some space for a few mistakes. And give your child a similar leniency.

Learn something from each mistake and ensure that you do something different the next time around.

Three Signs Your Child Is Learning Emotional Intelligence

How do we know that a child is becoming more emotionally intelligent? Let's examine three of the many potential signs of this.

1. They Readily Express Themselves

Now, this has little to nothing to do with a child's temperament. Even very quiet children will express their emotions in noticeable ways. While extroverted kids may be more verbal, introverted children might rather write, draw, or even sing about their feelings.

Sometimes, these expressions can happen so stealthily that you may not easily notice them in your child. But all kids with some level of emotional intelligence have a way (or a couple of ways) that they express their emotions.

2. They Listen to Others More

Here's another major sign that your child is improving their EQ. Suppose Kim and Rose, who are both 10 years old, are neighbors who are learning to become more emotionally intelligent. Here's what a conversation between them might look like initially.

Kim: "I have a big cat."

Rose could reply with something completely unrelated or self-focused, like, "My mom has a big restaurant."

As both kids develop their emotional intelligence, their conversation might turn out to become something like,

Kim: "I have a big cat."

Rose: "What's its name?" or "What color is its fur?"

As kids grow, they'll start to listen more actively to others and respond in emotionally appropriate ways.

In a related example, Rose might tell Kim that she's happy about visiting her mom's store after school, and Kim might be happy for her.

3. They Self-Regulate

Soon, you might notice that your child is taking some time to process their feelings. This can often be a slow process compared to your expectations, but it's a big step of improvement. So if you notice your child taking deep breaths where she might previously have spontaneously reacted angrily, you might acknowledge their behavior as showing traits of emotional intelligence.

Empathy Development

There's a saying that goes like this: "Walk a mile in someone else's shoes before you judge or criticize them."

This quote teaches empathy.

Empathy is the ability to be aware of others' feelings and imagine what it might feel like to be in their position (or shoes).

It's a key ingredient for building positive friendships and relationships. It reduces conflict and misunderstandings while leading to helping behaviors, kindness, and even greater success in life.

Thankfully, you can teach ANY child (regardless of their current emotional disposition) to develop empathy for others.

However, since children's cognitive abilities and life experiences develop over time, the most effective strategies to help children develop their emotions will depend on their age.

Let's look at some key strategies (with activities based on age) that can help parents and teachers teach children with ODD empathy.

Developing Empathy in Children Aged 3-5 Years

A child's abilities grow during their preschool years. This period is also the right time for them to master listening skills, understand different feelings, respond to others' feelings accordingly, and develop friendships.

Preschoolers also increase their moral awareness about fairness, as they can already better imagine how it feels to be the other person (compared to toddlers). However, although they know everyone has emotions, preschoolers are still developing in terms of how they react to the pains and difficulties of others.

This is why they may sometimes respond with inappropriate reactions, like nervous laughter or giggles, when someone hurts themselves. Gently reminding your preschooler how it might feel to be hurt and what they can say to help can teach them emotional intelligence.

For instance, suppose Jacques broke his toy unintentionally. It could help to ask 4-year-old Tina a question like, "Tina, how do we help Jacques feel better about his toy breaking?" Tina is likely to walk through Jacques' feelings and, possibly, suggest a way to cheer him up.

Developing Empathy in Children Aged 5-7 Years

As your child grows older, their cognitive abilities and moral awareness grow. They're also more capable of learning through games and more complicated conversations.

Let's check out some ideas on how to teach your older children to develop empathy and become less hurtful, vengeful, or vindictive in their relationships with others.

1. Use Visuals

Visuals can help teach a child to recognize various emotions and react appropriately to them, especially if your child has difficulty recognizing or labeling emotions.

Print out pictures from online that show happy, sad, or angry faces. It can also help to create more complex emotions like embarrassment, fear, disappointment, frustration, etc.

While showing your child pictures that show how people feel, it can help to ask about moments when they felt similarly. You could also provide similar examples from your life, teaching them that you understand how it feels to be in such situations—and that it's normal.

2. Embrace Diversity

A leading component of empathy is respecting people from different backgrounds. Allow your child to play with children of different races, backgrounds, sexes, ability levels, ages, etc. (of course, under moderate supervision).

You can also read books to them or watch shows that feature children with different backgrounds from your child. These materials can help the child concentrate on traits they share with others.

3. Teach Healthy Limits and Boundaries

Being compassionate doesn't mean your child should take on the problems of everyone else around them. Neither does it mean saying 'yes' or dropping their entire schedule to help others.

Teach your kids to understand and respect their boundaries and needs. For instance, if a child gives an unwanted hug, you can teach them to say, "I don't like that. Please don't touch me." Or, if another child calls your child the wrong name, teach them to say, "My name is… Call me … instead."

It can also help to teach your children that helping others shouldn't involve breaking any rules or doing anything they aren't comfortable with.

Lastly, respect your child's boundaries. If your child doesn't like to be picked up and thrown in the air, don't push it. You can say, "I understand you don't like me throwing you in the air. I won't do it again." By doing so, you model the way your child should expect others to behave when they say no.

Developing Empathy in Children Aged 7-11 Years

At this stage, your child can now read more advanced books and engage in high-level discussions about what the book's characters think, feel, want, or believe.

In one study, 110 children (aged 7 years) were enrolled in a reading program. The program randomly divided the students into two groups; the first group would engage in conversations about the emotional content of the stories, while the others would only produce sketch drawings about the stories.

After two months, the children in the conversation group demonstrated a greater development in emotion comprehension, empathy, and the theory of the mind. These positive results remained stable for six months.

Consider reading books with your children that are directly related to empathy. Ensure your children also read on their own and engage them in discussions about the feelings of the characters. Probe into how your kids could react in similar situations.

Besides reading helpful books that stir your child's emotions, engaging your child in cooperative discussions can go a long way in making them more compassionate.

Various unconnected studies have shown that successful experiences cooperating with others encourage us to cooperate in the future. You could encourage your child to engage in debates and discussions that teach them to consider others' perspectives.

Cooperative board games or activities like Legos, Stone Soup, Outfoxed, and The Secret Door can help your child spend constructive time with their siblings and peers.

And if your child seems to develop an interest in acting?

Get them involved in theater or acting classes. Stepping into someone else's role as many times as possible can increasingly help them build empathy. Similarly, young children tend to develop understanding and compassion for others as they play pretend or engage in similar activities.

Developing Empathy in Children Aged 12+ Years

At this age, your child is ripe to hold discussions with you about current events and develop empathy by reading newspapers and news magazines, or watching the news.

Suppose you hear about a hurricane raging in some part of the country or the world. It might help to ask questions like:

"How might the people involved in this situation feel?" "How would we feel if the hurricane occurred in our state?" "Is there anything we can do to help?"

You can also encourage your child to volunteer at something they're passionate about. Encourage them if they want to start a project or charitable organization to solve problems they feel strongly about.

What's important is that you let your kids explore the world beyond themselves while adding value to the community.

Remember 15-year-old L's story that I shared with you in this book's opening chapter?

Her family could have helped hasten her recovery from ODD behavior by encouraging her love for animals and requesting that she formally volunteer for an animal sanctuary, rather than create one in the home!

Most importantly, besides all the tricks and strategies I've shared for each age group, modeling empathy is very important. That could include offering caring gestures to others, such as a hug, listening attentively, or letting your child know you care when they're hurt or upset.

Breathing Exercises and Mindfulness

Various neuroscience studies have shown that breathing exercises and mindfulness can help people manage various issues like:

- Anxiety
- Depression
- Chronic pain
- Stress
- Trauma or post-traumatic stress disorder (PTSD)
- Difficulty focusing

Mindfulness is paying attention to what's happening around you. It often pairs with simple tasks people tend to gloss over in their daily lives, such as moving, eating, and, of course, breathing.

When connected with various daily tasks and routine body functions, mindfulness may help people decrease stress, improve their mood by strengthening their focus on the present, and allow them to feel less scattered about things or stuck in the past or future.

What's the Link between Mindfulness and Breathing?

Breathing is, well, getting air into and out of your lungs.

But mindful breathing? Mindful breathing is as easy as it sounds— allowing you to be mindful or present while breathing.

According to a 2017 study, mindful breathing helped autistic people reduce anxiety and depression. Another study discovered that mindful breathing helped people with borderline personality disorder (BPD) reduce feelings of shame.

Other research has shown that people who practice mindful breathing before performing a task make fewer mistakes. According to the researchers, this is because mindful breathing increases brain activity connected with tracking errors.

How to Practice Mindful Breathing with Your Child

The tips I will show you here are helpful for both adults and children. While I'll primarily speak to you, the parent, in this section, you can readily apply these exercises to your child as well.

Remember, the emotional health of you and your child is important if you intend to successfully lead your child and family out of the challenging circumstances that come with ODD.

The easiest way to do mindful breathing is to concentrate on inhaling and exhaling. While you can do this while standing, it's ideal to lie in a comfortable position.

Your eyes might be open or closed; you can maintain a soft gaze with your eyes partially closed without concentrating on anything in particular. While you can set a designated time for the exercise, it's helpful to practice it when you feel stressed or anxious.

Experts believe that regularly practicing mindful breathing can make it easier to do in difficult situations.

When trying to calm yourself in stressful moments, it can help to begin with taking an exaggerated breath by:

- Inhaling deeply through your nostrils for 3 seconds
- Holding your breath for 2 seconds
- Exhaling through your mouth for 4 seconds

Observe each breath without attempting to adjust it. While doing this, you may find your mind wandering or distracted by thoughts or bodily sensations. That's perfectly fine and normal. Once you notice, work towards bringing your attention back to your breathing exercise.

Breathing in this way, even for a minute or two, can help eliminate distraction, release negative thoughts, improve self-awareness, and quiet a racing mind. The more you practice this, the easier it gets, and the more you start noticing its benefits in your daily life.

Counting Your Way Out of Stress and Anxiety

Breath counting is a similar mindful breathing technique that can help you in the process. You might discover that it's amazingly difficult to maintain focus on the breath, but by counting them, you can stay on each breath.

Counting your breaths takes you out of thought loops that feed stress, anxiety, or other negative emotions.

Cognitive Behavioral Strategies for Kids

Cognitive behavioral therapy (CBT) is an effective treatment for many mental health disorders and can be useful for children starting from age six.

Common applications of CBT include mental health problems like:

- Anxiety
- Depression
- Social anxiety
- Panic attacks
- Attention deficit hyperactivity disorder (ADHD)
- Obsessive-compulsive disorder (OCD)
- Trauma and post-traumatic stress disorder (PTSD)
- Anxiety with autism spectrum disorder
- Mood disorders
- Eating disorders
- Insomnia

CBT observes our thoughts, emotions, and behaviors and how they're shaped by our own preconceived notions and the environment. CBT aims to help us learn to recognize illogical thought patterns that lead to negative behavioral outcomes and create new, logical thought patterns as replacements.

CBT therapists use various behavioral modification techniques to empower clients and give them lifelong tools they can use to manage mental health symptoms.

What Is CBT?

CBT is a form of talk therapy that helps people recognize unhelpful behaviors and thoughts while they learn to improve them. Therapy helps patients concentrate on the present and the future rather than the past.

But CBT is much more than just talk. Therapists will work to provide tangible ways for your child to exercise self-control and empower themselves. They will also teach your child skills they can put into practice immediately.

CBT is often provided alone, or in combination with medications or any other therapies your child might need. Lastly, the therapy is also helpful in treating behavioral disorders like ODD and helping patients improve specific symptoms.

Let's see some common CBT techniques to help your child relax better and overcome ODD symptoms.

Common CBT Techniques

CBT may teach your child any or all of the following techniques:

- Relaxation techniques to calm the body
- Journaling to track worries from home

- Mindfulness or grounding skills to focus attention during stress periods

- Practicing "cognitive restructuring" to transform unhelpful worries

- Using role-play to practice skills

- Experimenting in real life to test if their fears really come true

Explaining CBT to Kids

Explaining CBT to younger children is best done in simple terms. Some therapists use worksheets to help children visualize certain concepts toward better emotional management.

For instance, a worksheet may include drawings with blank thought bubbles that kids have to fill out. The therapist might ask the child what the person in the picture is thinking about.

These worksheets may also include stop signs to help the child recognize that they're about to go off on a tangent. Worksheets can help children and adolescents understand the connection between thoughts, feelings, and actions. They can also help children solidify what they've learned.

Lastly, CBT for children may involve checklists, planners, or a reward chart to help children remember and complete their tasks.

Finding the Right CBT for a Child

Although there are many therapists trained in CBT, it's important to look for one with enough experience working with kids. Here are some things to look out for when finding a CBT therapist for your child.

- Check their credentials: Search for a licensed counselor, family therapist, clinical social worker, psychologist, or psychiatrist. Licensure shows a professional is legally qualified to practice in your state.

- Experience: Search for a professional who has worked with kids or adolescents.

- Transparency: Look for a professional willing to state goals and offer a treatment plan after an initial assessment or session with you and your child.

Art and Play Therapy

If you have ever been to children's museums in cities like Washington D.C., Indianapolis, or Houston, you may have marveled at the astounding amount of activities available on site. They have a seemingly unending variety of activities and creative toys for kids of all ages.

Play is fun and enjoyable. But even more important, play has therapeutic effects. It helps us relieve stress and boredom and connects us with others in positive ways. Its therapeutic effects also regulates emotions, inspires creative thinking and exploration, and helps to boost a child's self-esteem.

This therapeutic effect of play makes it an attractive instrument for child therapy in treating various behavioral disorders like ODD.

Let's see what art and play therapy means and what to expect during a session.

What Art and Play Therapy Means

Children, especially toddlers and preschoolers, don't always have the ability to express issues troubling them. Besides the challenge of lacking the verbal skills to describe their feelings, children sometimes just don't know exactly how they feel—or simply feel unsafe to speak up about their deep-rooted emotions.

Regardless of the situation with your child, art and play therapy can help them overcome their obstacles because it builds on the natural way children learn and express themselves: playing and being creative. It provides a safe emotional distance from their challenges and can help bring suppressed feelings to the surface.

This then allows the therapist and parents to gain a better understanding of the child's inner world.

How Art and Play Therapy Benefits Your Kid

Art and play therapy is helpful in:

- Healing from past stressful and traumatic experiences: Therapy helps children to make sense of these events, cope and adjust to their current situation, and develop new and creative solutions to their challenges.

- Experiencing and expressing their feelings: This therapy supports the development of an adaptive perspective to a particular situation, regulates the intensity of their emotions, and increases their self-respect and self-acceptance.

- Learning new social and relational skills: It helps them develop empathy and respect for the feelings and thoughts of others through role-playing.

- Developing good decision-making skills (internal sense of self-control): It encourages kids to take responsibility for their actions, observe consequences, and develop successful strategies to make better decisions.

What to Expect During an Art and Play Therapy Session

During art and play therapy sessions, the therapist works together with the child in a playroom. The therapist chooses every toy and art material in the room to potentially symbolize different parts of a child's inner experience.

This could include things like:

- A small sandbox
- Stuffed toys
- Building toys
- Crayons and markers
- Indoor games
- Puppets and dolls
- Therapeutic stories
- Dance and movement (fans/scarves)
- Musical instruments

All these items help to encourage a child to explore their feelings, relationships, and other issues in a relaxed and imaginative atmosphere.

Art and play therapy is most appropriate for children between ages 3 and 12, with sessions typically lasting between 30 and 50 minutes.

Parents need to be actively involved in the therapy sessions to help it have the best effect.

As parents gain insights and understanding about their child's internal makeup, deep-rooted feelings, range of coping skills, and specific developmental level, they can maximize the support they give to their child.

Building Emotional Toolkits

When emotions run wild, thinking clearly can be one of the most challenging things to do. For children with "difficult" behavior, managing those emotions can be even tougher.

However, one way to help kids explore their emotions and find a path that works for them is to help them deliberately explore things that make them anxious, frustrated, excited, or calm—using emotional toolkits.

Let's explore what emotional toolkits are and how to create one for your child.

What Is an Emotional Toolkit?

An emotional toolkit refers to a range of techniques and tools that can help you cope with your emotions. An emotional toolkit can include everything from positive affirmations to journaling, and therapy, or objects that help enhance a child's emotional vocabulary and expression.

With that said, most of the techniques and tools I'll share in this subsection relate to helping your kid build an emotional toolkit that helps them self-regulate and better cope with challenging events.

1. Create an Emotions Chart

Kids experiencing ODD behaviors can find it hard to communicate their feelings, let alone know what to do during such difficult times. An excellent way to make things easier for them is to create a temperature gauge that lets them say whether they're in the "hot" or "cool" zone.

Once you get an idea of the emotions your child is experiencing, it could help to check in with them about what triggers they have for these emotions. Can you reduce their exposure to those triggers? Can being aware of these triggers reduce their intensity when they occur?

Perhaps the next technique on identifying cues might help you understand this better.

2. Identify the Cues

Emotions manifest in various ways in our bodies. For instance, developing anxiety might feel like nausea or butterflies in the stomach. Frustration or anger might feel like tense muscles or an increasing body temperature.

Work with your child to understand and explore signs and signals their bodies give them when they experience varying emotions. Here's an engaging way to do this.

Trace your child in chalk or on paper (and let them trace you). Next, using colors or pictures, allow them to label different body parts to describe their feelings.

Doing this can help them improve in their ability to recognize their body cues early, and possibly receive a signal that it's time to do something to calm down—before things escalate!

3. Pair Emotions with Coping Tools

You could also help craft an emotions chart that includes colors and faces that relate to various emotions. These tools can give kids a quick way to express their feelings without needing to use words.

You could also consider drawing a table that pairs various emotions with potential activities to help your child cope with them (coping tools). These potential activities could include:

- Drawing, crocheting, coloring, or singing
- Connecting with others (protects against isolation)
- Showering, lighting a favorite candle, having a cup of tea
- Working out, dancing
- Breathing, meditating, stretching

I've included an emotional toolkit template that mirrors what I just described in the workbook section to guide you in creating your own emotional toolkit table and pairing emotions with coping mechanisms.

4. Think about Sensory Inputs

Everyone, including children, has different sensory triggers and things they crave. For some, certain textures or sounds might be overwhelming or bothersome. For others, deep pressure or wrapping themselves in a tight blanket can be really calming.

Have fun with your child while they explore these varying sensory inputs, and figure out what irritates them and what helps them feel calm. Next, find ways to avoid the irritating inputs (as best as possible) and incorporate the calming inputs into your daily life.

Lastly, put together a sensory box or sensory corner with the things your child likes, such as a weighted blanket, music, essential oils, snacks, and more.

5. Play Around by Moving

Moving itself can be an incredibly helpful calming strategy. This time around, you aren't moving just to get some energy (although this can be helpful). Instead, you want to sense your body move through space.

Depending on your child's needs, stretching, bouncing, jumping, swinging, rocking in a chair, or doing similar movements can all serve different purposes in helping the brain and body feel calmer and more regulated. Check out how each of these movements make your child feel, and create a separate space your child can visit whenever they just need to move.

6. Keep Fidget Toys

Does your child need help concentrating their thoughts and attention? Fidget toys are excellent tools to ground them. Many times, looking distracted, disorganized, or emotionally overwhelmed is a sign of a powerful brain trying to pay attention to several things at one time.

Consider helping your child play with various fidget toys such as hair elastics, string that goes around their fingers, and other easy-to-use items in moments when they start feeling overwhelmed.

7. Build a "Pause" Plan

Pausing (also called distress tolerance) lets you take a break to wait out the intense urges, like the urge to throw things or scream, that often come with explosive emotions. Work with your child to make a plan;

write a list of 2-5 one-minute activities they can do during distress moments.

Pausing combines the practice of behavioral controls with implementing distraction techniques. Examples of these distress tolerance activities include walking up and down the hallway, coloring, sorting cards, counting windows, or taking deep breaths.

Practical Techniques for Anger Management

Anger can make people feel like they're at the mercy of an unpredictable or powerful emotion. Everyone, including kids, having challenges with anger management needs to learn to control their anger.

While anger is naturally a healthy, human emotion, it can lead to very difficult problems at work, in people's personal relationships, and in their overall quality of life if it gets out of control and gets destructive.

Anger varies in intensity from mild irritation to intense fury and rage. Like other emotions, it's often accompanied by physiological and biological changes. For instance, people's heart rate, blood pressure, adrenaline, and noradrenaline go up when they're angry.

How can you better manage anger in the home towards providing a more peaceful environment for everyone? Here are some helpful tips to do that.

1. Teach Your Child the Difference between Emotions and Actions

Teach your child to label their feelings so they can verbalize feelings of anger, frustration, and disappointment. Then let them know that the fact that they're angry gives them no right to hit.

Also help your child see that they're in control of their actions when they're angry.

Sometimes, aggressive actions stem from various uncomfortable feelings like embarrassment or sadness. You want to help your kids explore why they feel angry. For instance, maybe they feel sad about a canceled playdate or they're responding in anger because it helps them mask the real hurt they're feeling.

Talking about feelings and corresponding actions over time helps kids learn to recognize their feelings better.

2. Model Appropriate Anger Management Skills

Beyond speaking to them, the best way to teach children how to better manage their anger is showing them how you deal with your feelings when someone upsets you. Your kids will likely imitate your actions when you get angry.

Understandably, it's vital to protect your child from most problems of adulthood. However, it's healthy to show them how you handle anger and some other extreme emotions. Doing so helps them see not only that adults sometimes display explosive behavior, but that you understand how they feel and mean well for them by teaching them to manage their emotions.

Another way to model your emotional responses is to verbalize your feelings. For instance, you can say, "I'm furious that the gas man came later than the appointed time. But I'm still going to pay him the agreed-upon fee and do business with him again, hoping he doesn't disappoint the second time."

That way, you model two important morals: forgiveness and anger management.

You may also want to take responsibility for your actions when you lose your cool at home or in front of the kids. After things have died down, it helps to say, "I'm sorry you saw me yelling today when I was angry. Instead of raising my voice, I ought to have gone for a walk to cool off."

Hopefully, you won't have to explain yourself in this way too many times. But doing this can make your children see you as sincere or genuine and help them to trust you even more.

3. Establish Anger Rules

Most families have unofficial family rules about acceptable and unacceptable actions in reaction to anger. In some homes, slamming doors or raising voices isn't considered out of the ordinary, while others might have less tolerance for such actions.

It can help to write down household rules to guide your kids on expectations on how they should react when angry. For instance, you may want to address areas like name-calling, physical aggression, destruction of property, or verbal abuse.

4. Teach Healthy Coping Skills

Kids need to know the proper ways to deal with their anger. Instead of telling your child to never hit a sibling, how about telling them what to do during times of frustration or anger, like "Walk away from them when you feel angry, or use your words only."

You can also ask questions like, "What do you think you could do instead of hitting your brother?" That way, you can walk alongside them in identifying strategies that can help your child develop their EQ and become more compassionate.

Other healthy coping skills could include resorting to a "calm-down kit," such as a coloring book and crayons, lotion that smells good, or soothing music that can help your child calm their body and mind. Also, telling your child to consider taking time out to calm themselves before they get into trouble can be really helpful in helping them reduce anger.

Lastly, consider teaching your children problem-solving skills. These skills might help them solve problems without resorting to aggression or violence.

5. Don't Yield to Tantrums

Like in A.D.'s story with Miss T, his mom's leniency in the absence of his father encouraged his defiance, regardless of the fact that she was unhappy about his actions. Sometimes, children hold on to tantrums as they discover they are an effective way to get things done on their terms.

Don't give in to your child to avoid a meltdown. While it might be easier in the short term, in the long run, yielding too often to tantrums will only worsen ODD symptoms. Instead, work on connecting with your child so they can feel more confident that you'll meet their needs and that you mean well for them.

6. Offer Consequences When Necessary

There's no instilling discipline in a child without introducing some measure of positive and negative consequences. Give your kids positive consequences when they stick to the anger management rules and negative consequences when they break the rules.

Positive consequences, such as a reward system, can encourage your child to use anger management skills when they're angry.

And when they become aggressive, follow through with immediate consequences. Effective negative consequences may include loss of privileges, time-outs, or doing extra chores in favor of the target of their aggression.

7. Avoid Violent Media

If a child displays aggressive behavior, one way to help stem their actions is preventing them from viewing violent content. This could include violent TV shows, video games, or movies.

Concentrate on exposing them to books, games, and shows that exemplify healthy conflict resolution skills.

Note that children don't often enjoy displaying violent emotions. Rather, they're possibly reacting out of frustration and their inability to manage their feelings.

Instead of condemning a child's violent actions, walk hand-in-hand with your child towards responding appropriately to anger and other negative emotions that can impact their life at home or at school.

And if you still need help getting them through violent fits or rage, consider seeing their school counselor, a pediatrician, or a therapist for help.

It doesn't matter how wild your child might seem today; with the right principles, you can raise them to be a responsible and well-behaved individual with almost no trace of their current challenging traits.

Workbook 5

Creating an Emotional Toolkit That Pairs Emotions with Their Coping Tools

Emotion	Coping Tool
Anger	
Sadness	
Fear	
Depression	
Stress	
Guilt	
Anxiety	

Key Takeaways

- Studies have shown the relationship between a child's emotions and their mental, physical, social, and overall well-being.

- A child's EQ is how they become self-aware, control their emotions, motivate themselves, and relate to and empathize with others.

- Teach your child to develop their EQ by modeling good behaviors, as well as helping them define their feelings on a chart or spectrum.

- Breathing strategies, cognitive behavioral strategies, and art and play therapy can help children improve their emotional intelligence and reduce or completely cease disruptive behavior.

- Children are bound to struggle with managing their emotions at times, especially when dealing with behavioral challenges like ODD. However, with your guidance and care, your child's emotional management skills can improve with time.

- However, when it appears your children's emotional outbursts are getting beyond your management abilities, consider hiring a therapist or psychologist who's appropriately licensed and experienced with children.

- Lastly, understand that kids naturally don't enjoy feeling angry or having violent outbursts. Often, they're rebelling out of frustration and reacting to their inability to manage their own explosive feelings.

A Small Yet Significant Request Before You Continue!

I'm thrilled you've come this far in reading this book. I'm so grateful you chose my book from the many options available. Your journey through its pages means a lot to me.

I have a small favor to ask. Please take a few seconds to share your insights on Amazon.

Your review is more than feedback—it's a source of light for others seeking guidance in their relationship with their child.

What has stood out to you so far? How has the book influenced your perspective?

Your thoughts will not only guide others but also inspire the journey ahead. Your honest review will enrich many lives.

I can't wait to read your reflections on Amazon. Thank you for being a pivotal part of this supportive and transformative parenting community.

>> Leave a review on Amazon US <<

>> Leave a review on Amazon UK <<

CHAPTER 6

ADHD + CBT: A Combination for Better Days

"Behold, children are a heritage from the Lord, The fruit of the womb is a reward."

—Psalms 127:3 (NKJV)

"Everyone shines, given the right lighting."

—Susan Cain

ADHD   CBT

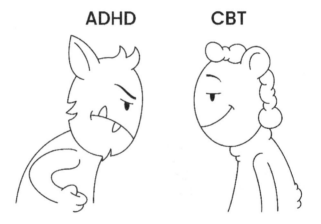

"It's hard to be enemies with you when you keep smiling."

Working through the twists and turns that come with attention deficit hyperactivity disorder (ADHD) is a task that takes its toll not just on the child but also on you. Working with an ADHD child requires the utmost diligence, dedication, and a great deal of mental stability.

In times past, the use of medication such as Adderall was the only and sole option available. While medications have been and still are effective for helping children focus and maximize their energies and attention span, cognitive behavioral therapy (CBT) provides a better way for children to live their best life without having to necessarily depend on medications, as well as equipping them with the principles required to break negative thought patterns associated with ADHD.

Addressing the Eleph-ANT in the Room: The Importance of Talk Therapy

Now that Sami knows she has ADHD, she can sense relief in her home. Her parents no longer wonder or scold her too much about how hyperactive her school says she is in class. Even her teacher seems to be a bit more understanding of her plight. Still, many times during the day, her frantic mind runs across thoughts of what this means for her. Will she ever get better and make real friends? What do other people think about her inability to get good grades? Will she forget to make it to the team tryout next week?

One of the major symptoms of kids diagnosed with ADHD is that they are constantly barraged with more trains of thought than the average person, especially the "unnecessary" kind of thoughts. Even when a child cannot focus on a single train of thought for long, it doesn't mean they don't think. The mind of someone with ADHD is like a disco with loudspeakers blaring a mixture of sounds that are so hard to ignore; they just get carried away with dancing to their heart's content until somebody comes to disconnect the power (i.e., asks them to say what they're thinking).

Diagnosing a child with ADHD is not enough because although the child understands they're different, they still need to process what that means in real-time. This is where CBT comes in handy, as it allows a child to talk about the things that go through their mind and put out fires of negative thought patterns that could trigger inattention.

Research has shown that when a child with ADHD is not off to the fairyland of other, more interesting stuff, they're constantly worried about how others view their psychological difference, and most times, this translates into low self-esteem, always worrying about how not to be different, or thinking about who will be the next person to snicker when impulsivity beckons. These thoughts can be described as ants (it is not necessary to pay attention to them unless they get in your pants) with an elephant's voice.

In therapy, a child gets to share some of the melody and lyrics of the songs from the loud, booming speakers in their head with someone professionally trained to reverse-engineer (help the child understand the underlying reason for why they do what they do, say what they say and feel what they feel). Therapy also helps disconnect some of the loudspeakers of thoughts that are not entirely true while reinforcing the child's ability to think positive thoughts.

Similarly, CBT provides short-term relief for depression and anxiety in children with ADHD, which some parents might not even know exists, especially in children whose symptoms include hypersensitivity. Between trying to discipline or keep the child fairly quiet and getting them to do their homework or study for their next test in school, the subtle signs of depression and anxiety likely go unnoticed. While the goal of CBT is not primarily to treat depression or anxiety, interacting with a therapist can unearth underlying issues, which in turn will help you enhance your child's mental well-being and give them one less thing to worry about.

Community and Teamwork

I remember listening to a TED talk where 34-year-old J spoke about her journey with ADHD. One thing that resonated with me was the fact that she met other people and realized she wasn't alone and that everyone with ADHD could play to their unique differences.

Raising a child with ADHD can be incredibly challenging, and it's no understatement to say it takes a village. This is because parenting an ADHD child often involves feelings of isolation, frustration, and guilt. A supportive community will give you a space to vent, share experiences, and receive empathetic understanding from others who "get it." This can alleviate emotional stress and prevent burnout.

Fortunately, CBT comes in group and personalized sessions, which makes it possible to meet other people who are also differently wired. The long-term result of this interaction is that it reduces the negative impact of thinking that your child was born on the other side of the universe. Better to go on a journey as a group rather than as an individual, right? This is not to say that personalized sessions aren't effective; not all people with ADHD are alike, and even in a group, everyone is on a very personalized journey.

For parents and caregivers, belonging to a community of other adults allows you to talk to someone who understands what it means to walk in your shoes, or at least a similar-sized shoe. The mental strain caused by caring for a child with ADHD can be really intense, and while you love your child deeply and totally, it can sometimes get overwhelming. Group CBT provides a way to interact with others who will listen to you as you offload some of that burden and provide encouragement from experience.

Also, sharing tips, strategies, and resources with other parents who have walked a similar path can give you the guidance you need. This collective wisdom can help you find better ways to manage ADHD symptoms and address specific challenges. Feeling out of place or judged by others is common for parents of ADHD children. A strong community will give you a sense of belonging and acceptance, breaking down the feeling of isolation and reminding you that you're not alone.

Teamwork involves building relationships with doctors, therapists, teachers, and other professionals involved in your child's care. A strong community builds communication and collaboration, leading to a more comprehensive and coordinated approach to supporting your child.

Every child with ADHD is unique, and every family goes through it differently. Being part of a community exposes you to a variety of experiences and strategies, broadening your understanding of ADHD and enriching your parenting toolkit.

Building community and teamwork also strengthens your own well-being. Feeling supported and equipped allows you to prioritize your own physical and mental health. Taking care of yourself is essential for effectively caring for your child, and a strong community can help you manage stress, practice self-care, and maintain a healthy balance.

Your kids are also not left out. ADHD can make it difficult for children to make and maintain friendships. A community provides a safe environment for them to connect with other children who understand their challenges, and this helps them build valuable social skills and friendships. Seeing other adults and children successfully manage ADHD can inspire and motivate your child. A community exposes them to positive role models, demonstrating that living with ADHD is not a limitation. Feeling accepted and understood within a supportive community will also boost your child's self-esteem and confidence, which in turn helps their overall development.

Teaching Emotional Regulation to ADHD Kids

It was craft time in Sam's class, and he was super excited to begin to draw different pictures and paint them in amazing colors. As his teacher began to explain what concept they had to play around, Sam began to share all the amazing ideas they could do for fun, without being asked by the teacher. He was so excited that he couldn't keep still enough to hear her finish. A few minutes later, he noticed two girls at the front were giggling to themselves while some gave him disapproving looks. Like a flip of the switch, his excitement crashed and a wave of sadness came over him, so much so that he started sobbing uncontrollably. The class that was meant to be fun had just turned into a consolation party.

Familiar with the situation but not sure what to do next, his teacher tried to keep control of the other children and asked them to be kind. She approached Sam and tried to help him calm down. It took about 30 minutes before order was restored to the class. By then, the crafts period was over and the opportunity for creative fun had slipped by.

Emotional dysregulation is a trait commonly observed in children with ADHD. It is characterized by extreme or inappropriate emotional responses to situations, stemming from a reduced ability to control emotional reactions in certain circumstances. In this case, a child might present with crying, quick mood swings, tantrums, and outbursts, as well as an inability to self-regulate after a meltdown. On the other side of the spectrum, the child might exhibit hyperexcitability, impulsiveness, and aggressiveness.

Scientifically, it has been proven that individuals with ADHD have an overactive amygdala, the part of the brain which is responsible for attaching emotions to experiences (Šimić et al., 2021). This is why emotional responses in ADHD kids seem to be more intense than normal, or inappropriate for the situation.

An overactive amygdala could also translate into the child focusing on the negativity in a situation or the worst possible scenario, as we see in Sam's story. His brain thought that the giggles from the girls in the front meant he was the dumbest person on earth—that he would never make a friend and would be alone forever. Hence the tears.

CBT helps children to cope with this by providing tools and strategies for emotional regulation. It employs the use of questions to help children understand their emotions better while also debunking negative thought patterns that can aggravate extreme emotional responses. When the child is encouraged to express what they feel in a calm manner that is easy to understand, they become more aware of their emotions. As a parent walks the child through the fears and thoughts that cause them to respond that way, they also get better at allaying fears, soothing anxiety, or explaining the situation more accurately.

CBT also offers strategies and teaches the child how to assist themselves in returning to a state of rest. An example of this is teaching the child how to breathe deeply, or teaching mantras to say when a train of negative thoughts hits. In Sam's case above, the teacher could take him to a quiet space and encourage him to take deep breaths, which could help calm him down or at least help shift his focus from the giggles to breathing exercises.

Let's look at another example of how CBT helps with emotional regulation.

Amos absolutely loves chocolate cake. His godmother invited his family to her birthday celebration, where the kids had a whole section to themselves and chocolate was in abundance. As soon as the car pulled to a stop and Amos spotted his favorite dessert, he couldn't wait to get out of the car. Once unstrapped from the car seat, he made his way over to the table and was pulling everything and everyone out of his way just to get to the head of the line.

CBT treatment for Amos could involve teaching him mantras such as "I can wait my turn for chocolate cake." Over time, consistent practice of these actions can help the child control their responses and actions.

ADHD and Social Skills

ADHD impacts the brain's executive functions responsible for planning, organizing, and regulating behavior. This can lead to difficulty paying attention to others in conversations, missing social cues, and appearing disinterested. Impulsivity is another core symptom of ADHD and can manifest in social settings as interrupting conversations, blurting out inappropriate comments, or acting without thinking of the consequences. This can be interpreted as rudeness or disrespect by peers.

Difficulty managing emotions like frustration, anger, or excitement can lead to outbursts or withdrawal in social interactions. This unpredictable behavior can be off-putting to others and make it harder to maintain relationships. ADHD kids may struggle to understand and interpret nonverbal cues like facial expressions, body language, and tone of voice. In social situations, misunderstandings and misinterpretations can occur, leading to confusion and conflicts.

If you have an ADHD kid or you've had to work with one before, then you know they don't like waiting their turn. They also dislike sharing attention or compromise, which can lead to conflicts and exclusion in group activities. Difficulty understanding how their behavior affects others and seeing things from another person's point of view can make it almost impossible to have healthy relationships.

These social misunderstandings can lead to negative feedback from peers, further impacting self-esteem and confidence in social situations. This creates a negative feedback loop that makes it harder for kids who have ADHD to develop and practice positive social skills. Other conditions often co-occurring with ADHD, like anxiety or depression, can add further layers of complexity to social interactions.

I need you to remember that every child with ADHD is unique, and their social skills challenges will vary depending on the specific symptoms they experience and the level of support they receive. However, understanding the root causes behind these behaviors can help you as a parent, educator, or other caregiver to provide targeted support and help your kid thrive socially.

To improve their social skills, teach your child to be a good listener by looking at the person talking, nodding to show they're paying attention, and asking questions to understand better. You can practice this at home by pretending to have conversations or using toys to represent different people talking. You can also help your child practice talking in a group by taking turns, staying on the same topic, and not interrupting. Simple conversation games like "I Spy" and "Finish the Sentence" can make this fun and engaging.

Explain the importance of body language—how our faces, movements, and tone of voice express feelings. Use picture books or act-out charades to help them recognize and use these cues appropriately. Teach your child healthy ways to deal with emotions like being upset, mad, or excited. Simple techniques like breathing slowly, counting to ten, or taking short breaks can make a big difference.

You can also encourage your child to think about how their words and actions might affect others. Role-playing different situations can help them understand different points of view. Make sure your child knows what's expected of them in different social situations. Communicate rules and guidelines to avoid confusion. Acknowledge and praise your child when they make an effort to use their social skills, even if they don't get everything perfect. Positive reinforcement helps build their confidence.

Choose environments with fewer distractions to help your child focus better on social interactions. This might mean finding quieter places for playdates or conversations. Be a good example by using good social skills yourself. Children often learn by watching, so modeling positive behavior is crucial. Talk to your child's teachers and other caregivers about the strategies you're using at home. Working together ensures consistent support across different settings.

You can also check out books and games that make learning social skills enjoyable. These resources often use stories and interactive activities to teach important concepts.

Beyond Symptoms; Bringing Out the Potential in Your Child

Michael Phelps, born on June 30, 1985, in Baltimore, Maryland, is an incredibly accomplished swimmer, holding the record for the most Olympic medals with a whopping 28, including an astonishing 23 golds. His story is not just about winning medals but about turning what was seemingly a disadvantage into an advantage.

During his early years, Phelps was diagnosed with ADHD. However, at the age of 7, he started swimming; it became a hobby and, gradually, a sport. By age 10, he had already established himself as a top-ranked young swimmer, finding a way to channel his energy positively.

Phelps's Olympic journey is nothing short of legendary:

- At the age of 15, he made his Olympic debut in Sydney in 2000.

- His first gold medal came in Athens in 2004.

- The Beijing Olympics in 2008 marked a historic moment where he won eight gold medals in a single Games.

- After accumulating 22 medals, Phelps initially retired after the 2012 London Olympics.

- Making a surprising comeback in Rio in 2016, he secured five more gold medals and one silver.

Surprisingly, Phelps credits his ADHD for helping him stay focused and energetic during intense competitions. Beyond his swimming career, Phelps retired in 2016 and shifted his focus to mental health. He established the Michael Phelps Foundation to contribute to mental health awareness.

To understand what makes an ADHD child special, start by watching them closely and spending time doing fun things together. Notice the things that make them happy, like building Legos, enjoying music, or playing with gadgets. These are clues about what they're good at and what they love.

Try different activities together, like drawing, playing sports, making music, or going outdoors. See how excited and interested they get in each one. Also, talk to them a lot about their dreams and what they enjoy. Listen carefully and show them that you think their interests are great, even if they seem a bit different.

ADHD kids tend to be super creative, have lots of energy, are able to focus really well on things they like, and think in creative ways. Whenever they do something good, even if it's small, tell them it's great. This makes them feel good and helps them want to try more things. Find ways to connect their strengths to real-life stuff. For example, if they love music, you can encourage them to join a band or learn how to make music. By doing this, you help them see how awesome they are and how they can do cool stuff with what they're good at.

Even though ADHD kids are great at some things, there are also things that can be a bit tricky for them. You can help by teaching them how to be organized, manage time, and plan things. This makes it easier for them to focus and do well. When they feel mad or frustrated, show them ways to calm down and handle those feelings. This makes it easier for them to get along with others and feel good overall. If things are tough, it's okay to talk to someone who knows a lot about ADHD, like a therapist. They can help with special ideas and support for both your kid and the family.

Enjoy trying out new things with your child and celebrate when they do well. If something doesn't go perfectly, that's okay—it's a chance to learn something new. Most importantly, make it all fun for both of you. By being patient and supporting them, you're helping them find out all the amazing things they can do.

Focus, Attention, and CBT

One of the major problems you might have to deal with in a child with ADHD is an inability to focus on specific tasks or thoughts for an extended period of time. It is not uncommon for a child to zone out of a science class when his teacher mentions the word "sunshine." As the rest of the class gets immersed in understanding the process of photosynthesis and what it means for plant energy, the kid is having an internal debate on how close to the sun Superman can fly, or if Superwoman will get there before him, and how the two of them will probably get roasted.

Just like how an overactive amygdala is responsible for the extreme switch of emotions expressed in ADHD, attention deficit has been linked to an unregulated or underactive prefrontal cortex (Alison, 2023).

The prefrontal cortex (PFC) is a region of the brain which is responsible for most of our cognitive abilities and executive functioning. Of course, it communicates with other regions of the brain to achieve this purpose. Neuroscientist Patricia Goldman-Rakic (1996) describes this functional process as "the ability to keep in mind an event that has just occurred, or bring to mind information from long-term storage, and use this representational knowledge to regulate behavior, thought and emotion."

In simple terms, the PFC is the part of the brain responsible for thoughts, analysis of those thoughts (whether it necessitates an action or not), behavior regulation, focus, and concentration. Alison (2023) illustrates the thoughts generated by the PFC as speeding cars; in a child with ADHD, the fastest moving car takes precedence at a particular time, until the next faster car drives past, and the next, and the next. This explains why a child with ADHD cannot seem to concentrate.

Incorporating CBT into treating ADHD, however, serves to assist the child by providing behavioral strategies that help to reduce distractions. These techniques help the child's ability to stay in the present instead of jumping to the shiny yellow speeding thought-car popping up in their mind.

CBT uses practical steps such as goal setting to help the child contain the overwhelm that comes with getting projects done. It teaches the skill of breaking down large tasks, such as cleaning a room, into smaller ones that can be finished quickly and effectively. This skill eliminates, or at the very least reduces, the risk of the child getting caught up with worrying about the "big" task and wanting to move on to do more immediate and simpler stuff like play a video game. For example, CBT involves turning "clean your room" into "pick up all the toys and put them in the blue basket," "take your dirty clothes to the laundry room," etc.

Besides goal setting, CBT encourages the child to use a to-do list or child-friendly planner to sort their thoughts as well as act as a reminder. There's no point in setting goals if you cannot remember them. CBT enhances a child's ability to work comfortably with lists that can help them keep an organized mind and provide guidance for their actions. A parent going grocery shopping could make a smaller list for their child so that the child can cross-check if both strawberries and blueberries should go in the shopping cart.

Another area focused on in CBT is time management skills. The easiest way to lose track of time is to get lost in so many interwoven thoughts. CBT attempts to help a child with ADHD regain a sense of timing so they can focus on the task at hand. By making use of alarms, wristwatches, and other related technologies, children are helped to stay in or return to the present so they can achieve their set goals.

Building Positive Self-Esteem

I am smart. I am bright. I am gifted. Breathe. I am smart. I am bright. I am gifted.

These were the words Lauren repeated to herself as she struggled to complete the essay homework she was given in school. It was due next week, and she had learned to get an early start on her homework these days.

She smiled as her mind drifted to how far she had come. A couple of months ago, the mere thought of having to write an essay would have scared the wits out of her or probably would have set off another bout of depressed mood.

After she received a medical diagnosis of ADHD, she had felt relieved to learn that she wasn't like the other kids because she was indeed different. But she didn't get why trying to finish up a writing assignment had to be this difficult.

Everyone said she had so much potential if only she could learn to do her assignments a little bit more carefully, but they could never know how hard it was for her to sit still to write. Or even get through reading reference material for the essays. They couldn't know how ashamed she felt about how everyone laughed because she forgot the submission deadline. Again.

Beep! Beep! The sound of the timer jarred her back to reality. Ten minutes had flown by so quickly. Adjusting in her seat, she took a deep breath again. *I am smart and can finish this in time. I can focus.* She wrote a few more words and reached for the atlas to once again check in which region of Africa Egypt was.

Her mantras were ways of helping prevent herself from going down the rabbit hole of self-debasement, which could trigger negative emotions. Her mom had helped her discover the power of positive self-talk as a coping mechanism against negative thoughts.

This was after she had learned more about ADHD, her peculiar patterns, and why she acted the way she did sometimes. Her mom had gone further to allow Lauren to express how ashamed, undeserving, and inadequate she felt—how it had affected her belief in her own worth and negatively impacted her relationships with others. Lauren knew she wasn't there yet, but each day promised improvements as she applied lessons learned from her mom, both on the good days and the not-so-good ones.

CBT can help create a better sense of self-perception. By combining the core principles of psychoeducation, positive self-talk, and cognitive reconstruction, CBT helped Lauren transition from a confused, ashamed girl into a child who understood and accepted her differences and saw herself as a healthy, worthy, and confident human.

Psychoeducation seeks to explain the concept of ADHD and the underlying processes of certain actions, thoughts, and emotions in a personalized manner so the child gains clarity on their differences. It also encourages the child to share how living with ADHD has altered their perception of themselves in an atmosphere of total acceptance and zero judgment.

Cognitive restructuring comes into play by helping the child see the inaccuracy in the thoughts or feelings previously shared without dismissing their feelings. It also involves a step-by-step follow-through process which enables the child to see the truth, understand and accept it so they stop beating themselves up. For example, the child might say, "I always embarrass myself because I always bring the wrong things to school. I'll never gain anyone's respect." A CBT therapist might then help the child see why they deserve respect even though they forget things.

Positive talk seals the deal as the child adopts mantras or affirmations such as "I am not a slob," "I can wait my turn to speak," etc. Again, as your child interacts with these techniques, the dividends of incorporating CBT into treatment will be reaped substantially over time.

Workbook 6

1. What challenges does your child face during daily routines, and how can you modify the routine to accommodate their needs better?

_____

_____

_____

_____

_____

2. Can you identify a recent situation where your child's thoughts, feelings, and behaviors were interconnected? How might a positive thought or behavioral intervention have influenced the outcome?

_____

_____

_____

_____

_____

3. What are one or two specific and achievable goals you can set as a family to support your child's well-being and development? How will you track progress toward these goals?

_____

_____

_____

_____

4. How can you incorporate short grounding exercises into your family's daily activities to help manage stress and enhance focus?

_____

_____

_____

_____

_____

5. Who are the key individuals in your support network, and how can you effectively communicate your family's needs to them? How might they contribute to your child's positive development?

_____

_____

_____

_____

_____

Key Takeaways

- Diagnosing a child with ADHD is not enough because although the child will understand that they're different, they still need to process what that means in real-time.

- A supportive community will give you a space to vent, share experiences, and receive empathetic understanding from others who "get it." This can alleviate emotional stress and prevent burnout.

- Building community and teamwork strengthens your own well-being. Feeling supported and equipped allows you to prioritize your physical and mental health.

- CBT can help recreate a better sense of self-perception for your child. By combining the core principles of psychoeducation, positive self-talk, and cognitive reconstruction, CBT can help transform your child into someone who understands and accepts their differences and sees themselves as a healthy, worthy, and confident human.

CHAPTER 7

Building Cooperation and Compliance

"My son, do not despise the Lord's discipline, and do not resent his rebuke, because the Lord disciplines those he loves, as a father the son he delights in."

—Proverbs 3:11-12 (NKJV)

"If you've never been hated by your child, you have never been a parent."

—Bette Davis

ODD

"So we're not grounded and she isn't even mad?
Have we lost our touch?"

Effective Discipline Strategies

Disciplining a child is never easy. However, it's sometimes the most loving thing you can do for them—IF you discipline your kids rightly.

That includes implementing effective discipline strategies that reinforce the impact you want without hurting your child while doing so.

If I could liken parenting tips to military artillery, these strategies exclusively serve the Special Armed Forces. This chapter is filled with all the hands-on special firepower necessary to prepare your child to become a more responsible and cooperative member of society.

We won't call them fighter jet weaponry per se, but like a military force determined to drive defiance from another, they include subtle missiles, FBI-grade spies, and even Navy Seals-level instruments to win your child over in the winningest way possible.

I guess you're ready, *already*! Here we go.

Establishing Routines and Structure

Adults aren't the only ones who go through the various changes that life brings. Children, too, go through these phases and sometimes even react to them more.

Children have less control over their lives than adults do and are often on the receiving end of the changes that life brings rather than the giving end. Whether it's a new daycare, school, or babysitter, a friend relocating, or new responsibilities, kids sometimes have to grapple with changes of varying difficulties. Not to mention the sometimes wild effect that puberty has on kids as they journey through adolescence.

However, your child can thrive when they know what to expect—even if they don't always like it. One way to help them know what to expect is to establish routines and structure.

By creating a structured environment for your child, you can help them feel safe and secure, which is a vital aspect of preventing behavioral problems.

Routines and structures are necessary for various reasons: to help children understand limits and boundaries; to help them learn self-discipline and experience frustration and delayed gratification; and to help them interact appropriately with the world around them.

Routines also help children learn independence. Once your child understands, for instance, that their mornings begin with brushing their teeth, getting dressed, eating breakfast, and packing their bag for school, chances are high you won't have to keep reminding them—or following them out the door, or always shouting for them to return for their homework.

This independence not only boosts your child's self-esteem as they become more confident in caring for themselves, it also reduces your child's chances of displaying disruptive behavior. They'll likely be less anxious about things happening around them. Instead of worrying about the events happening around them, they'd rather exercise their freedom and concentrate on managing their behavior.

Three Main Keys to Building Structure

Consistency, predictability, and following through are three vital elements you need to build the right structure for your child.

You may have heard this quote by Bruce Lee, the American martial artist and actor: "I fear not the man who has practiced 10,000 kicks once, but I fear the man who has practiced one kick 10,000 times."

Consistency involves doing the same thing every time. Predictability involves the ability to expect or know what will happen. Lastly, following through lets you enforce consequences (i.e., *say what you mean and mean what you say*).

Let's examine how to build a structure that includes these key elements by building effective routines and rules for your kids.

Creating Routines and Rules

1. Identify the Routines and Rules

Identify important daily activities and decide the order in which they should occur. Define important times of the day when these activities should occur and make a routine. Lastly, ensure the routine works for the entire family.

Create specific rules with well-defined behavioral patterns while avoiding vague rules like "Be nice" or "Be friendly." You can begin with one or two rules and include new rules as necessary. Too many rules will be difficult to enforce.

Lastly, set realistic rules and routines that fit your child's age and development. You, more than anyone else, understand your child's current routines, strengths, and daily schedule. Creating a realistic structure that perfectly matches your child's world is vital to helping them think and act in the direction you want for them.

2. Explain the Routines and Rules

Ensure your child understands what you want them to do and when you want them to do it. Speak with them about the rules and routines, and have them repeat them to you.

If you have trouble helping them remember or grasp the rules, try using simple charts with pictures that you can display in their room or somewhere else they can see them. All children will often need reminders about what to do, and repeating the rules is an excellent way to do so.

3. Follow the Routines and Rules

It helps when all family members follow the family routines or rules. That encourages your child to tag along, even when it doesn't feel exciting to them. And when they do (or don't) follow the routines, you want to implement the next tip.

4. Use Consequences

Implement positive consequences such as praise or some reward when your child follows the rules you set for them or even completes daily routines in a streak.

And if they don't? Implementing negative consequences like loss of privileges, time-out, or specially imposed home chores can help correctly reprimand a child and let them know you don't approve or like their actions.

Meanwhile, ensure that you set clear consequences for either following the routine or breaking the rules so your child doesn't feel wronged or treated unfairly when you implement them.

Regardless of who's enforcing a rule (whether grandparents or babysitters), it helps to provide a consistent message to your child. While your rules should be consistently enforced, you can make routines flexible to prevent boredom and also enhance your child's emotional and mental health.

The Power of Positive Reinforcement

When your child misbehaves, rewarding them might be the last thing that comes to your mind. However, through the lens of positive psychology, positive reinforcement can be the most effective behavior modification technique parents can use.

That's because it focuses on amplifying what is already good in our children, and in ourselves as their caretakers.

Positive reinforcement can motivate your child to become more responsible, do their chores, get along with their siblings, or complete their assignments without arguing or throwing tantrums.

Let's see how positive reinforcement works and how you can use it to modify your child's behavior positively.

How Positive Reinforcement Works

A type of positive discipline, positive reinforcement seeks to guide and shape children's behavior by concentrating on the positives while reframing errors as learning opportunities.

While negative consequences can help to discourage bad behavior, positive reinforcement focuses on the other side: identifying and rewarding positive behaviors in your child.

To do this, parents should be consistent, set limits, and be kind to their children. By rewarding good behavior, children are motivated to keep doing well—or even better.

You only need to look at adults and their paychecks to visualize this in a more personal way.

Adults go to work to receive a paycheck. There may be other rewards, like personal fulfillment. But their paycheck is largely the main positive consequence of going to work. And it motivates them to keep working.

Like adults, kids also receive motivation to keep up the good work when you provide them with positive reinforcement.

Reward behavior you want to see in your child more often, rather than just concentrating on their defiance, disobedience, or constant tantrums or arguments. They're also likely to develop good habits along the lines of behaviors you reward with your attention and gifts, with time.

Let's look at some ways to introduce positive reinforcement.

Various Ways to Introduce Positive Reinforcement

Whether it's being a good friend, completing chores, using manners, or complying with a request right away, there are various good behaviors you want your child to repeat.

You've learned to inform your child about what you want them to do and get them looking forward to your rewards.

Note that positive reinforcement doesn't need to involve a tangible item. Some helpful ways to positively reinforce a child's behavior include:

- Clapping and cheering

- Giving a thumbs-up

- Offering a special fun activity, like playing a game or reading a book together

- Offering praise

- Telling another adult how proud you are of your child while your child is listening

- Giving them a hug or pat on the back

- Giving a high-five

Now to a few tangible reward ideas. Suppose your child patiently helps their younger sibling with their homework; you could give them more screen time or more liberty with their night schedule on one occasion.

And if they clean their room without being asked, you could take them out to their favorite spot as a reward. They'll likely be encouraged to clean their room again or assist others in their work.

You can also introduce partial praise where they demonstrate partial obedience to your instructions. For instance, if you want your child to carefully put away their things when they're back from school and you find your child puts their socks away properly but forgets to hang up their coat, you can still compliment their partial obedience.

You can also compliment them when they, for instance, start following your instructions but take a detour afterward.

Remember, positive reinforcement seeks to make your child think the best about themselves, you, and the instructions you give them. And you can save them more goodwill by praising them as soon as they demonstrate good behavior (if you suspect they could derail).

Suppose your child struggles with doing the dishes. Don't hesitate to compliment them for getting started. This early compliment may give your child some sense of early success and motivate them to stick to the plan.

Positive Reinforcement: Frequency, Methods, and More

When your child is just starting to learn a new positive behavior or a specific skill, it's helpful to constantly provide positive reinforcement. If you reward them only once in a while or randomly, their behavior is unlikely to change.

Now, don't get me wrong. You don't have to offer your child a reward every time they clean up after a meal.

But younger kids are especially more likely to respond positively to frequent rewards.

Consider scheduling your rewards with intermediate ones coming in between bigger rewards. Intermediate prizes could be a sticker or token, while larger rewards could be an ice cream cone or more time on video games.

With time, you can space out your reinforcement as your child moves towards mastering a skill or positive behavior. Surprise reinforcements could also come in as vital maintenance.

Besides the frequency of introduced reinforcements, it's also helpful to reward children around situations or areas in which they behaved well.

Here's what I mean. If your kid helps you prepare lunch, you can let them choose what flavor of juice they want. If your child shares their toy with a sibling, you could let them stay up a bit later while playing.

This teaches the child in a very relatable way that one good turn deserves another, and can make the positive consequences more attractive and memorable.

To take it a notch higher, you can let your child decide what reward they would likely earn for constantly displaying a specific good behavior. This method gives the child a greater sense of agency and incentive, which could become another source of motivation for them.

Lastly, avoid unknowingly reinforcing negative behavior. It's easy to do this with your attention.

Even in negative situations, giving attention to a child who's constantly whining or throwing tantrums might reinforce their behaviors. Multiple "Stop this!" or "Don't go there!" could rather encourage them to keep doing things you disapprove of.

That's why psychologists think that ignoring can be one of the best ways to respond to attention-seeking misbehaviors in children.

Another way parents accidentally reinforce negative behavior is by giving in too easily. Suppose you instruct your child they can't stay up watching TV after 8 p.m., but your child keeps begging and pleading until you give in. You may have well reinforced their whining because the child learns that whining helps them get their desires fulfilled and encourages them to whine again in the future.

Ensure you don't reinforce negative behavior. Follow bad behavior with negative consequences and help them understand you're being intentional about getting the best for—and out of—them.

Implementing Effective Rewards and Consequences

Henry Cloud, an acclaimed American author, clinical psychologist, and New York Times bestselling author, once wrote about consequences and rewards:

"We change our behavior when the pain of staying the same becomes greater than the pain of changing. Consequences give us the pain that motivates us to change."

And I couldn't agree more.

Consequences and rewards provide the *pain* or *push* your child needs to become motivated to improve their behavior.

While we've touched on some ways to reward or punish your child's actions already, this chapter explores some of these methods and shows you how to effectively implement them.

I've Done That Already

Before seeking counsel or guidance, most parents, especially those of children with ODD, have tried it all. You've tried rewards. You've tried punishments. Whether you were less strict, or more strict, it may or may not have helped.

At some point, you possibly figured that seeing a psychologist or getting further counsel from a specialist was your last resort. And you've turned to that already.

While I perfectly understand where you are at the moment, most challenges of parenting ODD are often the result of how a plan is implemented rather than the plan itself.

For instance, rewards, when used correctly, can be effective. Conversely, when you don't use rewards well, it could all become useless.

The same principle applies to negative consequences for misbehaviors.

If you've wrongly implemented rewards or consequences and hit a brick wall as a result, you may have lost your child's trust.

It's time to work towards regaining your child's trust and review how you implement rewards and consequences in the future.

Regaining a Child's Trust

If you've lost your child's trust by not following through with punishments or rewards accordingly, it could be a challenging situation. You'll need to make a special effort towards rebuilding your child's trust while showing your child that you mean what you say and say what you mean.

It helps to admit at this point that interventions could take time to yield results, and your child's behavior could get worse before getting better. Children in these cases might doubt your willingness to use punishments or fulfill promises of rewards.

How to Implement Various Rewards

Now, there's a reason I'm addressing rewards before punishments. That's because positive reinforcements will do more to improve a child's behavior than negative consequences.

Let's look at how to implement various rewards like a token economy, as well as other creative options you might intend to use in encouraging your child's positive behavior.

A Token Economy

You've probably already benefited from, and offered, a "token economy," whether or not you know what it means.

Fiat money (or your national currency), for instance, runs off a form of token economy. In the family setting, a token economy means the parents give their children points for behaving well, which they can later exchange for rewards.

So, you could promise your child three points for helping in the garden for one hour, or five points for doing well on their next math test.

One benefit of a token economy is that your child can easily claim rewards (points) at any time. Implementing this correctly can allow your child to receive gratification instantly for behaving correctly.

By its nature, a token economy lets you provide frequent little rewards (points) to your child. That encourages your child to behave well often while working towards something larger that excites them.

However, it helps to introduce a token economy system that interests your child. That means your system should be easy for them to understand. It should also be exciting and rewarding to them.

Of course, you may also want to rename your token economy. Using the term "token economy" can sound like some complex academic term that complicates the entire learning process.

First, keep the system as simple as possible. Allocate points simply and understandably and record them somewhere obvious to your child.

It's an excellent idea to allocate points to things your child does daily. Think of allocating 1 point for waking up before 6.30 a.m. or 1 point for being ready for bedtime by 9 p.m.

Avoid making things complicated, or it can look too much like another chore or tough school assignment.

A token system that uses stickers to record points might appeal to younger kids. Think star stickers. Consider purchasing or printing a chart and some stickers from the internet to get started.

Consider asking your child to come up with their preferred list of rewards and their point costs. However, ensure that rewards aren't impossible to achieve. Avoid coming up with rewards that are too expensive or too cheap (children are wise enough to consider if something you're offering them is worth it).

The ideal token system lets your child get a frequent small reward while saving a few points to work toward something larger.

Tokens are just one category of rewards. Whatever form of rewards you choose to implement, ensure they follow the principles I've shared in this section so far.

For emphasis, rewards should be clear, have clear requirements, be given consistently and often, be realistic, and should be followed through on.

Implementing Negative Consequences the Right Way

Just as with rewards, there's a right way and a wrong way to use punishments. Using punishments incorrectly will make bad behaviors even worse.

Suppose you didn't use punishments for a long time or consistently earlier; a sudden implementation could make your child temporarily worsen their actions to test your limits and challenge you.

We'll consider how to use time-outs in managing your child's unwanted behavior.

Time-Outs

Time-outs are usually sufficient as a consequence for younger children to manage disruptive behavior. Here are helpful tips to help you implement them successfully.

1. Decide on a Location for Time-Outs

You want to choose a place where you can easily monitor your child closely and ensure they're distraction-free. With no phones, games, or toys, your child will likely feel the pangs of staying alone in a chair or mat doing *practically nothing*. Of course, a time-out with toys is more of a reward than a punitive measure—and one they might get to like soon.

2. Implement Immediately

If your child breaks a rule, it's time to send them for time-out right away. Delaying for an hour or so after the wrongdoing can make them disconnect the punishment from their bad behavior.

3. Explain the Punishment

In one or two sentences, tell your child why they're going to time out. Any explanation that's longer might easily be forgotten. "You refused to turn off the TV after your cartoon series finished; go to time-out for 10 minutes" is an example of what suffices.

4. Time the Time-outs

Set a timer so you and your child know exactly when their time-out ends. Specialists recommend that time-outs should last a minute per year of age. That is, 3-year-olds will incur 3 minutes of time-out, while 6-year-olds will have 6 minutes, and so on.

5. When It's Over

Move on after the timer rings. You could have a very brief conversation with your child, letting them know they did great by completing their time-out. Now, they have earned a clean slate.

How to Use Negative Consequences Effectively

1. Create a few simple and well-defined punishments for breaking clear rules. Children will have a hard time understanding a long or complex list of rules, with no chance of success if they don't exactly know the rules.

2. Always fulfill your promises. Otherwise, the threat of punishment will quickly become meaningless if you seldom implement punishments. It might be easy to feel sympathetic and let your child off the hook. But now is the time to put your foot down.

3. Avoid being excessive. Some parents have a habit of using extreme punishments when they're upset. For instance, grounding a kid for two weeks can hurt you as much as it hurts the child. After a few days, you could get tired of having a bored child in the home, and could eventually end the punishment early. That shows your child you don't mean it when you threaten negative consequences.

4. Never use corporal punishments. Hitting your child hard might get you what you want now, but it could cause trouble afterward. Your child might learn that hitting and violence are appropriate responses to their problems and become aggressive with other children, and even into adulthood.

5. Taking away privileges like the TV or phone can be very effective.

6. Don't take away "good things" from your child. By "good things," I mean things that can help them become better people overall. Does running motivate your child to get good grades in school so they can join the school's sprint team? Don't prevent them from practicing races. Does playing the guitar calm them down? Avoid taking it away from them when they're angry.

7. Avoid emotionally painful punishments like humiliation. Shaming and humiliating kids can irreparably hurt your relationship and cause significant distress and unhappiness that spiral into long-term consequences.

8. Don't punish out of anger. If you're angry, consider telling your child that you need a few hours to consider the consequences of their actions. Since the goal of these punishments is to help

your child learn a lesson correctly, it helps to be in a rational and calm state of mind to devise one.

9. Explain to your child why you're punishing them. Then help them learn from the experience by asking them to come up with strategies to not make the same mistakes again. Suppose they forgot to do the dishes—how can they remember next time?

Building new habits takes time. Your children might not change overnight or even in one month. Instead of impatiently anticipating small wins and changes, watch out for small wins and celebrate them.

The key to success, however, is to ensure you involve your child when setting up your token economy or time-outs. Remember, you want to be sure you select something that will motivate your child enough to work towards changing their behavior.

It can also help to begin with one or two attainable goals. Your limits and demands should feel challenging to the child, but not to the point of discouragement.

If you've been consistently using a reward system without positive changes with time, consider re-evaluating the system. Check the system for the following things: Is the reward something my child loves? Are my expectations appropriate? Are my demands or tasks clear? Am I stating the behavior positively? If not, make adjustments and reapply the system.

With a thoughtful and consistent approach to rewards and consequences, you and your child will likely be happy with the outcomes.

Collaborative Problem-Solving

Kids with problematic behavior are sometimes highly misunderstood and maltreated. Sometimes rewards and negative consequences don't get the job done and could worsen things. Fortunately, there's another way out: collaborative problem-solving (CPS).

Enshrining collaborative problem-solving as a norm in your family can be a game-changer in your parenting and your relationships with your kids. Not only can this approach help to shape your (presently challenging) child into a resilient, collaborative, problem-solving, empathic person, but it can also make the entire parenting experience incredibly freeing, rewarding, and peaceful.

CPS helps parents shift toward a more accurate and compassionate mindset that *their children will do well IF they can*, instead of the more popular notion that *they will do well if they want to.*

From this basic but powerful principle, CPS teaches kids to build skills like flexibility, problem-solving, and frustration tolerance. Going beyond just motivating kids to behave better, CBS begins with identifying triggers to a child's ODD-related systems and the specific skills they need to develop.

Next, the parent or caregiver works with the child to build those skills and develop lasting solutions to problems that work for everyone.

Here's a story that aptly describes CPS in parenting children with challenging behavior.

Mom walks into the room and finds 5-year-old Truce drawing on the wall.

Mom: I see you're having a great time here, Truce!

Truce: Yes, I am, Mom!

Mom: Obviously. But there's a little problem I'm sure we can work through.

Truce: Okay.

Mom: I don't want you to draw or write on the walls. I like keeping them clean. And it's a tough task to clean off all these pencil marks.

Truce: Wow, okay.

Mom: But I'm sure we can work together and brainstorm some ideas that will suit both of us. I like you flying your toy airplane all over the room, as it's lots of fun for you. And I want to also keep the walls clean. Do you have an idea that can work for both of us?

Truce: Yes! I'll finish drawing my airport on the wall and then I'll play some more and then I can help you do the cleaning.

Mom: That sounds quite creative. Thank you for opting to help me clean the wall. But the first part of your idea won't work for me because I don't want you to draw on the wall anymore.

Truce: Okay.

Mom: Here's my idea: how about you draw your airport on a piece of paper? I can help you if you want.

Truce: But I don't like drawing on paper.

Mom: Okay. Since we are both excellent problem-solvers, we can think of a way through this.

Truce: Yes! You help me draw a very big airport on that large whiteboard in your study and I can fly my airplanes on them? I want an airport with red lines, fire service, and a landing spot. Afterward, I can help you clean the wall. Is that fine with you?

Mom: Absolutely, that works for me. I love that idea. Let's get to it. *Mom high-fives Truce.*

Truce just amazingly solved a problem while meeting both his needs and his mom's. Of course, he later helped his mom clean the wall, with no force, threats, or yelling.

Parenting Styles That Promote Cooperation

Your parenting style could affect virtually everything from your child's physical health to their self-esteem and how they relate with others. Ensure your parenting style promotes cooperation, healthy growth, and development in your kids, because the way you discipline and interact with your children can influence them for the rest of their lives.

Psychologists have categorized parenting styles into four types. Parents can use one or more of these different styles, in various situations or contexts.

These styles are:

- Authoritarian
- Authoritative
- Permissive
- Neglecting (or uninvolved)

Each style has a different approach to raising kids, with its merits and demerits.

While there's no right parenting style, psychologists recommend the authoritative parenting style.

Let's examine each of these parenting styles and which style you might currently use in relating with your child.

Authoritarian

Authoritarian parents feel their kids should be seen and not heard. They often feel the kids must choose their way and none other. This parenting style also rarely considers a child's feelings.

When a child questions an authoritarian parent's rationale for saying something, the common reply goes along the lines of, "Because I said so." They never bring in their kids to get involved in solving challenges or obstacles. Instead, they make the rules and enforce the consequences, with little regard for what the child thinks.

Authoritarian parents may also use punishments instead of discipline. They'd rather make their child feel sorry for mistakes, instead of necessarily learning from or growing through them.

While children raised under this parenting style tend to follow rules often, their obedience can be costly. Children of authoritarian parents are at a higher risk of developing self-esteem problems because their opinions aren't valued at home.

Authoritative

Authoritative parents are nurturing, supportive, and responsive while setting firm restrictions. Notably, the authoritative parent goes beyond just telling their kids what to do; they do the harder work of modeling the behavior they expect from their children.

They attempt to control children's behavior by clearly explaining rules, discussing, and reasoning. While they listen to their children's viewpoints, they don't always *have* to accept them.

Children raised by authoritative parents tend to be energetic, friendly, cheerful, independent, self-controlled, cooperative, and achievement-oriented.

Permissive

In this parenting style, parents are warm but lenient. They fail to set firm limits, monitor their children's activities closely, or require appropriately mature behavior from their children.

The permissive parent sets rules but hardly enforces them. They don't give out consequences often. Also, permissive parents think that their children will learn best with little interference from them.

Permissive parents would usually rather take on the role of a friend than a parent. While they often encourage their children to speak with them about their problems, they don't put much effort into discouraging wrong behavior.

Children raised by permissive parents tend to be impulsive, rebellious, aimless, domineering, aggressive, and low in self-reliance, self-control, and achievement.

Uninvolved

Uninvolved parents don't ask their children to do their homework. They hardly know where their kids are or who they're with. Uninvolved parents also don't spend much time with their children.

While the uninvolved parent may be in the same home with the child, there tend to be few rules in the home. Kids may not receive much attention, guidance, and nurturing.

Uninvolved parents expect their kids to raise themselves. They don't devote much time or energy to meeting their kids' basic needs. Uninvolved parents may be neglectful, but they're often not intentionally doing so. For instance, a neglectful parent may be suffering from mental health issues or substance abuse problems. They may also not be able to care for their child's physical or emotional needs consistently.

Children raised by uninvolved parents tend to have low self-esteem and little self-confidence and seek other, sometimes inappropriate, role models to fill in the gap caused by neglectful parenting.

Setting Age-Appropriate Boundaries and Consequences

Some parents are often reluctant to set boundaries and consequences for their kids because they don't want to upset their kids or incite any arguments with their kids. However, failing to set clear limits could create more emotional challenges for children and make parenting more tasking.

Children need boundaries and consequences to help them learn how to self-regulate. Limits help them cope with intense feelings, build their resilience, and adapt to problems through adulthood.

However, there's a right way and a wrong way to set limits and boundaries. For regulations to be effective, they should be enforceable, consistent, easy to understand, and most importantly, age-appropriate.

Expecting a child to act in a way that doesn't reflect their current stage of development is setting them up for failure. In the same vein, setting overly challenging limits can hinder a child from developing confidence and autonomy.

Here are some guidelines for setting age-appropriate boundaries for your child.

Infants (Birth to 12 months old)

Although infants are too young to understand rules, they still need some structure. You can help your child feel secure and guarded by setting a schedule for feeding time, playtime, nap time, and bedtime.

Toddlers (1 to 3 years old)

Kids in this age range tend to express the desire to explore their environment and have poor impulse control as well as a limited ability to recognize others' points of view. This is why the rules you set for toddlers should make room for discovery while preventing unhealthy behavior.

One way to pique your toddler's interest and explorative instincts is to place fragile and potentially dangerous objects out of their reach so they can play freely. Without restricting your child's curiosity, concentrate on teaching them to share possessions and avoid aggressive displays like hitting or biting.

When your child needs correction, it's best to say something simple, like, "No biting." At this stage, they're still too young to understand explanations. You can then redirect your child's attention to something more positive. And when that doesn't prove effective, consider relocating your child from the triggering environment and letting them calm down.

School-age kids (6 to 11 years old)

Kids at this stage are bound to face more social and academic challenges as they enter their school years. As a parent, your role is to reduce the level of uncertainty in a child's life by giving them practical and predictable rules to follow.

Ensure your child knows what's expected of them every day. For instance, inform them of when they need to complete their homework, do chores, have screen time, or go to bed. It helps to provide a printed schedule and place it somewhere they can easily find it, such as on the fridge or on a wall in their room.

Tweens and adolescents (12 to 18 years old)

During this age category, parents should gradually cease closely monitoring a child's daily schedule. Instead, they'll do well to let them choose among a broad range of times for when they'll go to bed, do their homework, or complete chores.

Stepping back in this way is essential to allow your child to learn to manage their life independently. In place of rigid rules, teach and enforce strong moral values and conduct.

When parenting tweens and adolescents, it's important to remember that respect is reciprocal. Avoid belittling your child when they seem distant or are questioning your perspectives.

If it seems like your relationship with your child is becoming strained, working together with them on a "behavioral contract" may help.

Adolescents are often more willing to cooperate when they believe they are understood and are treated fairly.

Instilling discipline can be increasingly challenging as your child ages. If it's beginning to seem like you've lost control of your child, giving up isn't an option. Your child still needs your support, guidance, and insight to thrive. Consider hiring a trained professional such as a licensed family therapist or psychologist to help you identify difficulty points and learn better ways to relate and interact with one another.

The Power of Connection and Attachment

John Bowlby and Mary Ainsworth devised attachment theory in the mid-20th century. The theory suggests that the way people form attachments to their caregivers in childhood has a profound impact on their relationships throughout their lives.

Where children have a secure attachment style, they're more likely to form healthy and fulfilling relationships with others. An insecure attachment style, on the other hand, may cause the child to struggle to connect with others in a meaningful way.

What Exactly Is Secure Attachment?

Secure attachment involves feelings of safety and support in people's relationships with others. People with a secure attachment style can trust that their needs will be met and that their caregivers (and later, their friends, romantic partners, or other close connections) will be there for them when they need them. Such a sense of security also helps people explore the world around them, take risks, and forge deep connections with others.

When children experience physical or emotional neglect, it may lead them to develop an insecure attachment style, including being avoidant, anxious, or disorganized.

Meanwhile, Dan Siegel, a clinical professor of psychiatry at UCLA, developed a concept called the 4 S's of secure attachment. They are:

- Safe
- Seen
- Soothed
- Secure

While parenting never promises to be a piece of cake, parents can (and should) show up for their children.

Showing up or providing consistent support for a child may help them form a secure attachment to their peers and loved ones. To do this, parents need to pay attention to the four core support concepts called the 4 S's.

Here's what the 4 S's of secure attachment mean for parenting.

1. Safe

Children need to feel safe. Here, parents need to commit that they won't be a source of fear for their child. Caregivers should also reconnect with their children after any bouts of disagreements while apologizing when in the wrong.

Parents should also help to provide their children with a sense that their home is a haven. As adults, safety could mean being more free to openly express emotions and needs and develop a sense of trust in interpersonal relationships.

2. Seen

When children feel seen, they sense that caregivers and parents acknowledge them. Caregivers can help children feel seen by taking time out to understand what they may be going through and to learn their personality.

When children feel seen, they tend to form emotionally secure relationships in adulthood. They also feel comfortable being vulnerable and acting genuinely. They're also less likely to develop codependency in adulthood.

3. Soothed

"Soothed" children feel comfortable at all times. To help a child feel soothed, caregivers should concentrate on helping a child develop healthy coping strategies even in challenging moments.

One way parents can do this is by being present, calm, and empathetic to their children during emotional moments. Caregivers should also show affection to their kids and engage them during these stressful situations.

In adulthood, "soothed" children have a high likelihood of becoming emotionally intelligent adults who are better prepared to survive challenging situations. They're also more likely to adapt to change and offer support to others.

4. Secure

For the fourth S, parents and caregivers can help cultivate a sense of security and trust with their children. Parents do this by showing up consistently for their little ones.

Creating a secure place for your child and connecting with them also involves encouraging your child to understand and be unafraid of their emotions and recognize these emotions in others.

When children feel secure and well-connected, they are vulnerable and feel free to make mistakes and voice their opinions without fear of rejection or punishment. Secure children may also find it easy to establish trust with others while maintaining a sense of openness, empathy, and trustworthiness.

Handling Public Outbursts and Meltdowns

If you have a child showing symptoms of oppositional defiant behavior, you never know when public tantrums or outbursts will happen. You'll seemingly never be prepared for it, but sooner or later, your child will throw a tantrum in public and it will be epic. Sadly, reasoning with a child during the middle of an intense meltdown is practically of no use.

Standing back to pretend it isn't your child won't work, either. But how do you survive your child's public outbursts and meltdowns?

1. Stay Cool

Be cool. Start calm. Avoid yelling or screaming and keep your voice down.

2. Empathize

Hug them. It might sound simple, but a hug can make a lot of difference.

Also, try to empathize with your child. Often, when a child loses it, it's because they're hungry, angry, lonely, or tired.

If they want you to buy them a toy and you refuse, consider telling them they might get it at some future milestone like their birthday. Now, you don't give in, as that could send a message to your child that they can always get whatever they want as long as they can "make a show."

3. Don't Use Threatening Body Language

Avoid squaring up, getting too close, or sounding threatening in your demeanor to your child.

Instead, try to stay a few feet away, soften your shoulders, and relax your facial muscles. It can be tough, but try to avoid a power struggle with your child.

And when your child's struggles seem to trigger big emotions for you and you don't feel in control, step aside to a separate place to self-regulate. Take a few slow, deep breaths. The breaths should go deep into the diaphragm and should last for about 10 seconds.

Or you can simply count to 10. Doing this could trigger your parasympathetic nervous system and make you ready for the challenge ahead.

4. Avoid Setting Punishments in the Moment

A punishment is a fair (when proportionate) measure when a child breaks a rule. However, you want to wait until later when everyone is calm. Otherwise, you risk escalating the situation rather than de-escalating and encouraging cooperative behavior.

5. Wait It Out

Sometimes, a tantrum is like a whirlwind; you have to wait it out. Stay around so they're aware of your presence—and your resolve to wait till they're done.

Waiting it out close by can also help you ensure that they don't hurt themselves.

Dealing with Resistance and Defiance

Kids with ODD lose their temper quickly and often. They easily get annoyed and frustrated by other people, and are resentful, defiant, and hostile with adults while being bossy and pushy with other kids.

Unrestricted free time breeds aggressive behavior among children. In an unstructured environment, children can become annoying, destructive, or threatening to other children and to adult authority figures.

In many of these situations, parents often get the blame for their child's defiance or oppositional behavior. Even worse, parents sometimes put more blame on themselves, or feel isolated and incompetent.

But how do parents deal with defiance and resistance in their children towards restoring peace in the home?

1. Create an Effective Structure

When dealing with resistance and defiance in children, it helps to create a structure around addressing your child's defiant behaviors.

They're possibly struggling against doing their homework or getting up early enough in the morning. Screaming at the child to get out of bed won't work.

Instead, you need to show your child that they have a problem that needs a solution.

So, you might tell your child, "Getting up late after your alarm has gone off makes you miss your bus. How can you avoid this?"

Setting the right structure for your child could also involve developing behavior contracts. These contracts help to remind children that they can earn more privileges if they behave responsibly.

For instance, if bedtime is a challenge, the behavior contract could help by attributing little rewards or "points" to kids for getting to bed on time.

2. Avoid Power Struggles

Fighting for power will only make the defiance worse. Instead, offering "if...then" warnings can help turn the behavior around.

Offer one warning only and ensure that you follow through with consequences when necessary. Giving in will only encourage more defiance because they don't think any *actual* consequences will follow if they defy or resist your orders.

3. Provide Logical Consequences

Logical consequences include things like loss of privileges or time-outs. It helps to be consistent with instilling these logical consequences, as consistency helps to reduce defiant behavior.

4. Seek Professional Help

Dealing with a child's ODD behavior can sometimes get out of hand. When you feel your discipline strategies aren't effective enough, consider getting professional help.

Workbook 7

Practice collaborative problem-solving with your child at least twice in two weeks. Observe your child's reactions to your attempts.

What do you think was the result of the CPS session? Is there a reason to celebrate? Are there any methods or strategies you need to revise for better results next time?

Key Takeaways

Implement positive reinforcement. Utilize collaborative problem-solving and effective consequences to encourage cooperation.

Be consistent with your routines and let your child know you expect them to follow them.

While you reinforce positive behavior by offering scheduled rewards related to their behaviors, ensure you don't accidentally reinforce negative behavior by giving in too early or paying attention to tantrums.

A token economy will help you implement rewards and will be as effective as you make it. Take it seriously and your child will likely get involved.

Children feel securely attached and connected to parents and caregivers when you help them feel safe, secure, soothed, and seen. While tantrums and outbursts may break out at any time, and anywhere, the best way to address them involves empathetically calming down yourself and your child, or waiting it out if other attempts to pacify fail.

PART 3

Thriving Together

Mrs. C was a mom to two kids—an 8-month-old girl and a 4-year-boy. While parenting children around this age range can be stressful for anyone, Mrs. C and her husband, who worked as a software engineer in Massachusetts, had been having acute challenges in the home.

Tim, their older child, was increasingly consumed by the tantrums and obsessions that are often related to ODD and ADHD.

Tim had shown early signals of ODD from birth. As a baby, he would cry a lot and was never a good sleeper. He outgrew this as he neared his first birthday and seemed happy for a while.

However, he soon began to show weird signs as a toddler. For instance, he'd pick up trash and put it underneath the stroller. He appeared to be having fun, and he did this obsessively.

At this point, Mrs. C and her husband were surprised at their child's behavior, wondering if every parent had similar experiences.

"Yeah, yeah. Kids often act like that." "All toddlers have tantrums," were the answers they heard from other parents.

But the challenge was the intensity of Tim's behavior; it was overwhelming.

Soon, Tim started displaying sensory issues, like not liking to have his hair combed, his teeth brushed, or how his blankets felt.

But that was just the beginning. The tantrums got worse and worse. Tim would soon start acting violently with his peers. He became more obsessively compulsive about things. He could throw tantrums for as long as two hours, and they were quite violent. His tantrums and violent behavior seemed to grow with his strength.

Mrs. C and her husband started seeking different solutions, including consulting with a developmental pediatrician who diagnosed him with autism. The pediatrician's diagnosis perplexed Tim's parents because their son was quite verbal.

Dissatisfied with the pediatrician's diagnosis, Mrs. C and her husband went on to see a psychologist, a pediatrician, and a naturopath. They got a diagnosis of ADHD and obsessive-compulsive disorder for their son.

Stimulants and other non-medical interventions wouldn't work (Mrs. C and her husband deferred giving their child drugs), and the tantrums got more violent.

But the challenge with Tim's behavior went beyond just affecting his parents' relationship with him.

It also affected how much care their 8-month-old baby got, as Tim seemed to take all his parents' energy and concern. Mrs. C was developing symptoms of intense stress, while her husband was finding it a bit hard to concentrate at work.

Once, Tim kicked a pregnant woman in the stomach. The family had to stop going out often, including to family functions.

Tim had a very low appraisal of himself. One day, while sobbing amid his tantrum, his mom heard him mutter while crying, *"I'm just never going to be happy, ever again."* It was heartbreaking for his parents to hear him mourn his behavior in self-pity and resignation.

It was at this point, when Tim was five years old, that a friend recommended a mental institute to Tim's parents.

Mrs. C and her husband hoped their visit to the doctor would be a one-off visit, followed by advice on medications and possibly follow-up on the phone.

To their surprise, the psychiatrist gave Tim an ODD diagnosis and recommended parent-child interaction therapy. It would last for three months, each session occurring once a week.

Initially, Mrs. C's husband felt the therapy was too expensive, besides the fact that the family would have to travel four hours to the city where the mental institute was located.

However, after the first three weeks, Tim started to improve.

The therapist recommended a family-based therapy that caters to the well-being of all family members toward creating a nurturing home where everyone thrives. Since Tim's behavior affected every member of the family, the therapist noted that holistic care for everyone in the home was necessary to build the right foundation for long-term success, not just for Tim, but for his younger sibling and parents.

Like Tim's psychologist had explained, the best approach to dealing with oppositional defiant disorder involves creating a nurturing home, building emotional resilience and self-care for parents, and zooming in on the child to help them become a successful person when they grow up.

How do parents of children with behavioral challenges like ODD create a thriving environment that checks these boxes?

I've carefully shared the answer in the final three chapters of this book.

While Chapter 6 addresses the relationship between the family environment and ODD, Chapter 7 addresses the emotional well-being of parents, and the final chapter ends with a game plan for long-term success for you, your child, and your family.

Let's look at how parents of children like Tim can help their children (and themselves) overcome challenging behavior and become a source of joy to themselves, their families, and society at large.

CHAPTER 8

The Family Environment and ODD

"Seek the Lord and His strength; Seek His face evermore!"

—1 Chronicles 16:11 (NKJV)

"Children feel nurtured and safe when we create a world for them that is orderly and predictable."

—Anonymous

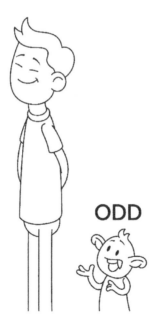

ODD

"I'm beginning to think you're outgrown me."

Creating a Nurturing Home
Creating a Nurturing Home Environment

Various studies have shown that when children are given the right environment, they're better suited to adapt to their experiences in adulthood.

Like seeds that thrive in a greenhouse that contains rich soil with good drainage and the right proportions of lighting, water, and protection from the wind, children need a healthy environment as well. And when it's time to transplant them into the world, they'll not only be hardy enough to survive, they'll also be vibrant enough to thrive.

Our home must become like a greenhouse, with the rich soil of our resources, the sunshine of our protection, the water of our love, and our protection from the winds of stress that weaken them.

Understanding Your Child's Unsaid Words

Children may have some significant control over their behavior, thoughts, and actions, but they have very little control over their environment. They have to depend on their parents to meet their basic physical and emotional needs.

That means it's important to provide the most nurturing physical and emotional environment possible for your kids.

Sadly, children sometimes are too young to identify or speak about their emotional needs or stresses. However, one way they communicate their needs and stresses is through their behavior.

Your child's behavior is always saying something. And when they act out, they're typically calling for help.

They could be telling you, "I need some space to move around," or "I'm overstimulated."

When you tell a child to "Stop acting like that," they're probably hearing, "Stop trying to tell me what's wrong with you or what you need."

That said, many years of professional and parenting experience have shown that when parents take the time to work towards figuring out what their kids' behavior is communicating, one of the best areas to look at is their environment.

Suppose a child melts down at a grocery store after you break the news they won't get the bicycle they were promised today. Is the child's public outburst a manipulation or are they communicating that they can't handle the disappointment in addition to the sensory overload from the fluorescent lights and the hum of the refrigeration units?

Everything in your child's environment, including the actions of people around them, the lighting, the food they eat, and the emotions of others, influences how they grow, develop, think, feel, and behave. Here are some things you can do to improve your child's environment and help them behave better.

1. Handle Conflict Well

Expressing anger and displeasure via loud yelling, flared tempers, and wild outbursts can create inner stress in children. Remember, your children will learn various behaviors by watching you, including how to handle conflict.

Would you be glad if your children took after your conflict resolution skills? Handling conflicts wisely and calmly can go a long way in directing your children appropriately.

Additionally, resolving conflict maturely signals stability to your children. They learn that even when people disagree, relationships can emerge unbroken.

2. Give Them Time

Children feel cared for and important when you give them time and attention. If they have to compete with your screen time and cellphone, they might think you care more about your social media reputation than your reputation in their eyes.

When your children are around you, it can be helpful to put down your phone. Ask them intriguing and engaging questions. Hug them, and possibly leave your phone where it won't disturb you.

3. Accept Your Child

Nurturing a child and accepting them are not mutually exclusive. One way to show your child that you accept them is through your words.

Despite their sometimes weird or disruptive behavior, it won't hurt to commend your child a few times. How about, "You are such an awesome kid," or "You know, your mom and I are so glad to have you as our son."

Another way to show your acceptance of your child is to support their interests—even if you don't like them. Don't allow your children to feel like they've disappointed you because they're not what you expected or hoped they would be.

4. Set Boundaries

Again, structures are among the most important elements to create a nurturing family environment for your child. That's because children feel nurtured and safe in a predictable and orderly environment.

Among many things, this means you want to set consistent rules with your kids and be consistent with implementing them. It also helps to explain to your children the "whys" behind all rules. They'll learn from the process of deciding what's important to you and your family.

5. Love

There's no building a predictable, peaceful home without the ingredient of love. Tell your children you love them. Carve out time from the day to play with them. A nurturing environment begins and ends with love.

Sibling Rivalry and ODD

If you're raising an oppositional defiant child, you probably have lost count of the times they've given their siblings violent headbutts or smacks. What begins as a minor altercation could quickly escalate into a full-blown fight that quickly gets out of control.

While sibling rivalry is a remarkably normal feature of family life that can sometimes push kids to become and do better, too much competition, squabbling, and fighting can also be hurtful. Sometimes, the impact of sibling rivalry could have lasting effects on children's self-esteem and perspectives about their family relationships.

According to a 2021 study on family dynamics, sibling bullying is linked to a lower sense of competence, life satisfaction, and self-esteem in young adults. Another related study found that children who were bullied by their siblings were twice as much at risk of depression and self-harm in early adulthood.

You may not think of physical and verbal fights between siblings as bullying, but they can feel that way to your children.

Why Things May Be Heating Up Between Your Defiant Child and Their Sibling(s)

Low frustration tolerance and resentful feelings are two possible reasons why your defiant child may be having constant aggressive behavior with their siblings.

All kids have some challenges with tolerating frustration. However, kids with oppositional defiant disorder experience these challenges more. These kids will almost always fight to gain control of any situation, regardless of who they're up against. To them, giving in to another child, especially a sibling, is unthinkable.

Moreover, siblings of ODD children are often aware that the intense stress level in the home is connected to the defiant child. Defiant children often deliberately annoy or aggravate others, whether it's to get revenge for a perceived wrong behavior or just to overcome boredom.

They often find it challenging to accept responsibility for their wrongdoing. And like we saw in A.D.'s story (in the opening of Part 2), a defiant child's irresponsible actions directly hurt other kids in the home.

Consequently, siblings may start to resent the defiant child, making them feel hurt and angry. This clash of emotions could get things heated on both ends of the sibling rivalry, as the kids battle between failing to take responsibility and being named the disruptive child.

So, what can you do to better manage sibling rivalry and turn it into healthy and helpful interactions?

Strategies for Managing Sibling Rivalry

1. Avoid Comparisons

Every child is unique. While comparisons are inevitable and natural, it's important to not compare your kids in a way that makes other children seem better than the defiant kid.

2. Be Aware of Your Biases

It's completely understandable and normal that you're proud of one child and find it impossible to feel the same about the other. However, be aware of that and ensure that you're careful about what you say and do.

As much as possible, work towards broadcasting through your actions that you love and appreciate all your children.

3. Be Aware of How Life Events and Stages Can Affect Siblings

Children are typically nicer than adults. But they also sometimes display symptoms of jealousy when another sibling seems to get most of the attention.

Even something exciting, such as winning an award or a new baby, can feel tough to a brother or sister. And they might need some extra love.

Meanwhile, an older teen sibling might need some privacy and need to be left alone by their younger sibling. Both of them might need some coaching and attention from a parent to avoid them hurting.

4. Spend Some Individual Time with Each Child

Each child in the home should feel like they're a priority and that you appreciate their interests. And when you need to spend some more time with one of your kids for a special reason, such as an emotional or medical problem, speak to the other kids about it.

5. Create Regular Family Times

Spend time with everyone in the family doing fun things to bond. Think game nights or family outings. It could help to rotate among your kids who chooses the game or activity the entire family participates in. That way, each child knows their parents value and appreciate their choices.

6. Ensure Restitution

If one of your kids harms their sibling or takes something from them, ensure a consequence follows their action. While your ODD child can be quite a handful, don't let them hold other family members hostage for fear of retaliation.

Find some form of restitution to compensate the child who was wronged by the ODD kid (or the other way around) and then follow through with the plan.

7. Have Ground Rules on Recognizing and Setting Boundaries in the Family

Everyone deserves respect and kindness in the home, whether or not they seem to have special needs. It's okay to disagree or even fight, but it's not okay to be mean.

Let your child know that too, and teach them to set these boundaries for the people around them.

If someone is deliberately provoking them with their actions or words, they have the right to ask them to stop or walk out. Suppose someone is following your child; they're crossing their boundaries and should be reported to the right authorities.

Create these ground rules, write them down and place them where everyone can see them, and stick to them. And if sibling rivalry is becoming a challenge in the home, speak with a professional.

Consistency in Parenting Styles

How confusing would it be for an ODD child to have parents who are constantly moving the goalposts?

One day, Mom lets them watch TV till 9 p.m., while the next day she gets angry after they'd just begun watching their 7 p.m. show. Mom thinks it's fine to leave the dinner table without finishing your veggies but Dad insists they must swallow every pea.

Whether it's one parent that's inconsistent, or it's both parents at opposing poles on certain actions, they still spell inconsistency in parenting styles.

Why You Should Practice a Consistent Parenting Style

1. Older children (especially) can learn to use inconsistent parenting styles to their advantage. They could play each parent against the other and sometimes use examples of inconsistent parenting as an excuse to push the boundaries.

2. When kids have repetitive experiences, it helps to strengthen the connections in their brains and tells them what to expect from their parents, family, and caregivers.

3. Predictability helps children develop deeper emotional stability. It also helps them develop emotional security and trust, which reduces their chances of misbehavior.

4. When a parent is inconsistent with their practices, it can cause children to develop problems attaching themselves to you. For instance, they could find it challenging to look up to you as a reliable source of comfort since there's little predictability or structure. This poor attachment can link to other social, behavioral, and emotional problems.

5. Lack of consistency can also motivate a child to gravitate towards a good cop/bad cop situation where kids run to one parent for warmth and care when wronged while painting the other black.

6. Worse still, differences in ideas on how parents should discipline and nurture their kids can lead to marital crises, which can in turn affect children's emotional, behavioral, and social outcomes.

Creating Consistent Routines

Routines are actions that happen about the same time and in the same way every day. They help a child feel safe and secure, resulting in fewer behavioral issues.

When you have consistent routines like taking a bath, putting on pajamas, brushing teeth, or reading a book just before bedtime, your child is likely to predict what happens next in the home, *ceteris paribus*.

This ambiance of predictability helps your child develop independence as they grow older. For instance, they're likely to begin learning to wash their hands or brush their teeth before going to bed without nagging and reminders.

Creating Consistent Expectations

Setting inconsistent rules or expectations for a child confuses them. They're likely to keep testing your limits, trying out what they can or cannot do, or how far a certain behavior is allowable.

Inconsistency is also likely to create power struggles and get both you and your child stressed and frustrated.

Remember, children are often still in the cause-and-effect stage where they're learning things they can *make* happen or the consequences of their actions. It helps to be as consistent as you can in how you respond and react to your children's words and behavior.

If you threaten to leave the store if your child doesn't stop throwing a tantrum because you refused to purchase a toy—don't purchase the toy, and leave the store if your child insists on putting on a show.

With older children, have a conversation with them, allowing them to ask related questions around the limits you set for them. Every child or family situation is different. However, by creating an open environment where they can discuss your expectations of them, you can keep fostering a healthy relationship with them based on trust.

Handling Necessary Adjustments

It's best to stick to established routines. However, routines can sometimes change due to decisions made in discussion with your partner or other changes in the routines in the home.

If there's a need to make adjustments or introduce major changes to the routine, share it with your child before doing so. This helps them prepare mentally so they don't have to be anxious or surprised about the change.

More importantly, if unwanted disruptions occur, work towards getting back on track as soon as possible.

Handling Challenging Situations: Homework, Mealtime, and Bedtime

As children grow and develop their mental and physical faculties, they tend to learn to be independent and to say no. During this developmental phase, you'll often find them resisting schedules such as bedtime or homework or trying to short-circuit the process.

However, while stubborn behavior can be normal in children, children with ODD often take theirs to a fiercer level.

With that said, if you're parenting a child with ODD, you have probably observed that mealtime, bedtime, and homework are some of the most challenging situations you'll find yourself in.

Here, I'll share some hands-on tips for helping your child cope with these challenges.

Preparing Your Child for the Next Task

One way to do this is to institute a routine. For instance, the routine could involve putting away toys, a final drink of water, or letting them know they should start preparing for homework or bedtime.

Of course, as you introduce the routine, your child will likely resist. Common objections to bedtime or homework could include, "I'm hungry" or "I want another movie."

It's helpful to address all these issues before moving to the homework desk or their bedroom. You can help prepare their mind by telling the child ahead of time that they're having the last snack, drink, or watching the last movie before their next task.

Keep Routines Short, Predictable, and Consistent

When you impose a predictable homework or bedtime routine, your child already knows what you expect of them. A typical routine could include putting on their pajamas, brushing their teeth, or getting their books out of their backpack.

Using a firm but warm tone is helpful to keep your child accountable when moving through homework and bedtime routines.

With that said, avoid making routines too long. Work towards keeping them under one hour. One way to shorten it is to break down the routine and have some of the tasks completed earlier (or later) in the day.

Reduce Exposure to Electronics in the Hour before Bedtime or Homework

It helps to reduce your child's exposure to electronics in the hour before bedtime or homework to increase their chances of properly concentrating or of sleeping soundly.

If you can't prevent your child from using a tablet or other electronic device before bedtime, consider lowering the volume or dimming the device's backlight. You want to ensure the content on the device is calm and soothing, not violence-inciting, fast-paced YouTube videos or action movies.

Instead, use audiobooks or soothing songs that help your child calm down before bedtime.

A similar situation is applicable to preparing your child for homework. Reducing screen time can help the child's mental preparedness for the task ahead.

Keep Calm

Keeping calm regardless of your child's violent behavior during bedtime or when they have to do their homework can go a long way in helpfully managing the situation.

Raising your voice or getting frustrated can make the child view homework as a dreary event or become more scared of bedtime routines. Alternatively, doing something calming for both you and your child can help you better prepare for the routines.

Think soft music, singing a nighttime song, or reading a book together. If you can turn these routines into times when you and your child both feel calm, it will become something you both look forward to every afternoon or night.

Avoid Foods and Drinks with Caffeine

Some caregivers don't know that most chocolate contains caffeine. That's why it helps to avoid giving your child chocolate-containing foods just before bedtime or homework hour. Ensure your child doesn't sneak in any sips of soda; if your child could possibly access soda outside your control, consider moving it out of their reach.

Boosting Good Table Manners at Mealtime

Toddlers can make quite a mess when they eat. Others would rather eat their food on the run than sit down at the table. Or, when they can, some kids don't mind wasting food by squashing it in their hands, throwing it on the floor, or leaving most of the food uneaten.

Of course you know that eating while running could cause them to choke, apart from being antisocial. And that food costs money, time, and effort to prepare.

But getting angry with your child for wasting food or worrying about whether they're eating enough won't do it. Ironically, defiant children are sometimes glad to see you anxious or angry. So, losing your temper doesn't teach your child proper table manners.

Instead, use some of the tips I've shared earlier in this chapter, such as being consistent with your parenting style and being patient with your child's growth process. That said, how do you inculcate table manners in a defiant child? Here are some helpful tips to try.

- Set up a predictable mealtime routine that helps your child remember that they should sit down at an appropriate table without distractions like TV or video games.

- Rather than fighting them over table manners, work towards making mealtime fun and enjoyable to your child. One way to do this could be involving the kid in important family discussions.

- Be realistic about the meal's timing; don't serve the meal too late.

- If your child is a toddler, present the foods in easy-to-eat ways such as in pieces or strips.

- Don't force your child to finish everything on their plate. It's sometimes better to waste a few leftovers than engage in a fight just because they failed to eat after becoming full.

- Explain the benefits of good table manners, such as avoiding the risk of choking or the ability to be understood when they speak without having a mouthful of food.

- Introduce consequences if your older kids deliberately waste food, including taking away their plate. You can then offer them a healthy snack later on if they're hungry.

- Compliment your child whenever they display the desired behavior using rewards like stickers or stamps. Avoid bribing them with candy, chocolates, or desserts.

Addressing Sibling Dynamics

A child spends half of their free time with siblings. Meanwhile, siblings also engage in some sort of conflict with each other eight times per hour, on average, and 70% of families report physical violence between siblings. Studies have also shown that 70% of parents demonstrate their preference for one child over another.

Granted, sibling rivalry could take various forms, such as arguing, name-calling, tattling, physical fighting, taking one another's belongings, and the like. But these conflicts can be exhausting, frustrating, and upsetting, especially when younger children or kids with ODD and other disruptive behavior are involved.

Here are helpful strategies to help minimize sibling rivalry in the home and help your kids get along.

1. Assess Sibling Conflict towards Managing It Effectively

Assess conflict levels between your kids as soon as they occur. Whether it's mild or moderate, stay out of it. Of course, if the fight approaches greater severity, then it's time to save the day.

2. Create More Time for Siblings to Bond

Siblings sometimes don't want to spend time together. Parents have the responsibility to instill this relationship and set the pace for their children.

One way to do this is setting time aside during weekends just for the kids. Try to get them to have some special time together, without your presence (or at least only while you're within earshot).

Helpful examples could be a kids-only movie night or getting them to write and perform for the rest of the family. The aim is to boost a feeling of camaraderie and togetherness among them.

3. Schedule Quality One-on-One Time

Schedule times to spend regular, quality hours with each child individually. Doing so helps to create more potential for healthy interaction between siblings, as each child increasingly feels they don't need to compete to be worthy of your special attention.

4. Establish Equitable (Not Equal) Rules

Treating your kids the same way could do them more harm than good. That's because each child is unique in their developmental phase or needs.

While your 15-year-old son might have to do his laundry, your 7-year-old daughter might only have to place her dirty clothes in the laundry bag.

Tailor your rules, consequences, and expectations for each child to meet their unique situations. That way, you can set up your kids for success individually as they learn from your rewards and consequences.

5. Give Your Children the Benefit of the Doubt

Avoid stereotyping certain behaviors to your older child or your ODD kid. Sometimes, even the most troublesome child in the pack is 100% innocent. And the oldest child may not always be the bully.

Give each child the benefit of the doubt, remembering that everyone has a role in every interaction or its outcomes. That way, you're less likely to misjudge a child prematurely, while boosting an equitable environment where everyone feels loved and noticed.

6. Set Healthy Boundaries

Set healthy boundaries on what's obtainable among your children across physical, social, and emotional lines. And once you notice a child teasing the other or taking play too far, it's time to intervene and draw the line. For instance, separate them when the kids appear no longer in control of their actions.

7. Make Teamwork Exciting

Whenever possible, it helps to put your kids on one team. As the kids work towards a single goal, they learn to work together and collaborate, increasing their chances of getting along.

8. Encourage Win-Win Negotiations

If a conflict comes about, your first response should be to honor both sides. Dismissing the significance of what the kids are fighting over might overtly or subtly dig into the situation or escalate it.

Validating what they're angry about can also encourage them to find your intervention helpful and compassionate. After validating the bone of contention, give each child some time to express their perspective.

As each child listens to the other person share how their sibling hurt or wronged them, they're likely to learn more empathy and prepare for win-win situations.

Support your kids in choosing creative ways to ensure everyone has a satisfying answer to their problem. For instance, schedule a specified amount of time to have control of the TV remote if it's become a common cause of conflict among your kids.

9. Avoid Taking Sides

While most parents have favorites, and you might have yours, avoid displaying them. The more you refrain from displaying favoritism, the more secure your children will feel.

Avoid comparing one child to another. They might grow to resent the (perceived) best-loved child. One way to help promote a good relationship among siblings is to ensure they don't feel you're treating them differently, or unfairly. That way, you can raise them to avoid blaming others and reduce the chances of sibling rivalry.

Balancing Attention Between Siblings

If you have a child displaying ODD symptoms, you might sometimes feel guilty for leaving other kids in another room while you tend to the disruptive child. With other demands competing for your time and attention, it can be challenging to create enough time to make everyone feel loved and cared for.

How do you balance attention between children in the family, particularly when the disruptive child's behavior is already inspiring the other children to tread a reactionary but unpleasant path?

Here are some ideas for improving balance in your home and helping each child feel special and appreciated for who they are.

Talk openly about it in a non-embarrassing way. "Your little sister is having some real difficulties right now. I know that means I'm spending more time with her, but that's not because I love her more. We'll get through this, and while we're at it, how can I make you know how special you are to me?"

Make time to do special things with the other kids. How about a special swim date for Dad and son? Or a manicure day for Mom and daughter? Or going to pick out a new outfit for your child as a family? Your children are likely to notice your efforts at ensuring everyone feels equitably loved and will appreciate them.

Lastly, avoid assuming that the other kids will understand. Put yourself in their shoes and try to imagine what it feels like to think a sibling is getting more attention, even when that isn't the case!

Don't Ignore Your Older Child

Don't ignore your older kids. As your older child increases in independence, it's easy to assume they won't need you as much. And that should be the case, to an extent. They should be able to use the bathroom, prepare their own food, or entertain themselves without your help.

But don't let their increasing self-sufficiency deceive you into thinking they don't want your attention anymore. While a younger or more challenging child will likely need your help more, your older child still needs your time, even in the easiest ways.

Think about ways you can spend time with them, such as asking them to help with your younger or problematic kid, when you can. You could also schedule a later bedtime for them than their siblings so you can review their day's homework or read a book together. They'll appreciate your meeting their needs, and recognize that their sibling isn't your priority *at all times*.

Pay attention to the attention balance. Ensure you're open and honest while letting all your children know how much you care about their feelings.

Family Therapy and Its Role

Family therapy is a form of group psychotherapy (talk therapy) that works towards improving interfamilial relationships and behaviors. Therapists use family therapy to help families adjust to life milestones like aging, relocation, or family-based relationship conflicts.

Mental health professionals also use family therapy in treating certain mental health or behavioral conditions. For instance, family therapy could involve engaging all or multiple family members in treating oppositional defiant disorder in one child in the home.

Besides ODD, family therapy can also help treat other mental health conditions like:

- Anxiety disorders
- Eating disorders
- Mood disorders
- Schizophrenia
- Substance use disorder
- Conduct disorder
- Disruptive mood dysregulation disorder (DMDD)
- Personality disorders, like borderline personality disorder

Types of Family Therapy

The choice of family therapy depends on your family's unique needs and circumstances. Therapists may also combine elements from various therapeutic approaches in the best way they can to meet your needs.

Here are some types of family therapy your therapist might suggest to you in helping a child grow through oppositional defiant disorder.

1. Couples Therapy or Marriage Counseling: Here, the therapist addresses you and your partner to help you determine the causative factors behind your problems and provide helpful solutions. Issues may relate to communication, raising kids, finances, understanding your partner's mental health condition, and more.

2. Structural Family Therapy: This type of therapy considers the inner relationships, boundaries, and hierarchies that make a family unit (or structure). This therapy concentrates on fostering direct interactions among family members as its primary way to create positive change. It helps family members discover alternatives to problematic patterns in their interactions, rather than receiving instructions on what to do.

3. Systemic Family Therapy: The foundation of systemic family therapy considers the family's issues in their various contexts. For instance, the therapist will consider how one family member functions as a partner in a romantic relationship, or as a parent to their child, and vice versa. Other possible contexts include cultural, religious, and political views or socio-economic status. According to this philosophy, context is the

most significant factor in the family's psychological development and emotional health.

Psychotherapy

Psychoeducation is also a crucial part of family therapy. It involves mental health professionals teaching families about mental health conditions. It also involves basic information about the condition (in this case, oppositional defiant disorder), its prognosis (outlook), and potential treatment options.

Finding a Family Therapist

Finding a family therapist can be a time-consuming task. Speak with trusted people around you, such as your primary healthcare provider or a friend or family member, to give you a referral for a therapist.

Also, consider searching for family therapists online through local and state psychological associations. Ensure your family therapist is licensed to practice in the state as a mental health professional. It's also helpful to seek someone experienced with attending to children's behavioral conditions.

Benefits of Family Therapy

Various studies have studied the effectiveness of family therapy in helping children with mental and emotional health conditions, such as depression, adolescent substance use, and obesity. These studies show significant improvements in relationships among family members, while also showing it can help children function better at school.

Here's what the numbers look like. About two-thirds of respondents report an improvement in their overall physical health. In child-parent cases, about 73% of parents report that their child's behavior improved. Meanwhile, almost 90% of people report an improvement in their emotional health.

Risks of Family Therapy

While family therapy has its upsides, it isn't for everyone. For instance, if one or more members are reluctant to participate in the therapy, it can create conflict in the home.

Family therapy will more likely work if participants are open and honest with the therapist; are committed to making positive changes; and show readiness to follow up on the agreed-upon action plan.

Workbook 8

Playing kids versus parents

Schedule a moment for an all-family fun session. I suggest you play a game where kids team up against the parents. It could be any game, from indoor sports to board games.

Ask your kids what they think of the event, and possibly ask for their suggestions for subsequent family fun times.

Key Takeaways

Creating a nurturing home, maintaining consistency in parenting, and incorporating family therapy to foster cooperation are important in helping your child's behavior improve.

When children are given what they need to build a solid foundation in their early years, they have more strength to deal with life's experiences in adulthood. And a solid foundation includes the right environment.

Kids need consistent routines, rewards, and consequences for undesirable behaviors. Consistency might take a long time, but being consistent in your response can help them improve and adjust their disruptive tendencies.

Mental health professionals use family therapy, a talk therapy that caters to all family members, in treating certain mental health or behavioral conditions. Family therapy is most likely to work when all participants show readiness to follow up on agreed-upon action plans.

CHAPTER 9

Self-Care for Parents

"Rest and self-care are so important. When you take time to replenish your spirit, it allows you to serve others from the overflow. You cannot serve from an empty vessel."

— Eleanor Brownn

"Come to me, all you who are weary and burdened, and I will give you rest. Take my yoke upon you and learn from me, for I am gentle and humble in heart, and you will find rest for your souls. For my yoke is easy and my burden is light."

—Matthew 11:28 (NKJV)

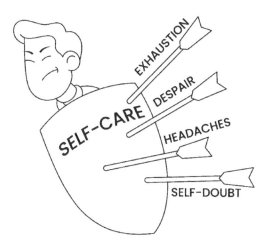

Emotional Resilience and Self-Care for Parents
The Parental Stress and Emotional Exhaustion Cycle

Dr. C, a clinical psychologist resident at a Boston hospital, understands the terrain of parenting while working on a personal level. After moving to Boston with her three kids to begin her residency, she had to function solo until her husband could join them.

She had to manage her budding career and her kids' well-being—all during a worldwide pandemic. Consequently, she had to often neglect her self-care. Soon, perpetual exhaustion, a high level of irritability, and burnout became a constant schedule in her daily routine.

What Burnout and the Emotional Exhaustion Cycle Feel Like

Burnout is a form of exhaustion that occurs because parents have been through emotional, physical, and mental stress. It happens when parents feel overwhelmed and are unable to meet life's demands.

In 2019, the World Health Organization recognized burnout syndrome in its International Classification of Diseases as an occupational condition connected to various health conditions like substance use, changing sleep habits, and fatig ue.

Experts would say burnout occurs in stages.

In the first stage, parents experience overwhelming exhaustion. Depending on the child's age, parents may experience various forms of exhaustion. For instance, parents of toddlers and younger kids tend to be more physically tired, while parents of teens may experience emotional exhaustion due to conflicts with their children.

During the pandemic, many parents had to focus on childcare and homeschooling during the day, often delaying their jobs till the evening. This made them more likely to be irritable and stressed the following day.

Sadly, these burned-out parents tend to cope with chronic stress by attempting to plan how to get everything done. That approach, experts say, complicates the challenge and can disrupt sleep, exacerbate anxiety and irritability, and become a loop that repeats itself daily.

When they don't find relief or respite, the next stage sees burned-out parents distancing themselves from their kids to preserve their energy. Of course, this, in turn, can hurt their feelings as well as their children's feelings, and possibly worsen the cycle's effects.

The third phase is when parents begin to notice a loss of fulfillment in parenting. These parents will likely make statements like, "I like my child, but I just can't stand being around them anymore."

Whether a burned-out parent spanks or yells at their child, they not only harm their kids but can create a vicious cycle of emotional exhaustion. Parents who experience this often feel ashamed and end up later ruminating on their behavior. Incidentally, they also wake up the next day more tired and sensitive to the feelings of their children and themselves, further compounding the situation.

Symptoms of Parental Burnout and Emotional Exhaustion

The symptoms of parental burnout build on one another. Sadly, parental burnout isn't like occupational burnout, where people can change jobs to get some relief. Consequently, people undergoing parental burnout may experience suicidal ideation and escapism.

Burnouts can also cause parents to be violent towards their children or neglect them, even against their ethics or philosophical leaning.

Signs of burnout include:

- Irritability

- Emotional exhaustion

- Lack of motivation

- A sense of despair

- Headaches, neck pain, and muscle aches

- Feelings of helplessness, hopelessness, or self-doubt

- Isolating behaviors

- Detachment from others and pleasurable activities

Why Parental Burnout Is Becoming More Common

Parental burnout isn't a new phenomenon. Parents have experienced this condition for decades, especially as women entered the workforce in droves over the last hundred years. Due to the COVID-19 pandemic, today's parents are also experiencing heightened levels of stress and anxiety.

Medical reports claim that more parents are reporting experiencing bouts of parental stress and the emotional exhaustion cycle. And there were various reasons for this prevalence, including loss of jobs, homes, or incomes leading to additional stress and anxiety.

As other studies corroborate, other reasons for burnout include financial insecurity, lack of support, and social isolation.

Research also shows that parents with poor coping skills are at risk of experiencing burnout frequently. Similarly, people with low frustration or poor resilience skills are more susceptible to experiencing burnout.

Overcoming Burnout and the Emotional Exhaustion Cycle

If you constantly neglect your feelings to satisfy your child, it can result in cycles of parental burnout and emotional exhaustion. Fortunately, there are some things you can do to overcome burnout.

Let's look at a few of them.

1. Speak with Your Partner

One of the first things you can (or should) do when experiencing burnout is speak with your spouse or loved one.

Explain your experiences to them in an honest way. Don't be afraid to admit you're struggling or overwhelmed. Share your needs with them, if possible, outlining concrete details about them.

2. Get Adequate Sleep

Sleep is vital to your mental health. Getting adequate sleep can be difficult, especially if you have a newborn or young child at home. However, if you can prioritize sleep, don't hesitate to do so.

You can consider having what psychologists call twenty-minute power naps at different times during the day. These naps can help reduce stress and restore your emotional, physical, and mental well-being. They can also improve your focus and help you better regulate your feelings.

3. Rest When Possible

When you feel overworked or overwhelmed, take a few minutes to rest. And there are various ways to rest, such as having a warm cup of coffee or tea. You could also consider sitting on the sofa, watching cartoons with your kids or listening to music.

Feel free to be as creative as possible. However, you'll do well to get as much rest as possible.

4. Build a Support Network

It's amazing to have a supportive partner or spouse when battling with overcoming emotional exhaustion. However, many parents need more help. Others lack the required resources or at-home support.

An excellent way to extend your support network is joining parenting groups. They may help you feel understood, seen, and heard. You could also hire a childcare provider or sitter, especially if you think you need a break.

Consider speaking to a psychologist or therapist if you still feel overwhelmed. Sometimes, just speaking with others can help you gain a better perspective or new insights that helps you to be happier.

5. Be Patient with Yourself

Raising challenging kids is both difficult and rewarding. Feelings of exhaustion and frustration can (and do) happen, and most caregivers will experience parental burnout at one time or another. It's normal. However, how you treat yourself matters.

Allow yourself to *feel* your feelings. You don't have to face everything all alone and be Superdad / Supermom.

Don't forget that you're still human and vulnerable. You aren't the source of all the problems in the home. And you can't fix everything that's wrong. Be patient with yourself. Be kind.

6. Exercise

After going through feelings of exhaustion, the last thing you might want to do is spend another stretch of time working out or burning calories in a gym—at least, not until you learn how helpful exercise is to people experiencing burnout.

Research has shown that exercise can actually increase your energy levels. It can also help to reduce stress.

7. Practice Self-Care Daily

While it might sound impossible sometimes, practicing self-care every day is one of the best things you can do for yourself.

Take two minutes every morning to breathe and think about you. Journal if you have the time, or walk down the road.

Bathing at the end of the day can also help you unwind.

Strategies for Managing Parental Stress

Parenting is no walk in the park.

From late night feedings to tantrums and outbursts or homework, raising little humans is challenging.

Not to mention that you often have to place your child's needs ahead of yours.

The effect of this could be parental stress that sometimes affects various other aspects of your life.

How do you deal with the parental stress that comes with parenting children with ODD?

Ration Your Exposure to Negative Thoughts and Negative Media

It's natural for people to start looking for patterns when going through a challenging situation like parenting ODD. You're likely convinced that your child's next move will be problematic. And you'll likely pay more attention to potential threats when you're feeling upset, angry, or alarmed.

When stressed, people tend to focus on the negatives. Sadly, your biases and fear may graduate into self-fulfilling prophecies. And assuming the worst can make you liable to provoke negative behavior from others within and outside the family.

Avoid exposing yourself to negative emotional content, as your current stress levels may inspire you to focus more on upsetting images, threatening words, and negative feedback. You're also more likely to replay or recollect negative memories or worry about the future, leading to a downward spiral of deteriorating mood.

These thoughts activate the stress circuits in the brain, leading to more anxiety and gloom. Meanwhile, a single trigger such as an unpleasant reminder, an angry comment, or a distressing anecdote could be sufficient to set the process in motion.

Overdosing on threatening and bad information doesn't just enhance your current stress levels, it can also affect your ability to think constructively and solve problems. Consequently, you could hurt everyone, including your children, your family, neighbors, and coworkers.

Switch off disturbing media. Avoid people who may want to judge you or be hostile or rude to you, particularly for events connected with your stress. Consider taking a new route to work if it could mean avoiding noise, pollution, hostility, and other factors that stress you.

Concentrate on the Positives

You've already seen how negative images can trigger your stress response on a downward spiral. The opposite trend is also true. People can induce good moods when they concentrate on positive content.

This is why you want to seek out pleasant social interactions, concentrate on your child's smiles, and seize chances to demonstrate physical affection to them. Concentrate on your favorite memories, read entertaining and uplifting stories, share jokes, and take some time out with the family pet.

Researchers have proven that these activities can help to distract your brain from stress towards calmness and healthier living. Additionally, concentrating on others' acts of kindness and social support, including those performed by strangers, can help deactivate the stress response.

Budget for More Time

Everyone experiences time pressure, but some parents find it particularly difficult.

According to a study in Scandinavia, moms are more burdened by time pressure than dads. And most women affected by time pressure are usually financially stressed, highly educated, or lacking in social support.

You may think that changing your schedule is costly. However, consider that the stress that comes from time pressure can be toxic, and several studies have showed that people often underestimate how long future tasks will take.

Thankfully, your family will likely benefit from adjusting the overall expectations for the schedule. Suppose running late is hurting your degree of self-fulfillment; start preparing for the day earlier without assuming your child is trying to get in the way.

Reappraise after Bad Things Happen

Sometimes it doesn't matter how many great thoughts you think. Sometimes, stressful things happen. Yet there's a lot you can do to cope with the situation.

First, studies show that people handle stress better when they reconsider situations from a different angle.

Psychologists found that HIV patients have better quality of life when they concentrate on the good things they experience, such as their personal relationships. While you may not be in that category, it's certain that the littlest bit of positive thinking can make a significant difference in how you feel.

Studies show that parents who use cognitive reappraisal are less likely to overreact or be counterproductive when disciplining their kids.

A good practice is to conduct a positive reappraisal to help you bounce back. By positive reappraisal, I mean you review events after things have settled a bit to learn from the experience.

What if the negative situation doesn't seem to have any silver lining or any potential lesson to learn? Try to view the situation with more objectivity and detachment and stop dwelling on your personal emotional reactions.

Now, this isn't the same as suppressing your feelings (bottling up your negative feelings could hurt you even more). However, it involves stepping outside to see the big picture.

For instance, you might need to concede that tough times have their season, even though they don't (or shouldn't) last.

Balancing Your Needs with Your Child's Needs

To adequately care for a child, parents and caregivers need regular a refresh through social, emotional, and practical supports. These support systems can help you and your child flourish.

Conversely, their absence could lead to heightened stress and struggles that have a high possibility of building up or being ignored instead of being resolved. And consistent buildup of stress could lead to poor social, emotional, and physical health in parents and children.

Fortunately, there are various ways to replenish yourself, ranging from practicing self-care to connecting with other parents.

Self-Replenishment Essentials for Parents

1. Eat Healthy Foods

Depending on your demography (male, female, nursing mother, etc.), there are various healthy foods nutritionists would recommend for your health. However, nutritionists generally advise that people drink enough water, eat a diet rich in fruits and vegetables, and avoid eating meals late at night.

Consider speaking with your personal healthcare provider or nutritionist for helpful information on how you can maintain a proper diet.

2. Exercise Regularly

Again, everyone likely has exercises that appeal more to them than others. And some exercises may also benefit you more than others, depending on what your typical day looks like.

Whether it's taking frequent evening strolls or subscribing to a gym for monthly workouts, find a suitable regimen that matches your daily schedule and helps you replenish your energy sufficiently.

3. Take Naps During Your Day

Naps as short as twenty minutes during the day can help you recover from the stress of work and family life and refocus on your personal needs. These brief sleeps can also be helpful breaks to rewind over the day and mentally prepare to effectively carry out the remaining tasks of the day.

4. Practice Self-Care

It could be a cup of tea, some juice, or a fortnightly spa day. Whatever you need to stay happy or effective may just be worth it—not just for yourself, but for you to be a better colleague, spouse, or parent.

5. Avoid Overscheduling

Research shows that people are likely to overestimate how much they can do over a specified period of time. Understand that you're likely to be among this class of people and modify your next schedule appropriately.

And if you still don't manage to do the dishes, mop the floor, and complete the leftover tasks from the office before the next morning? Don't beat yourself up over it. Things happen.

6. Leave the Home

Take a walk down the street or in a park not far from your home. Go alone if necessary, or with your spouse. It can help relieve the stress or tension that could build up after the day's activities.

7. Enjoy the Present

Yes, you may be having a tough time raising your kids. However, it's also a season to be proud of, and to be enjoyed. Children help us shift our priorities to what matters most. So, enjoy the highs and lows of your day, remembering that it won't last forever, anyway—with the hope that you and your kids will come out just fine.

8. Connect with Other Parents and Caregivers

Connecting with communities where parents and caregivers provide support and encouragement for one another can provide you with so much love and support that could lessen your stress levels and leave you lighter.

You'll also be better prepared to discover new ways of viewing existing problems and reconnecting with and updating your own internal parenting compass. This can also help you discover effective parenting skills that suit your family needs.

Letting Go of Guilt: No Such Thing as Perfect Parenting

"Mommy, hug and kiss!" Sarah was already late and stood the risk of not beating the traffic on the way to the office if she didn't leave now. But her little daughters were running towards her with determination. Their goal was to ensure they got at least one more hug and kiss before letting her go. And they must get them.

Sarah crouched down, trying to avoid their sticky mouths on her office-ready dress.

"Mom, will you pick us up from daycare?" her older child asked.

"Not today," she replied. "But I'll be back before dinner, all right?" While the answer seemed satisfactory, a feeling grew increasingly in Sarah's heart as she approached the car. She recognized the feeling all too well: mom guilt.

Many mothers, whether or not they work outside the home, understand what it feels like to think they aren't living up to the expectations they had about the kind of mother they'd be.

It could be getting takeout instead of cooking dinner, shouting instead of answering patiently, or getting bored solving math homework for the thousandth time.

It doesn't matter what you feel guilty about. While one parent could feel badly about their children not playing enough sports, another parent feels guilty that their child spends too much time playing sports.

But why do parents constantly compare to see whether they measure up?

Unclear Expectations

Parenting is one thing nobody understands until they run into it—and even then, they know surprisingly little. It's no doubt one of the most challenging jobs in the world, yet parents have no real way of knowing whether they're doing well.

Many parents worry that there are no clear goal posts for what they need to do to be great parents. And when your child keeps throwing up challenging behavior typical of kids diagnosed with ODD? The guilt is almost always in your face.

Cut it out. Nearly every parent feels just like you do.

Besides, no one's going to give out a parent-of-the-year award!

Of course, you could feel like a failure after every time your child is being a jerk. But it isn't worth the guilt.

What if the things you're putting most of your energy into hardly register with your kids? Your kids might not care that you spent hours trying to get them a "perfect" dance costume. And they may not be so impressed that you made their sandwich into the shape of their favorite cartoon character.

The best way to truly impress your kids? Just be there for them. Spend time listening to their stories. Play their favorite game with them.

Do They Feel Safe and Loved?

You definitely never expect your child to be perfect. Why should you be a perfect parent?

Whether you like it or not, you're still learning and growing as a parent. Of course, there are some things you should feel guilty about. That's also fine.

But there are many other times, especially after an intensely busy day, when your guilt explodes for almost no reason at all.

During these times, it can help to ask, "Are my kids alive? Do they feel safe? Did I tell them, 'I love you'?"

If the answer to all these questions is yes, then it's time to let go of all your guilt.

Your children feel safe and loved—and they know that completely. And that's what really matters. That's what they'll most often remember when they reminisce on their childhood, and you definitely shouldn't feel guilty about that.

Self-Care Techniques

Self-care refers to a set of conscious actions people take in order to promote their own physical, mental, and emotional health.

Self-care could take various forms, from getting enough sleep every day to stepping outside for a few minutes for some fresh air. It could also involve taking some time out to do things you enjoy.

Self-care is helpful to build resilience toward the life stressors you can't eliminate, such as work or family life. Parents are better equipped to live their best life after they've taken the adequate steps to care for their mind and body.

Sadly, many people tend to view self-care as a luxury they should have only once every six months rather than a priority. As a result, they're often left feeling overwhelmed, ill-equipped, and too tired to handle the challenges life throws at them.

Why Self-Care Is Important

Research has shown that an effective self-care routine is beneficial in various ways. Some of these include:

- Improved happiness
- Increased energy
- Reduced burnout
- Stronger interpersonal relationships
- Reduced stress and improved resilience
- Reduced anxiety and depression

According to the World Health Organization (WHO), self-care is vital because it can promote health, prevent disease, and help people better cope with illness. The global organization has also linked specific forms of self-care, such as exercise, to different health and wellness benefits, including a longer life.

Types of Self-Care

Psychologists have classified self-care into at least five major classes: physical, emotional, social, mental, and spiritual.

Every parent needs to find a balance between these types of self-care to appropriately care for their health and children's well-being. You may also need self-care in one specific area of your life toward restoring balance or finding relief from a stressor in your life.

Let's examine what each of these types of self-care means and how to achieve them in your home.

1. Physical Self-Care

You need to care for your body appropriately if you want it to run efficiently. Remember that there's a strong link between your body and your mind. As you care for your body, you're likely to feel better in other areas of your health as well.

Physical self-care could range from how you fuel your body to how much sleep you're getting and how many physical activities you involve yourself in. Attending medical appointments, taking prescribed medication, and managing your physical health are all part of physical self-care.

Here are helpful questions you can ask to assess your physical self-care routine:

- Are you getting enough exercise?
- Does your diet adequately fuel your body?
- Are you getting enough sleep?
- Do you feel like you're taking charge of your health?

2. Emotional Self-Care

Emotional self-care helps you have healthy coping skills against uncomfortable emotions like sadness, anxiety, and anger. This may involve doing activities that help you acknowledge and express your feelings safely and regularly.

It could be talking to your partner or a close friend about your feelings. It could be setting aside time for leisure activities that help you express your feelings.

To assess your emotional self-care activities, consider questions like:

- What activities do you incorporate into your life to make you feel recharged?

- Do you have healthy ways to process your emotions?

3. Social Self-Care

While it can be hard to make time for friends and you may end up neglecting your relationships as life gets busy, socialization remains vital for self-care.

Your connections are vital to your well-being. And the best way to maintain these close relationships is to put time and energy into building them.

There's no specific number of hours you need to spend with friends and family. Everyone has different social needs. You'll want to figure out your social needs and build adequate time into your schedule to create an optimal social life.

You may ask yourself these questions to assess your social self-care:

- Are you getting enough one-on-one, in-person time with friends?

- Are you consciously working to cultivate your relationships with friends and family?

4. Mental Self-Care

Your thoughts and the way you think can immensely influence your psychological well-being, and by extension your overall health.

Mental self-care involves doing things to keep your mind alert, such as puzzles or learning about a subject that amuses you. Reading books or watching movies that inspire and fuel your mind might also be excellent ideas.

Self-compassion and self-acceptance can help you maintain healthier inner dialogue. A couple of questions to consider when considering your mental self-care include:

- Are you making sufficient time for activities that stimulate you mentally?

- Are you doing proactive things to help you be mentally healthy?

5. Spiritual Self-care

While many people tend to overlook the importance of spiritual self-care, it's highly important in helping you feel whole, balanced, and happy.

Here are some questions to help you check how well you're paying attention to your spiritual welfare.

- How often do I meditate?

- What activities help me feel calm in my spirit?

- Do I prioritize being alone and connecting with God from time to time?

Decluttering, meditating, taking a walk in nature and more are great steps to get started with spiritual self-care. It's really up to you to decide what activities you're most comfortable with

Finding Support and Community Resources

You and your partner want the best for your kids towards nurturing their growth and development. One of the best ways to help you overcome the stress, financial strain, and social isolation that comes with parenting ODD is to connect with other parents and kids.

You want to get the right information and emotional support to help you learn about enhancing your child's behavior and overall well-being. The expected result is improved outcomes for you, your partner, and the kids.

What Community Support Systems Can Offer You and Your Family

Fortunately, the U.S. has tons of support and community resources for families and parents with various needs. These resources range from online platforms containing large databases of helpful support structures to walk-in community centers in your neighborhood, city, or state.

Here are some of the offerings you can get from various support and community resources around you.

- Information about disabilities, diagnoses, and resources (how to access services)
- Parent-to-parent support among people with similar previous or current experiences

- Workshops and support groups with training and strategies you can explore

- Social activities for the entire family

- Family advocacy and policy development—helping parents contribute to family and disability-related policies and programs

There Are So Many Resources

Now, while that earlier statement about the thousands of support and community resources available might sound like good news, it can have a negative effect too.

Some parents become overwhelmed and find it challenging to navigate the service system for their child and find social and emotional support for themselves.

For instance, if the platforms aren't user-friendly enough for easy navigation, or the preferred resources are distant from home, or there might just be too many resources to know which to select for your situation, it can be difficult.

In such situations, it can help to consult a professional psychologist or your family doctor on the most appropriate support structure for your family. Or you could contact organizations like the National Parental Helpline or similar governmental resources for helping children with challenging kids.

When Do I Seek Support?

Every parent needs some form of support in raising their kids, whether they're raising toddlers or young adults who are about to leave the home.

Getting support may include basic activities like speaking with a friend or family member whose child is older than yours or chatting with your parent about your child.

However, it might be imperative to seek some form of more comprehensive or professional help with parenting your child in situations when you need to:

- Understand a new diagnosis
- Transition your child into early intervention preschool; public school; post-secondary education; or employment
- Relocate the family to an entirely new location or state
- Advocate for educational rights and services
- Plan your financial needs while having a special needs child
- Find special services like building a ramp or inclusive summer camps
- Obtain parenting strategies and education
- Help your child deal with stigma or bullying
- Balance the needs of typically developing siblings
- Raise a prematurely born infant

Maintaining a Positive Outlook on Your Parenting Journey

Parents are almost always searching for ways to change their children's behavior into some mold that works perfectly for them.

However, successful parenting isn't about achieving perfection. Instead, it's about working towards that goal and become good, positive parents to our kids.

That's because, sometimes, trying to change *yourself* rather than your children might be the final straw that'll break the back of your child's ODD behavior.

What if you stopped trying to change your kids, and just began changing *you?* What if you changed your parenting style, expectations, and philosophy? What if you just chose to not take everything too seriously?

Adjusting your thoughts and feelings about your parenting struggles can help you become a calmer and more positive parent.

Making a little change to your perspectives here and there can help you actually enjoy your kids more, and—better yet—your child(ren)'s actions will follow your lead.

Here are a few little changes that can help to produce stronger and more positive relationships with your kid(s).

Change Your Lens

Rethink about what your child possibly wants to get out of the actions you consider "bad" or "defiant." Maybe your child's high-pitched shriek that gets under your skin is actually just to get your attention or reaction.

It might sound weird, but kids are fine with negative attention when they just need any response from you. So, your angry reaction is only enhancing their behavior.

Next, reconsider why you think this action bothers you so much. Do they embarrass you in front of others? Have you tagged it as "bad" behavior just because older folks think it is unacceptable?

What if the behavior is more_developmentally appropriate than extraordinary? Looking at things in a less stressful way can help you stress your kids less about changing, and possibly fast-track their growth process.

Reduce Your Expectations

Understandably, you want to raise your kids the best way possible into becoming the best they can be.

But sometimes, we tend to forget that kids are still *kids*. If your child is showing too much childish behavior, first consider that that behavior is somewhat common among other kids.

Sometimes, during the holiday season for example, your child might be overwhelmed by large gatherings or having to eat and sleep at different times from regular school hours. Or your child may be introverted or shy. Try to reduce your expectations of your child, and it'll do at least one thing for you: create less room for frustration.

Remind Yourself It Won't Last Forever

Do you remember how horrific your first weeks were after having a newborn baby? You hardly slept, feeding a little baby every couple of hours.

That stage might have felt like it wouldn't end for you, but it did. And so will each phase of parenthood.

If your 3-year-old will only eat spaghetti and milk or your 12-hours-a-night sleeper just started waking up at midnight, remember that this won't last forever.

Coach Instead of Control

Instead of seeking to *control* your child's behavior, how about *coaching* them through authoritative parenting? Consider yourself to be your child's life coach—someone who will be there to encourage them and make good decisions and model appropriate behaviors.

Share the Emotional Responsibility

You're possibly already asking your partner to drop off your son at school or help change your baby's diaper, right? Sure. But how often do you share your emotional responsibilities as a parent?

Whenever you feel overwhelmed by all the feelings that come with being a parent, or are getting worried about how your kid is performing in school, share your emotions with your spouse or partner.

You can't (and don't need to) carry the weight of the home alone.

Workbook 9

Look out for online support and community resources in your city or state that help with parenting children with ODD.

Find the resource(s) that best suits your needs and participate actively on the platforms or at sessions.

Ask relevant questions about caring for yourself and your family and get answers from people with significant experience working with children who have behaviors similar to your child's.

Share your experience with others as you help your child (and your family) become the best they can be socially, physically, mentally, and emotionally.

Key Takeaways

Prioritize your well-being and manage the guilt and stress that comes with parenting through self-care, stress management techniques, and self-compassion.

There's no perfect parent. And there's no perfect child either. So, cut out the dad/mom guilt.

While your ODD child might be quite a handful, trying to change their behavior to suit your situation may not work.

Replenishing yourself through self-care is essential for your child's health and growth. And that's achievable through physical, social, and emotional resources and support structures.

Self-care also helps you build resilience toward the life stressors you can't eliminate, such as work or family life.

There are various resources online and onsite with communities and support systems to help parents and families with tough kids better understand and overcome their situations. Seek the opportunities that best suit you, and when you've found them, participate actively in them towards improving your family's experiences.

CHAPTER 10

Long-Term Success

"For I know the thoughts that I think toward you, says the Lord, thoughts of peace and not of evil, to give you a future and a hope. Then you will call upon Me and go and pray to Me, and I will listen to you."

—Jeremiah 29:11 (NKJV)

"We may not be able to prepare for the future of our children, but we can at least prepare our children for the future."

—Franklin D. Roosevelt

"Can you take a break from being so supportive?
It's exhausting!"

Preparing Your Child for Success
Celebrating Progress and Small Wins

Celebrating your child's small wins and progress motivates them to keep going and accomplish even bigger things.

Whether you're trying to ensure your kid completes their homework daily when they return from school or cleans their room every week, begin by celebrating the next time they do their "favorite" chore or obey your less important instructions.

While I can't promise that your child will start improving dramatically within two weeks after you start reading this book, you can always expect to see a little progress that's worth celebrating.

The Progress Principle

Professors Teresa Amabile and Steven J. Kramer of Harvard Business School discovered the Progress Principle. The principle, in summary, posits that small wins add up to bigger ones.

It claims that making progress in meaningful work is the most important thing that can boost a person's positive emotions, motivate them to move forward, and give them the perception of accomplishment.

According to the principle, solving little problems can lead to an extraordinarily positive inner life. In the workplace, this sense of accomplishment drives performance, creativity, and productivity and gives you the power to make each day the best it could be.

Why You Want to Celebrate Your Small Progress and Tiny Wins

Celebrating progress and small wins with your child is about finding meaning in little successes. Taking time to celebrate the littlest wins in your child's behavior or self-care therapy helps you appreciate the efforts invested and the progress made. Let's now examine why celebrating little wins is important for parents, families, and children.

Motivates a Positive Outlook

You're likely to stay motivated and positive as you appreciate each progress and win, no matter how small. It also helps you see the good things in your life and your child's world and maintain a rather optimistic view about parenting an ODD child.

Builds a Stronger Family Bond

Celebrating little wins can help to bring families together, especially when you do this alongside your spouse and other family members. It reinforces the idea to everyone that you are all in this together.

This sense of togetherness creates a stronger bond between family members and creates a supportive chain where everybody helps each other through life's highs and lows.

Increases Your Confidence

Celebrating little wins is a great confidence booster for you and your family. Acknowledging and celebrating your achievements, regardless of their size, can help you recognize your (and your child's) capabilities and strengths. As your confidence increases, it can help you tackle tough challenges with ease.

Celebrating Success with Your Child

When a child demonstrates a little improvement or experiences a small win, the feeling of accomplishment (which could result from you celebrating them) keeps them motivated.

Success can be found when you begin to recognize small wins, celebrating what your kids have done so far to encourage them toward completion.

Of course, remember that successful parenting also affects you. You'll be motivated towards doing more to improve your child's behavior as you celebrate their (and your) wins in character, skill, and other areas. The tiny wins may seem insignificant, but they carry lots of weight and meaning in our lives.

Here are various ways to celebrate.

1. Take Time to Reflect

Reflecting on the small successes can help you appreciate and celebrate your kids. After each day or week, take some time to think about the things that went well and those that made you proud.

2. Give the Kids Some Kudos

Give your kids kudos for the strong (you just have to call it that!) effort they've put into their work so far, rather than the perceived outcomes. The effort they put toward attempting to obey you or listen to you is in itself a small win. That's particularly important because while your kids might be growing in self-confidence (or their confidence in you), you don't want to berate them for their little roadblocks or bumps.

3. Treat Yourself

Don't hesitate to treat yourself when you achieve your small wins. Treating yourself helps to enshrine the milestone and possibly encourages you to look forward to the following weeks or months in your child's life.

Treat yourself to something you enjoy, such as your favorite meal, movie, or a day out with your family.

4. Share the Success

Consider sharing the success about your child's behavior or parenting experience with others. It can help to spice up your celebration.

Speak with your family and friends about the little success you've achieved. It can also help to use social media to share your accomplishments and inspire others to share and celebrate their little parental wins.

Encouraging Independence and Responsibility

When your child was younger, you likely often heard them scream every now and then, "Let me do that!" Your 5-year old kid wanted to take out the trash, bake cookies, and mop the bathroom.

But now, your formerly helpful child is possibly nowhere to be found.

It doesn't happen to all kids, but many children shift into a new phase. Picking up their toys or hanging up their coat after school becomes a dreadful task. And playing has become so much more important than their homework.

As they approach the teenage years, you'll find your child displays another level of independence. But this independence isn't exactly the way you might desire. Teens insist they want to have their academics, social relationships, and their life in general under *their* control.

Of course, your child's display of independence (or the absence of it) can skyrocket with ODD-like behaviors in the background.

You think your child might ruin their reputation and the family's image if they keep skipping school or going out with bad friends. But your teenager thinks you're just an old-fashioned and unintelligent parent.

That said, regardless of what your child thinks they need, you have the right to teach your kids responsibility and independence.

Remember, parenting is a lifelong commitment that won't always be easy, even as your child grows and improves their character to make you and the family proud. Let's look at some tips to help your child become more confident and self-reliant and to boost their self-esteem.

Give Them Some Space

Kids need space to learn and develop. And chances are low that they will ever become more independent if you actually don't give them the chance to *be*. Encourage self-reliance in your kids by giving them ample opportunities to explore without being overly supervised.

Are your kids playing in another room? Allow them to play without you. And if you must check on them, be discreet about it. If their play spirals into a conflict, give them a chance to resolve their differences productively before intervening.

Are you walking alongside them on a sidewalk? At your discretion, allow them to walk a little ahead of you. When you can, send them out to get the mail if your mailbox is some distance away. Give them the chance to order or pay for their lunch while you watch them from a safe point.

The goal is to find at least one way daily where your child can accomplish something on their own, without your direct supervision.

Offer Choices and Freedom—with Limits

Provide reasonable levels of freedom that lets your kids make choices. Doing so builds your child's confidence in their decision-making skills and helps them build a sense of responsibility.

It could also involve asking your child to choose whether they'll walk home from school with a friend or choose whether to wear a red or blue shirt. Allowing your kids to make their own choices gives them more significant opportunities to think on their feet, with or without your presence.

Moreover, letting your child make their own decisions helps you show your kids that you value their ideas, wants, needs, and preferences. The more practice you give them in making choices for themselves, the better.

However, remember that giving your child too many options can get them overwhelmed.

So instead of asking them what they want to do after doing their homework, how about asking them to choose between going to the playground or hiking? You want to offer two or three options you're comfortable with. That way, you're free to say yes to all their options.

It'll help to provide some buffer (in the form of supervision, rules, or guided choices) when giving them new freedoms.

Admit that mess-ups can happen. But it just means your child isn't quite ready for the new privilege. In that case, be prepared to intervene and keep them behaving responsibly or safely.

Thankfully, losing the privilege can also serve as a natural consequence. That way, you'll lean toward helping them build the necessary skills to explore their freedom in the future when they're ready, instead of concentrating on their past wrong behavior.

Believe in Your Child

Your kids need to know that you believe in them. Encourage them with positive words like, "You're a smart kid. You know how to do this." By doing this, you're also preparing your kids to gain greater self-esteem as you spur them towards independence and responsibility.

One way to allow your child to think positively about themselves is by modeling the behavior in yourself. Remember, your kids see themselves in you and will be more impressed if you appear self-confident as a dad or mom.

Let Your Kids Fail and Experience the Consequences

Life is full of opportunities to succeed and make mistakes. Sometimes, kids won't learn until they hurt themselves in some way. Resist the temptation to constantly hover over your child or telemonitor them.

If your child is bent on making a negative choice, consider helping them experience the natural or imposed consequences of their actions. An 'F' in school—especially their first—sends a very clear message that they need to study harder or that your warnings are proving true. It hits differently from when you were trying to hound your child to study so they don't fail.

And if your child chooses to stay out longer than your curfew limits, they lose the privilege of going out the next weekend. You can be sure they'll likely think twice (or more) before staying out late the next time.

Peer Relationships and Social Skills

One of the most important factors in a child's development is how they get along with others. In fact, good social skills are necessary for success in life.

These skills include working well with others, making good friends, or acting appropriately in various social situations. It also includes what they say to others, how to keep friends, and more.

How kids and adolescents function socially can affect their academic performance, behavior, interpersonal relationships, and participation in extracurricular activities.

Researchers from Penn State University discovered how children can successfully navigate the social world of peers, benefiting from their friends while also overcoming the stress that could arise from peer conflicts.

Peer relationships, the study shows, provide a unique context for kids to learn a slew of vital social emotional skills, like empathy, cooperation, and problem-solving strategies. That means, among many other things, that there are things your child would rather learn from their peers than at home.

However, these relationships can also contribute negatively to a child's social and emotional development through bullying, exclusion, and deviant peer behavior.

Lastly, the Penn State study discovered that children experiencing difficulties with their peers often need extra systematic and intensive social coaching.

It might seem like you have little control over how your child relates with their peers and friends. On the contrary, there are several ways parents and caregivers can positively influence their child's social skills to develop healthy relationships and friendships.

Here are ways to help your child become more socially savvy based on psychological science.

Toddlers and Preschoolers

Your child can learn good socialization skills as early as toddlerhood. In fact, that's an excellent time to begin, as research shows that children with good social skills have a higher chance of staying in school, being happy in future relationships, and remaining healthy.

Here are ways to help toddlers become better socially.

- *Show your kids how to take turns.* Use play times as a chance to show them how to take turns rather than allowing them to dictate every activity to you. For instance, suggest looking at a book together after they suggested playing with stuffed toys. You can help them build flexibility as you involve them in such interactions so that when they're with their peers, it isn't entirely strange to them.

- *Structure playdates.* Your child is likely to improve their social skills if you positively involve yourself in their world. Help your kids organize social opportunities such as playdates. It can also help to help them decide when, with whom, and what they do together.

Young Children

If your kids are coming into kindergarten and elementary school, they're still quite self-focused. It's the right time to help them to begin thinking about others. Remember, younger kids typically think in concrete terms. It'll help to suggest highly skill-driven activities that tell them exactly what to say and how to say it, for instance.

Here are some ways to help them.

Help them Act with Kindness

Ask your child what they did to ensure other kids feel happy in a given activity. While doing so, you can quietly advise them on acts of kindness to execute towards others. For instance, suggest that they invite another kid sitting alone to join them on the playground.

Encourage Them to Take Another's Perspective

If your child loves playing with a certain toy, speak with them about inviting one or two other kids to play with the toy with them. This exercise helps them accept other people's differences and also gain empathy.

Middle Schoolers

Two social aspects of your child's social life become prominent as your kids get into middle school. One centers on their peer groups, while the other relates to the development of one-on-one friendships. Some ways to help kids in this age group include:

Encourage Them to Develop Friendship Skills

Great friendships have a number of common denominators, including disclosing vulnerabilities, nurturance, trust, and loyalty. You want to help your child understand and demonstrate these qualities and also choose the right friends to share them with.

Boost Their Self-Confidence

Middle-school children also need to learn how to maintain their self-confidence against the threat of peer exclusion. This is the stage where kids will likely experience some form of bullying from their peers. Teach them that they're not victims of bullying because of their own faults, but because bullies just have challenges with controlling behavior. It's also a great time to guide them toward making their own decisions about peer issues while letting them know that you're there to support and counsel them.

Teens

As kids grow into the teenage years, their peer relationships grow more sophisticated as they possibly enter romantic relationships, deepen friendships, and experience increased peer pressure. Here's how to help them navigate this complex social period.

Teach Them to Honor Themselves

Teaching your child to value and nurture their own identity can go a long way in building their social skills. It also reminds them not to buckle under peer pressure or environmental demands. Research has shown, however, that your kids will eventually end up creating values somewhere at the midpoint between their parents and peers' desires.

Normalize Their Insecurities

Most teens are concerned about their social identity. You want to remind them that they're not alone; virtually everyone else is just as worried as they are. Telling them that can also encourage your teens to empathize with their peers, as they too are possibly dealing with lots of complex issues.

Preparing for Transitions and Future Challenges

Life is a process of continuous change; it unfolds like a river, flowing into the future not quite known or seen. And it isn't any different for your child. As your life goes through various situations, your child is possibly going through the transitions with you or experiencing their unique changes physically, mentally, socially, and emotionally.

As your child journeys through life, they're likely to discover and rediscover their identity, beliefs, and unique lifestyle. Their experiences will likely shape their perspectives, expectations, and ultimately their identity.

So, whether it's moving across culture, class, age, or location, the birth of a sibling, the death of a loved one, or a serious illness in a family member, children also experience events that could split their world open.

Now, you don't have to wait until you change your child's school or welcome another baby to teach your child how to overcome transitions. Here are some ways to help your child feel safe, adjust, and build resilience against the big changes.

Give Them Time to Prepare

Of course, some changes (like the passing away of a loved one) don't give you time to prepare. However, when preparation is possible, give your child lots of warning about the imminent future change. That gives them time to process and start accepting the change.

It also gives you time to familiarize your child with the unknown. If you're moving into another home, consider taking your child along with you to the new house/school. You could also invite your child to meet the teacher, get a brief tour of the classroom or even learn from the teacher what a typical day at the new school is like.

If you're welcoming a baby, show your child pictures of themselves as babies. Speak about what to expect when the new baby arrives and all the ways your kid can be a great big sister or brother.

Listen to Their Concerns

While you might want to remind your child about the bright aspects of the big change coming, take time to address their questions and concerns. That way, you can work through the emotions they're going through.

Many times, children just want you to understand and empathize with them. It'll help to acknowledge and validate their feelings without being too quick to deter them or shield them from their emotions.

For instance, tell them something like, "Moving to a new place can seem scary or sad. It's fine to feel that way. But we can handle this together."

Help your child label their emotions if they seem to struggle with identifying their feelings (such as sad, nervous, worried, scared, or anxious). Helping them put a name to the feeling makes it less overwhelming and easier to manage.

Give them some tips ahead of time on how to manage their anxieties or worries. For example, it's okay to fill them in on various activities that you'll still do together even after the new baby comes, including hugging or kissing them when they need it.

If they're anxious about moving to a new school, think of a comforting strategy that roleplays potential scenarios and conversations to get them less anxious. Work to ensure your child feels heard and recognized.

Keep Routines Intact

One of the ways to help your child cope with big changes is to ensure—as much as possible—that routines stay the same. As you've seen again and again in this book, consistency and stability can help your child build resilience and sufficient emotional intelligence in the new era.

So, avoid changing your child's crib, for instance, if your child is already anxious about losing attention to their new sibling. Maintain bedtimes and mealtimes. Ensure the structure feels safe for kids. You want to provide as much safety as possible to your child through the changing situations.

If you're changing homes, consider painting the new room like the child's former room. Allow the child to play with the same toys, read the same books, and repeat as many family rituals as possible.

Give Them Options and Request Their Help

During major life changes, children tend to feel they have no control over events. However, you can allow your child to make the right choices by letting them choose the wall color for their new room, cook the first meal in the new house, or decide their first outfit on their first day at the new school.

The same goes for requesting your child's assistance. Kids want to contribute and feel valuable, responsible, and helpful in the home, regardless of how they demonstrate that ubiquitous desire.

Ask your child for suggestions for the new baby's name or for additional input on the new house. Depending on your child's age, they can help with moving boxes, packing items, or doing other things to assist with the relocation.

Of course, there are plenty of ways to make your child feel more responsible or more special and important in the new season.

Note that your child likely feels helpless at this moment. But you can help them address this feeling by providing subtle opportunities to allow them to help you and make decisions.

Connect and Play with Them

Here's another vital factor that should remain consistent in your child's relationship with you through the changes.

Help your child know that regardless of what happens, you'll still be by their side, and nothing is going to happen to the bond you share with them.

While you might be coping with the new changes and the extra stress that comes with them, it can help to set time aside (as little as 10 minutes) daily to give your child your undivided attention.

Put the phone away, make eye contact with them, and maintain a playful and affectionate ambiance while spending this period with them.

It can help to watch a movie together, play a video game that your child enjoys, or share a meal at your child's favorite restaurant. That way, you're able to bond with your child in a more personal way by engaging in the activities they enjoy.

A little additional attention and parent-child play time can help to reassure your child of your love and care. It also helps your child better cope with other changes in their lives.

Speak with Them about Other Changes

Engage your child in age-sensitive discussions about their life's journey thus far.

What changes have already taken place in their lives? It could include getting a new pet, joining a soccer team, or starting a new grade in school.

Speak with them about why these changes occurred. What was good or not so good about these changes? What did your child learn from these experiences? How did they go through it, and what coping skills did it teach them?

Taking lessons from their past can help your child feel stronger and more prepared for the next one.

Similarly, you can draw a "before" and "after" picture for your child, showing to them changes they've successfully moved past. Speak with them about the experience of that change, asking some of the questions above and others you may think of yourself.

After walking them through these changes, you'll possibly help your child see that the once-terrifying changes are part of everyone's lives. They therefore no longer need to feel scared or overwhelmed by them.

That way, you're preparing them to put the current transition or big change into perspective.

Their situation may feel scary now, but you and your child can adjust to the changes together. Along the way, they'll also learn new strategies and skills for handling the changes that inevitably occur in life.

Advocacy and Reducing Stigmatization

People with behavioral disorders like oppositional defiant disorder are often faced with stigmatizing behaviors from other members of society. This response often comes as people anticipate behaviors that those with ODD could suddenly display.

Sadly, such stigmatizing behavior comes from people around them who should protect, nurture, and guide them toward constructive behaviors.

These stigmatizing behaviors range from avoidance to reduced quality of life or even unfair treatment from the criminal justice system. Those with ODD also sometimes wrongly suffer from restrictions on social facilities and reduced roles in their lives and community participation.

Researchers say that social stigma and discrimination can worsen mental health problems and stop people from getting the help they need.

Other harmful effects of the stigma associated with ODD behaviors include:

- Feelings of shame, hopelessness, and isolation

- Self-doubt (the belief that you'll never overcome your illness or achieve what you want in life)

- Reluctance to seek help or get treatment

- Lack of understanding from family, friends, etc.

- Fewer opportunities for employment or social interaction

- Bullying, physical violence, or harassment

Helping ODD Kids Deal with Stigma

Do you want to have an ODD child who's battling any of these stigmatizing behaviors (or more) because of behaviors they're likely to exhibit? Are you trying to help your child to overcome stigma and fight for their rights despite their behavior?

Here are some helpful tips to work with.

1. Provide them with the necessary mental health treatment. Don't let the fear of being labeled with a child suffering from mental illness stop you from getting the help you need.

2. Don't believe the lies. Your child's situation likely leads you to various information online and offline (from specialists, family, and friends). The truth is, not all this information will be true. But constantly listening to ignorant information can force you to believe it or negatively influence the way you feel about yourself. Note (and teach your child) that mental health conditions aren't a sign of weakness and are rarely something you can deal with on your own. Consulting a mental health professional is an excellent start on your child's (or family's) road to management or recovery.

3. Never hide or isolate yourself. Many people with mental health or behavioral conditions want to isolate themselves from others, especially in the face of stigma. Encourage your child to reach out to people they trust—coaches, family, friends, or religious leaders. Of course, you expect them to include you in that list of people they can turn to easily for support.

4. Connect with others. Where necessary, consider leading your child to join a mental health support group, either virtually or in person. You may not call these groups exactly what they are in front of your child to reduce feelings of shame or embarrassment in them. But groups of people who are heavily misunderstood by others can help them deal with feelings of isolation and make them realize that they're not alone in their experiences.

5. "You are not your illness." Ensure that your child doesn't define themselves by their illness as other people would. Rather than saying, "I'm a defiant kid" or "I'm disruptive," teach them to say, "I have ODD." The subtle difference can make a lot of impact on your child's self-esteem.

6. Avoid personalizing people's judgments. Many of these hurried judgments are biased and based on a lack of understanding more than anything else. Whether it's from their friends, peers, or neighbors, these judgments often arise prematurely from people who didn't take the time to personally get to know them. So, teach your child to not accept these judgments as having anything to do with them.

Advocating for the Rights of ODD Kids

The United States as a whole and each state in the country have existing legislation against discrimination in compliance with international conventions and regulations that protect the rights of people with mental illness.

If you parent a child struggling with ODD and need to get them the help they need, you aren't alone. Schools sadly don't always inform parents about available support structures.

In A.D.'s story earlier in this book, his recovery and better management began as his school intervened in his situation and convinced his parents to schedule sessions with a psychologist.

1. Obsessively Document Everything

One way to easily navigate the complicated school system and its bureaucracy is to obsessively document all milestone events around your child's case. That includes the details of all conversations—whom you spoke with, the date and time it happened, and what you discussed. Other important documents to keep include your child's report cards, written communication with their school, and, where applicable, paperwork showcasing a 504 plan and Individualized Education Program (IEP).

2. Boldly Request an Evaluation

Avoid being scared of requesting an evaluation from your child's school on their social performance. These evaluations can help to reveal your child's strengths, weaknesses, and the kind of services they might require to perform optimally.

Often, parents are scared of requesting evaluations for their kids because they're worried that evaluations must always result in some kind of service they're not comfortable with. However, you're never obligated to consent to recommended services. An evaluation only provides information. And it's never harmful to have more information about what's best for your child.

3. Communicate Adequately

The better you communicate with your child's school, the better the outcomes your child experiences. Keep open communication with the school staff, especially if you're concerned about anything happening with them or at school.

Also, learn how to speak to your children, asking questions like, "Tell me one thing you learned today" after school. That way, you can help your child learn where they might be struggling, which is a vital step to help them learn where they might need additional help.

4. Understand Your Rights—and Your Child's Rights

Is your child in a public school? You have more power than you might think. However, to effectively advocate for your child, it helps to deeply understand the rights available to you as a parent. Consider looking up these rights through your state's Department of Education and similar organizations that publish detailed factsheets for parents.

Goal Setting for a Bright Future

Scientists say that 92% of people fail to achieve their goals. And most of these people may have never learned to effectively set their goals.

But how do you set the right goals for your child's future? Positive goal-setting is about making challenging but achievable goals that your child feels motivated and energized to pursue.

The trick is to find the right level of challenge to meet your child at their current level or situation. Walking your child through the right goals can help them better participate in school while building valuable life skills.

Set Achievable Goals

While it's helpful to set challenging goals, ensure that they're not out of your child's reach. You know your child best and understand how much challenge they can handle.

But suppose you're not sure; begin small and build up their resilience gradually. To make the goals easier to achieve, break them down into smaller steps that let them experience a sense of achievement along the way to keep them interested.

Set realistic goals for them so they can experience the sense of accomplishment that comes with achieving goals.

A goal could be as little as "I'll get to class on time daily" or "I'll get no lower than B's in all my courses this year."

Make the Goals Actionable

Define how your children can make their goals happen. It's not enough for your child to say, "I'll make it onto the school's long-distance racing team" without including how to reach that goal.

It might be better to add, "I'm going to make it onto the school's long-distance racing team by spending 45 minutes daily practicing ball drills and showing up at practice twice a week." That way, it becomes clear what the child needs to do.

Create Time-Specific Goals

Setting the right timeframe for goals can help motivate your child as they track their progress and monitor how close they are to reaching their goals. Help your child set realistic timeframes that aren't too far or too soon in the future so they have a better chance of attaining them.

For instance, suppose your child wants to become better at reading. Help them pursue reading at least one book each month. At the end of the year, they'll have read 12 books.

This is helpful for setting not just short-term goals, but long-term success goals.

Create Their Goals, Not Yours

It can be challenging to step back and allow your child to make their own choices. That's because kids are more likely to take responsibility for achieving their goals if it's their goals, not yours.

Your child might come up with some weird goals. The process of negotiating and guiding them toward an achievable goal is necessary for their mental development, but you want to guide them towards goals that reflect their identity and positively pique their interest.

Record Their Goals and Speak about Them

Your child's goals could be about many things, from arriving at school before the bell rings to asking for help when they need it and speaking kindly to peers and teachers. Whatever their goals are, they're more likely to stick to them if you record them and talk about them as often as possible.

Allow them to position their goals where they deem fit, such as on the fridge, the wall in their room, etc. At the right time, regularly speak about them with your child so everyone can effectively track and celebrate any wins while providing any support they might need to get them going.

Workbook 10

Creating SMART Goals for Your Child's Future

Whether you have a toddler, a middle-schooler, or an adolescent ODD child, you can set SMART (Specific, Measurable, Achievable, Realistic, and Time-bound) goals to set them up for success later in life.

Work with your child to create SMART short-term and long-term goals that align with their (and your) needs.

Let them know about the goals, and place them in a comfortable place that lets you track and measure their progress in line with the goals.

Key Takeaways

Teach your child to be independent and responsible by giving them some space and offering them some amount of freedom with measurable limits.

Prepare your child ahead of transitions by giving them time to prepare, listening to their concerns, and keeping routines intact.

Understand your (and your child's) rights appropriately to identify and defend them against discrimination if they're struggling with ODD. You have the right to request an evaluation of your child's social behavior. However, you're not obligated to accept any recommended service.

Your Review Can Inspire Change!

Dear Valued Reader,

Congratulations on completing our book! Your journey through its pages is a testament to your commitment, and we're deeply grateful for your participation in our narrative.

Now that you've turned the final page, we invite you to share your reflections. Your insights hold the power to guide future readers embarking on their own journeys. An honest review from you shines as a beacon, revealing the treasures within our book. It celebrates the moments that captivated you, the wisdom that resonated, and the doors it opened in your life.

Your feedback is more than just a review; it's a compass that helps fellow adventurers navigate the vast sea of literature, particularly moms and dads on their own unique paths.

Dedicating just a minute or two to leave a review on Amazon can cast ripples across the reading community, fostering a world of inspired readers.

We eagerly anticipate your stories and insights! Below are the links to share your invaluable experience. Every word you offer lights the path for others.

With our sincerest appreciation,

The Team at SpreadLife Publishing

SpreadLife Publishing

 Leave a Review on Amazon US

Leave a Review on Amazon UK

Conclusion

As I pen down the parting words in this self-help parenting manual, I can't help but recollect several stories of young people – kids and adolescents – globally who were diagnosed with ODD/ADHD and have gone on to become well-behaved, successful adults.

This book contains a few of those success stories, but there are thousands of success stories out there all across America of such kids who've turned out great later in life. If these stories are anything to go by, your child's behavioral condition isn't hopeless. If you're taking the right steps, chances are high that your child *will* get better, learn to better manage their behavior and become responsible members of the society, rather than develop worse conditions.

You've seen that some ODD/ADHD cases occur due to genetic causes, while others are largely due to environmental factors, such as the mental health of their parents. Regardless of their predominant factors, psychologists recommend a family-based therapy approach to treating ODD/ADHD.

Family-based approaches refer to methods that address the mental, emotional, and physical health conditions of all family members. So, where a parent requires emotional assistance themselves, the right therapy helps them effectively manage their emotions while guiding the child toward constructive behaviors.

After attempting to help you understand ODD/ADHD in the first part, the next part runs into empowering caregivers and parents of ODD/ADHD kids with the right strategies to deal with the behavior.

First, the strategies involve communicating rightly with your child about their condition. And that includes separating your child from their behavior and seeing the possible best about their future. Even more, it involves helping your child view their situation from the most optimistic point of view possible.

Since ODD/ADHD behavior is mostly tied to emotional management and expression, showing you how to build emotional intelligence in your child became of prime importance in the second part.

Emotional intelligence (EQ) involves teaching your child to become self-aware, control their emotions, motivate themselves, empathize, and effectively relate with others.

While empathizing with your child about their behavior, it's vital to seek various ways to effectively instill discipline in your child. These effective discipline techniques include setting routines and structures, positive reinforcement, as well as rewards and consequences that truly pique your child's interests.

Remember, the ultimate goal is to help groom your child to become an independent, responsible, and successful member of the family and the society at large.

That's why, in the third part, I show you how to create a nurturing home for kids exhibiting ODD/ADHD behavior without compromising your own emotional or physical health. Lastly, there's no denying the need for SMART goals **(this language is too common)** when crafting your child's path to success. Yes, SMART goals**(this language is too common)** chart the course for anyone who intends to achieve success in life, and that includes successfully parenting ODD/ADHD.

How has this book helped you already on your parenting journey or in understanding how to raise kids diagnosed with ODD/ADHD effectively? Is there any feedback, comments, or suggestions on the lessons shared in this book that you'd like to have me hear?

Kindly feel free to share them with me via the Amazon page where you purchased the book.

Remember, you're not alone in this.

Till we meet again,

Adios.

References

Abraham, Kim (2023)
The Odd Child and Sibling Fighting: 5 Survival Tips

https://www.google.com/url?sa=t&source=web&rct=j&opi=8997844
9&url=https://www.empoweringparents.com/article/odd-child-and-
sibling-
fighting/&ved=2ahUKEwja6firiLSBAxU8QUEAHWexDhsQFnoEC
BYQAQ&usg=AOvVaw0LE7t-weT8bkUwOa-B45N

Akyurek, Gokcen et al. (2019)
Stigma in Obsessive Compulsive Disorder

https://www.google.com/url?sa=t&source=web&rct=j&opi=8997844
9&url=https://www.intechopen.com/chapters/65312&ved=2ahUKE
wiIrL-
5jbSBAxWqW0EAHQ_DA3EQFnoECCwQAQ&usg=AOvVaw29d
ddpnXA8griNv9Wp1-7C

Ashley, Abramson (2023)
The Impact of Parental Burnout

https://www.google.com/url?sa=t&source=web&rct=j&opi=8997844
9&url=https://www.apa.org/monitor/2021/10/cover-parental-
burnout&ved=2ahUKEwjv8Z6zirSBAxUzQUEAHWodBEwQFnoE
CBAQAQ&usg=AOvVaw0UtIOdkVfR4w2vzbGQxYl3

Astair, Alison (2023)
Sibling Rivalry - 12 Tips on Bringing Some Balance

https://www.google.com/url?sa=t&source=web&rct=j&opi=8997844
9&url=https://www.aloveforlanguage.com/en/articles/general-
interest/sibling-rivalry-12-tips-on-bringing-some-
balance.html&ved=2ahUKEwiK5-
34ibSBAxXIX0EAHQZjBJYQFnoECAwQBQ&usg=AOvVaw0Sb4
GmgWOg5bMk4Dha1gxV

Bell, Amy (2019)
Shed the Guilt, There's No Such Thing As Perfect Parenting

https://www.google.com/url?sa=t&source=web&rct=j&opi=8997844
9&url=https://www.cbc.ca/amp/1.5373882&ved=2ahUKEwix7YaMi
7SBAxWvTUEAHT5JBMwQFnoECB0QAQ&usg=AOvVaw3NC1
gLnhLH60_0ZOMhyE9o

Broennimann and Lorenz (2021)
How to Enforce Boundaries

https://www.google.com/url?sa=t&source=web&rct=j&opi=8997844
9&url=https://www.wikihow.com/Enforce-
Boundaries&ved=2ahUKEwjk8cWRjrSBAxWAXUEAHZYpCf8QFn
oECA0QBQ&usg=AOvVaw2QZM7dqR_TJiiYHzeoLTx3

Ceder, Jill (2021)
How to Be a More Positive Parent

https://www.google.com/url?sa=t&source=web&rct=j&opi=8997844
9&url=https://www.verywellfamily.com/ways-to-make-parenting-
easier-
4101922&ved=2ahUKEwjytKXJi7SBAxWpVEEAHcvvB0sQFnoEC
BoQAQ&usg=AOvVaw2qpLALsYwEb2Pl8mGIk8kk

Ceder, Jill (2022)

Why Does Consistency Matter in Parenting

https://www.google.com/url?sa=t&source=web&rct=j&opi=8997844
9&url=https://www.verywellfamily.com/why-does-consistency-
matter-in-parenting-
4135227%23:~:text%3DConsistency%2520means%2520purposely
%2520choosing%2520how,you%2520can%2520give%2520your%2
520kid.&ved=2ahUKEwi_4bW_iLSBAxVxXUEAHeWyC8AQFnoE
CAwQBQ&usg=AOvVaw1_ugjUWvBokPPtbLmCAYpO

Cherry, K (2023)
How Family Therapy Works

https://www.google.com/url?sa=t&source=web&rct=j&opi=8997844
9&url=https://www.verywellmind.com/family-therapy-definition-
types-techniques-and-efficacy-
5190233&ved=2ahUKEwjxo4KIirSBAxWsVUEAHQMtAEMQFno
ECCsQAQ&usg=AOvVaw2Qn7424GxJHEhxLmY1-oUn

Cullins, Ashley (2023)
7 Key Strategies to Manage Sibling Rivalry

https://www.google.com/url?sa=t&source=web&rct=j&opi=8997844
9&url=https://biglifejournal.com/blogs/blog/key-strategies-manage-
sibling-
rivalry&ved=2ahUKEwiv96_kibSBAxXVVEEAHcijCBAQFnoECCI
QAQ&usg=AOvVaw22qZeyOoiSoRb0nHd9rjTk

Dewar, Gwen (Retrieved October 2023)
Parenting Stress: 12 Evidence-Based Tips for Making Life Better

https://www.google.com/url?sa=t&source=web&rct=j&opi=8997844
9&url=https://parentingscience.com/parenting-stress-evidence-based-

tips/&ved=2ahUKEwi374vIirSBAxX4U0EAHfxGD8QQFnoECBkQ
AQ&usg=AOvVaw0GCR23hA1T5xNsnnFfPBzx

Gallo, Allana (2023)
6 Little Things You Can Do Every Day to Make Your Child More
Independent

https://www.google.com/url?sa=t&source=web&rct=j&opi=8997844
9&url=https://www.parents.com/kids/development/little-things-you-
can-do-every-day-to-make-your-child-more-
independent/&ved=2ahUKEwiZjJPcjLSBAxUVVEEAHQDRDKYQ
FnoECBsQAQ&usg=AOvVaw0Qiix-j3eKEZwXCYy6a1k4

Gongala, Sagari (2023)
How to Deal with a Stubborn Child

https://www.google.com/url?sa=t&source=web&rct=j&opi=8997844
9&url=https://www.momjunction.com/articles/effective-ways-to-
deal-with-stubborn-
kids_0076976/&ved=2ahUKEwjh99DUibSBAxWHT0EAHRVSCE
oQFnoECBwQAQ&usg=AOvVaw12kp49ZCMH06XXOSZHcPic

Hamburgh, Rin (2019)
Why We Need to Banish 'Mummy Guilt': There's No Such Thing As
a Perfect Parent

https://www.google.com/url?sa=t&source=web&rct=j&opi=8997844
9&url=https://www.thenationalnews.com/lifestyle/family/why-we-
need-to-banish-mummy-guilt-there-s-no-such-thing-as-a-perfect-
parent-
1.947417%3FoutputType%3Damp&ved=2ahUKEwix7YaMi7SBAx
WvTUEAHT5JBMwQFnoECBgQAQ&usg=AOvVaw3RbJlbq6IYH
jpksiMHUnn0

Ho, Leon (2023)

How to Celebrate Small Wins to Achieve Big Goals

https://www.google.com/url?sa=t&source=web&rct=j&opi=8997844
9&url=https://www.lifehack.org/396379/how-celebrate-small-wins-
achieve-big-
goals&ved=2ahUKEwixxfLEjLSBAxXYQUEAHelrC_UQFnoECCw
QAQ&usg=AOvVaw2JxqttaZasi8OSa602JOI

Lee, Katherine (2021)

How to Encourage Independence in Your Child

https://www.google.com/url?sa=t&source=web&rct=j&opi=8997844
9&url=https://www.verywellfamily.com/encourage-independence-in-
your-child-
620721&ved=2ahUKEwiZjJPcjLSBAxUVVEEAHQDRDKYQFnoE
CC4QAQ&usg=AOvVaw0RVNkpeAxk0E5ZdQEQRzID

Leo, Pam (Retrieved October 2023)

Creating More Nurturing Environments for Children

https://www.google.com/url?sa=t&source=web&rct=j&opi=8997844
9&url=https://www.naturalchild.org/articles/guest/pam_leo3.html&v
ed=2ahUKEwj397GdiLSBAxXnTkEAHWGqB2cQFnoECEgQAQ&
usg=AOvVaw37soI9abWticJr33dFTNmT

Li, Pamela (2023)

Top 10 Good Parenting Tips - Best Advice

https://www.google.com/url?sa=t&source=web&rct=j&opi=8997844
9&url=https://www.parentingforbrain.com/how-to-be-a-good-parent-
10-parenting-

tips/&ved=2ahUKEwjytKXJi7SBAxWpVEEAHcvvB0sQFnoECCcQ
AQ&usg=AOvVaw0n0USsO5gEvzuKgRm7qUs9

Lonczak, Heather (2019)
What Is Positive Parenting: 33 Examples and Benefits

https://www.google.com/url?sa=t&source=web&rct=j&opi=8997844
9&url=https://positivepsychology.com/positive-
parenting/&ved=2ahUKEwjytKXJi7SBAxWpVEEAHcvvB0sQFnoE
CCoQAQ&usg=AOvVaw3wowlfnRCHcHhFaaJeFABt

McCarthy, Claire (2022)
Sibling Rivalry is Normal - But Is It Helpful or Harmful?

https://www.google.com/url?sa=t&source=web&rct=j&opi=8997844
9&url=https://www.health.harvard.edu/blog/sibling-rivalry-is-
normal-but-is-it-helpful-or-harmful-
202212062861&ved=2ahUKEwja6firiLSBAxU8QUEAHWexDhsQ
FnoECC8QAQ&usg=AOvVaw2x-YeqnN-hZPzIBBDdzbs9

Nash, Jo (2018)
How to Set Healthy Boundaries and Build Positive Relationships

https://www.google.com/url?sa=t&source=web&rct=j&opi=8997844
9&url=https://positivepsychology.com/great-self-care-setting-healthy-
boundaries/&ved=2ahUKEwjk8cWRjrSBAxWAXUEAHZYpCf8QF
noECBQQAQ&usg=AOvVaw2pP8HcGAbqCYawPXZ2B2KD

O'Connor Gail (2023)
Got Mom Guilt? Here's How to Let Go of Feeling Like You're Not a
Perfect Parent (Because That Doesn't Exist)

https://www.google.com/url?sa=t&source=web&rct=j&opi=8997844
9&url=https://www.womansworld.com/posts/parenting/got-mom-

guilt-heres-how-to-let-go-of-feeling-like-youre-not-a-perfect-parent-because-that-doesnt-exist/amp&ved=2ahUKEwix7YaMi7SBAxWvTUEAHT5JBMwQFnoECBsQAQ&usg=AOvVaw39q5rO1jRKAJAkOVLtRVIP

Raypole, C (2021)

How to Set Boundaries with Your Parents and Stick to Them

https://www.google.com/url?sa=t&source=web&rct=j&opi=89978449&url=https://www.healthline.com/health/mental-health/set-boundaries-with-parents&ved=2ahUKEwjk8cWRjrSBAxWAXUEAHZYpCf8QFnoECCYQAQ&usg=AOvVaw1X1X0lD5IJNgd2tb45_iCO

Scott, Elizabeth (2023)

5 Self-Care Practices for Every Area of Your Life

https://www.google.com/url?sa=t&source=web&rct=j&opi=89978449&url=https://www.verywellmind.com/self-care-strategies-overall-stress-reduction-3144729&ved=2ahUKEwjm-ZKni7SBAxWGLcAKHeeUC_MQFnoECCYQAQ&usg=AOvVaw0LnVx8TOEQjJdQK_kV6uAM

Sylvester, Rachel (2022)

'Dyslexia Is My Superpower': How Learning Differently Helped Richard Branson Become a Rule-Breaking Billionaire

https://robbreport.com/lifestyle/news/richard-branson-dyslexia-1234727547/

Wilds, Hayley (2023)

11 Incredible Strategies to Improve Sibling Relationships

https://www.google.com/url?sa=t&source=web&rct=j&opi=8997844
9&url=https://thecenteredparent.com/11-incredible-strategies-to-
improve-sibling-
relationships/&ved=2ahUKEwiv96_kibSBAxXVVEEAHcijCBAQFn
oECCYQAQ&usg=AOvVaw2IWZ-vHdwoIx0uRWrXapkw

Zapata, Kimberly (2023)
Dear Exhausted and Burnt Out Parent: We're Here to Help

https://www.google.com/url?sa=t&source=web&rct=j&opi=8997844
9&url=https://www.healthline.com/health/parenting/parental-
burnout&ved=2ahUKEwjv8Z6zirSBAxUzQUEAHWodBEwQFnoE
CB0QAQ&usg=AOvVaw2VR320pRqzW2TuToOEdRhx

OTHER REFERENCES
(Retrieved October 2023)

https://www.google.com/url?sa=t&source=web&rct=j&opi=8997844
9&url=https://www.sparktheirfuture.qld.edu.au/positive-goal-
setting/&ved=2ahUKEwiFjvHbjbSBAxWSQkEAHdyYA0QQFnoEC
CgQAQ&usg=AOvVaw0oaAVBcKtUFH3gC2Iy9-jh

(Retrieved October 2023)

https://www.google.com/url?sa=t&source=web&rct=j&opi=8997844
9&url=https://biglifejournal.com/blogs/blog/goal-setting-for-
kids&ved=2ahUKEwiFjvHbjbSBAxWSQkEAHdyYA0QQFnoECBw
QAQ&usg=AOvVaw1lra61AdSvxABNmP_dr22h

(Retrieved October 2023)

https://www.google.com/url?sa=t&source=web&rct=j&opi=8997844
9&url=https://mycll.org/for-parents-and-teachers/social-skills-and-
peer-

relationships/&ved=2ahUKEwiBgfT3jLSBAxVPSkEAHefNDNgQF
noECBQQAQ&usg=AOvVaw3WrT_OmPTne9xhZ1Ip9Km1

(Retrieved October 2023)

https://www.google.com/url?sa=t&source=web&rct=j&opi=8997844
9&url=https://wp.nyu.edu/steinhardt-appsych_opus/peer-
relationships-protective-factors-and-social-skill-development-in-low-
income-
children/&ved=2ahUKEwiBgfT3jLSBAxVPSkEAHefNDNgQFnoE
CBcQAQ&usg=AOvVaw0w4tno0K_0lFIXbFwjmdH3

(Retrieved October 2023)

https://www.google.com/url?sa=t&source=web&rct=j&opi=8997844
9&url=https://www.extraordinarykidstherapy.net/blog/the-
importance-of-celebrating-tiny-wins-as-a-
parent%23:~:text%3DCelebrating%2520tiny%2520wins%2520can
%2520help,overcome%2520the%2520challenges%2520we%2520fac
e.&ved=2ahUKEwixxfLEjLSBAxXYQUEAHelrC_UQFnoECA4QB
Q&usg=AOvVaw20XkiCPanYOPJFuUzdWFfv

(Retrieved October 2023)

https://www.google.com/url?sa=t&source=web&rct=j&opi=8997844
9&url=https://www.childwelfare.gov/topics/preventing/promoting/pa
renting/&ved=2ahUKEwjq_aW4i7SBAxU8QUEAHWexDhsQFnoE
CBoQAQ&usg=AOvVaw1DTfaTqslDRhS4Pyh4bCT5

(Retrieved October 2023)

https://www.google.com/url?sa=t&source=web&rct=j&opi=8997844
9&url=https://preparedparents.org/tip/celebrating-small-

wins/&ved=2ahUKEwixxfLEjLSBAxXYQUEAHelrC_UQFnoECA0
QAQ&usg=AOvVaw2VkhRyzm4JsSVy9k3rTJro

(Retrieved October 2023)

https://www.google.com/url?sa=t&source=web&rct=j&opi=8997844
9&url=https://ready4k.com/blog/trauma-informed-
education/connect-families-to-
resources/&ved=2ahUKEwjq_aW4i7SBAxU8QUEAHWexDhsQFno
ECBwQAQ&usg=AOvVaw1z_jHx_qRYJMSO2WXnewC_

(Retrieved October 2023)

https://www.google.com/url?sa=t&source=web&rct=j&opi=8997844
9&url=https://firstchanceforchildren.org/resources/community-
resources/&ved=2ahUKEwjq_aW4i7SBAxU8QUEAHWexDhsQFno
ECBsQAQ&usg=AOvVaw0qc8L25Wd2DPofEtRcfWHN

(Retrieved October 2023)

https://www.google.com/url?sa=t&source=web&rct=j&opi=8997844
9&url=https://www.nimh.nih.gov/health/topics/caring-for-your-
mental-health&ved=2ahUKEwjm-
ZKni7SBAxWGLcAKHeeUC_MQFnoECA8QBQ&usg=AOvVaw2
Ui0OI56mwszflgv4nubv2

(Retrieved October 2023)

https://www.google.com/url?sa=t&source=web&rct=j&opi=8997844
9&url=https://members.believeperform.com/product/how-to-create-
a-nurturing-home-environment-for-children-during-
lockdown/&ved=2ahUKEwj397GdiLSBAxXnTkEAHWGqB2cQFn
oECBUQAQ&usg=AOvVaw05B6n2Imoo9-pUzxgoZw8h

(Retrieved October 2023)

https://www.google.com/url?sa=t&source=web&rct=j&opi=8997844
9&url=https://www.allprodad.com/creating-a-nurturing-
environment-for-your-
kids/&ved=2ahUKEwj397GdiLSBAxXnTkEAHWGqB2cQFnoECA
wQBQ&usg=AOvVaw1hmqUyYR0rL3Xwxq3UBdXF

(Retrieved October 2023)

https://www.google.com/url?sa=t&source=web&rct=j&opi=8997844
9&url=https://ibpf.org/articles/50-ways-to-start-practicing-self-
care/&ved=2ahUKEwjm-
ZKni7SBAxWGLcAKHeeUC_MQFnoECCsQAQ&usg=AOvVaw0
CCdnr1OUFUAzYopeQZ5bf

(Retrieved October 2023)

https://www.google.com/url?sa=t&source=web&rct=j&opi=8997844
9&url=https://childdevelopmentinfo.com/how-to-be-a-
parent/angry_child/stress/&ved=2ahUKEwi374vIirSBAxX4U0EAHfx
GD8QQFnoECA8QAQ&usg=AOvVaw1cBdimnEnwrVRj5XLJ40L
y

(Retrieved October 2023)

https://www.google.com/url?sa=t&source=web&rct=j&opi=8997844
9&url=https://www.attachmentparenting.org/strive-balance-your-
personal-and-family-
life&ved=2ahUKEwjck97wirSBAxV0WUEAHRx3AHIQFnoECCY
QAQ&usg=AOvVaw3HmC2VC2E_97T2CSxfIYAL

(Retrieved October 2023)

https://www.google.com/url?sa=t&source=web&rct=j&opi=8997844
9&url=https://www.newportacademy.com/resources/restoring-

families/parental-burnout/%23:~:text%3D%25E2%2580%259CParental%2520burnout%2520is%2520a%2520state,chronic%2520anxiety%252C%2520and%2520illness.%25E2%2580%259D&ved=2ahUKEwjv8Z6zirSBAxUzQUEAHWodBEwQFnoECA0QBQ&usg=AOvVaw1iHbHrrhwnwiRat9hB2aCp

(Retrieved October 2023)

https://www.google.com/url?sa=t&source=web&rct=j&opi=89978449&url=https://www.goodtherapy.org/blog/faq/what-is-the-purpose-of-family-therapy/amp/&ved=2ahUKEwjxo4KIirSBAxWsVUEAHQMtAEMQFnoECCoQAQ&usg=AOvVaw1r9759POJF1BHYReEQHicM

(Retrieved October 2023)

https://www.google.com/url?sa=t&source=web&rct=j&opi=89978449&url=https://sleepingshouldbeeasy.com/balancing-childrens-needs-fairly/&ved=2ahUKEwiK5-34ibSBAxXIX0EAHQZjBJYQFnoECCoQAQ&usg=AOvVaw1Nqiwl84MSrjYK3Fnb7bhg

(Retrieved October 2023)

https://www.google.com/url?sa=t&source=web&rct=j&opi=89978449&url=https://30seconds.com/mom/tip/amp-14621/Balancing-Attention-With-Kids-What-to-Do-When-One-Child-Needs-More-Time&ved=2ahUKEwiK5-34ibSBAxXIX0EAHQZjBJYQFnoECCcQAQ&usg=AOvVaw3uy8dQNWR-awUi4xdMWTqn

(Retrieved October 2023)

https://www.google.com/url?sa=t&source=web&rct=j&opi=8997844
9&url=https://www.empoweringparents.com/article/oppositional-
defiant-disorder-and-sibling-fighting-7-things-i-know-
now/&ved=2ahUKEwja6firiLSBAxU8QUEAHWexDhsQFnoECBc
QAQ&usg=AOvVaw1siQhNfLWrBUUAKDxzYd4u

(Retrieved October 2023)

https://www.google.com/url?sa=t&source=web&rct=j&opi=8997844
9&url=https://www.melbournechildpsychology.com.au/blog/working
-together-the-importance-of-consistency-in-
parenting/&ved=2ahUKEwi_4bW_iLSBAxVxXUEAHeWyC8AQFn
oECCYQAQ&usg=AOvVaw2p7pJ1S-g3Gl9h2TdhpsYt

(Retrieved October 2023)

https://www.google.com/url?sa=t&source=web&rct=j&opi=8997844
9&url=https://health.clevelandclinic.org/sibling-
rivalry/amp/&ved=2ahUKEwiv96_kibSBAxXVVEEAHcijCBAQFno
ECA0QBQ&usg=AOvVaw3lW2IkoZ9t8W4pE4wrvD3A

(Retrieved October 2023)

https://www.google.com/url?sa=t&source=web&rct=j&opi=8997844
9&url=https://www.uhhospitals.org/blog/articles/2022/03/how-to-
stop-having-bedtime-battles-with-your-
toddler&ved=2ahUKEwjh99DUibSBAxWHT0EAHRVSCEoQFnoE
CC8QAQ&usg=AOvVaw322RbVcMg7mUJR4MAIISsy

(Retrieved October 2023)

https://www.google.com/url?sa=t&source=web&rct=j&opi=8997844
9&url=https://limetreecounseling.com/healthy-boundary-

counseling/%23:~:text%3DBoundaries%2520with%2520consequenc
es%2520help%2520everyone,the%2520boundary%2520put%2520i
n%2520place.&ved=2ahUKEwiT5vyAjrSBAxXlW0EAHZWPCGM
QFnoECAwQBQ&usg=AOvVaw2f925pbcWdRzkOUID0UBQu

(Retrieved October 2023)

https://www.google.com/url?sa=t&source=web&rct=j&opi=8997844
9&url=https://news.sanfordhealth.org/parenting/the-power-of-
consistency/&ved=2ahUKEwi_4bW_iLSBAxVxXUEAHeWyC8AQF
noECB0QAQ&usg=AOvVaw2vyLhOP_aBg4T3kJa56aFk

(Retrieved October 2023)

https://www.google.com/url?sa=t&source=web&rct=j&opi=8997844
9&url=https://empathicparentingcounseling.com/blog/how-to-enjoy-
parenting/%23:~:text%3DCultivate%2520a%2520positive%2520par
enting%2520mindset%2520by%2520practicing%2520gratitude%25
2C%2520self%252Dcare,understanding%2520their%2520needs%2
520and%2520interests.&ved=2ahUKEwjytKXJi7SBAxWpVEEAHcv
vB0sQFnoECBIQBQ&usg=AOvVaw2bVzn6LfoQFbCz9Hb7ZGYj

Boylan, Khrista (2007)
Comorbidity of Internalizing Disorders in Children with Oppositional
Defiant Disorder

https://www.google.com/url?sa=t&source=web&rct=j&opi=8997844
9&url=https://pubmed.ncbi.nlm.nih.gov/17896121/&ved=2ahUKE
wjyl7Ci97OBAxV7WkEAHQ9EBEgQFnoECBoQAQ&usg=AOvVa
w0p043bCmPFdup_mFfw_ro0

Geng, Caitlin (2022)

What to Know about ADHD and ODD

https://www.medicalnewstoday.com/articles/adhd-and-odd#:~:text=About%2060%25%20of%20people%20with,risk%20of%20having%20both%20conditions

Holland, K (2019)

What Oppositional Defiant Disorder (ODD) Looks Like in Children

https://www.google.com/url?sa=t&source=web&rct=j&opi=89978449&url=https://www.healthline.com/health/childrens-health/odd-in-children&ved=2ahUKEwiXzM3s8rOBAxVERUEAHaOwA44QFnoECCkQAQ&usg=AOvVaw3nh9T6lVnISca33ayflNaD

Lin et al. (2019)
Family Risk Factors Associated with Oppositional Defiant Disorder Symptoms

https://www.google.com/url?sa=t&source=web&rct=j&opi=89978449&url=https://www.frontiersin.org/articles/10.3389/fpsyg.2019.02062&ved=2ahUKEwjp9cGO87OBAxXeRUEAHWW9CKoQFnoECB0QAQ&usg=AOvVaw0NH3I3jYl_Dwh-aOnujzST

Lovering, N (2021)
Treating Oppositional Defiant Disorder

https://www.google.com/url?sa=t&source=web&rct=j&opi=89978449&url=https://psychcentral.com/disorders/oppositional-defiant-disorder-treatment&ved=2ahUKEwjMn9zY9LOBAxUwVEEAHb8HAM4QFnoECCYQAQ&usg=AOvVaw3timX0_M6PFtzIIA_I8Ae-

Mayo Clinic Staff
Oppositional Defiant Disorder

https://www.google.com/url?sa=t&source=web&rct=j&opi=8997844
9&url=https://www.mayoclinic.org/diseases-conditions/oppositional-
defiant-disorder/symptoms-causes/syc-
20375831&ved=2ahUKEwii06uw8rOBAxVZVUEAHdtGDs8QFno
ECBoQAQ&usg=AOvVaw2rrD215Wog8l24krf741Gk

Raypole, C (2019)
Dispelling 6 Common Myths about Oppositional Defiant Disorder

https://www.google.com/url?sa=t&source=web&rct=j&opi=8997844
9&url=https://www.goodtherapy.org/blog/dispelling-6-common-
myths-about-oppositional-defiant-disorder-
0117197/amp/&ved=2ahUKEwiZvZ2n87OBAxWlWEEAHbN4Co
YQFnoECAwQBQ&usg=AOvVaw1qSReFxY3D4DKnF6V7kYp3

The Recovery Village (2022)
Conduct Disorder vs Oppositional Defiant Disorder

https://www.google.com/url?sa=t&source=web&rct=j&opi=8997844
9&url=https://www.therecoveryvillage.com/mental-health/disruptive-
behavior-disorder/conduct-disorder-vs-
odd/&ved=2ahUKEwjso5aA87OBAxVnSkEAHTaZCsEQFnoECBs
QAQ&usg=AOvVaw3SCvEsAKHZRb_kkOELIMKa

Shishira, Sreenivas (2022)
ADHD vs ODD: Similarities and Differences

https://www.google.com/url?sa=t&source=web&rct=j&opi=8997844
9&url=https://www.webmd.com/add-adhd/childhood-adhd/adhd-
odd-similarities-

differences&ved=2ahUKEwjso5aA87OBAxVnSkEAHTaZCsEQFno
ECCsQAQ&usg=AOvVaw085-27gsnKcZo7t8ffzbaa

Studaker-Cordner, M and Abraham, K
ODD Kids and Behavior: 5 Things You Need to Know as a Parent

https://www.google.com/url?sa=t&source=web&rct=j&opi=8997844
9&url=https://www.empoweringparents.com/article/odd-kids-and-
behavior-5-things-you-need-to-know-as-a-
parent/&ved=2ahUKEwjWwfy08bOBAxVXYEEAHfmjDUoQFnoE
CB4QAQ&usg=AOvVaw13ZvYg78mgLlM94AuGccQb

Thompson, Hilary (2021)
Oppositional Defiant Disorder: When Your Kid Isn't Just "Difficult"

https://www.google.com/url?sa=t&source=web&rct=j&opi=8997844
9&url=https://www.todaysparent.com/family/discipline/oppositional-
defiance-disorder-when-your-kid-isnt-just-
difficult/&ved=2ahUKEwjWwfy08bOBAxVXYEEAHfmjDUoQFno
ECBsQAQ&usg=AOvVaw0MmRJyjwb96UTJMIxestiC

WebMD Editorial (2022)
Oppositional Defiant Disorder

https://www.google.com/url?sa=t&source=web&rct=j&opi=8997844
9&url=https://www.webmd.com/mental-health/oppositional-defiant-
disorder&ved=2ahUKEwjWwfy08bOBAxVXYEEAHfmjDUoQFno
ECCoQAQ&usg=AOvVaw1L4SBq-2O4lCA6_9G-9nUd

https://www.google.com/url?sa=t&source=web&rct=j&opi=8997844
9&url=https://nathensmiraculousescape.com/out/writing/oppositiona
l-defiant-disorder-

assessment/&ved=2ahUKEwiCubPF9bOBAxX2VUEAHXjCAbAQF
noECCgQAQ&usg=AOvVaw1MMJBgKfsBovAmYCleJmRW

https://www.google.com/url?sa=t&source=web&rct=j&opi=8997844
9&url=https://growingearlyminds.org.au/tips/oppositional-defiant-
disorder/&ved=2ahUKEwj73aSB9rOBAxUiWkEAHZzQAeoQFnoE
CC8QAQ&usg=AOvVaw1-tlNYXmCkN6IHSNlPbJca

https://www.google.com/url?sa=t&source=web&rct=j&opi=8997844
9&url=https://www.crossroadstopathwaysllc.com/post/nurturing-
connection-and-understanding-supporting-children-with-
oppositional-defiant-
disorder&ved=2ahUKEwj73aSB9rOBAxUiWkEAHZzQAeoQFnoE
CBUQAQ&usg=AOvVaw0hAOZjgTTtnEl4BS_fEo3r

https://www.google.com/url?sa=t&source=web&rct=j&opi=8997844
9&url=https://www.aamft.org/Consumer_Updates/Oppositional_Def
iant_Disorder.aspx%23:~:text%3DEffect%2520on%2520Families%
2520%2526%2520Relationships,do%2520not%2520work%2520wit
h%2520ODD.&ved=2ahUKEwjp9cGO87OBAxXeRUEAHWW9C
KoQFnoECAwQBQ&usg=AOvVaw1S5M1ALM38QewY1ofZydvu

https://www.google.com/url?sa=t&source=web&rct=j&opi=8997844
9&url=https://edgefoundation.org/common-myths-about-
oppositional-defiant-disorder-
odd/&ved=2ahUKEwiZvZ2n87OBAxWlWEEAHbN4CoYQFnoEC
BIQAQ&usg=AOvVaw17OWyVVN9Lg9zkcl60BCn9

https://www.google.com/url?sa=t&source=web&rct=j&opi=8997844
9&url=https://raisingchildren.net.au/school-age/health-daily-
care/school-age-mental-health-

concerns/odd&ved=2ahUKEwir_52b9LOBAxWjSkEAHS8IB1AQFn
oECCcQAQ&usg=AOvVaw38Um9i_Fo5cEmWMTKIjuJr

https://www.google.com/url?sa=t&source=web&rct=j&opi=8997844
9&url=http://www.differencebetween.net/science/health/difference-
between-conduct-disorder-and-oppositional-defiant-
disorder/&ved=2ahUKEwjso5aA87OBAxVnSkEAHTaZCsEQFnoE
CDMQAQ&usg=AOvVaw3I2-9KQ7sZpI7gYp6qO_WW

https://www.google.com/url?sa=t&source=web&rct=j&opi=8997844
9&url=https://www.betterhealth.vic.gov.au/health/conditionsandtreat
ments/oppositional-defiant-disorder-
odd%23:~:text%3DAround%2520one%2520in%252010%2520chil
dren,deficit%2520hyperactivity%2520disorder%2520(ADHD).&ved
=2ahUKEwiXzM3s8rOBAxVERUEAHaOwA44QFnoECA8QBQ&
usg=AOvVaw2JCsb4NhKHsX9LCie4q42s

https://www.google.com/url?sa=t&source=web&rct=j&opi=8997844
9&url=https://www.hopkinsmedicine.org/health/conditions-and-
diseases/oppositional-defiant-
disorder&ved=2ahUKEwiXzM3s8rOBAxVERUEAHaOwA44QFno
ECB8QAQ&usg=AOvVaw2kuHtylNsxs1tzkyn76ziS

https://www.google.com/url?sa=t&source=web&rct=j&opi=8997844
9&url=https://www.nationwidechildrens.org/conditions/oppositional
-defiant-
disorder%23:~:text%3DIt%27s%2520not%2520known%2520what
%2520causes,inconsistent%2520or%2520overly%2520harsh%2520
discipline.&ved=2ahUKEwii06uw8rOBAxVZVUEAHdtGDs8QFno
ECBAQBQ&usg=AOvVaw1QkY7zq5-HOGh05fTzQubN

Busch and Oakley (2017)
Emotional Intelligence: Why It Matters and How to Teach It

https://www.google.com/url?sa=t&source=web&rct=j&opi=8997844
9&url=https://amp.theguardian.com/teacher-
network/2017/nov/03/emotional-intelligence-why-it-matters-and-
how-to-teach-
it&ved=2ahUKEwi9moKsgLSBAxUZXEEAHQUDDYQQFnoECC
IQAQ&usg=AOvVaw3GLVmfXCn6oXl7gtAPZ8PP

Cameron, Brittney (2023)
The Power of Positive Reinforcement

https://www.google.com/url?sa=t&source=web&rct=j&opi=8997844
9&url=https://youthfirstinc.org/the-power-of-positive-
reinforcement/&ved=2ahUKEwjU6J7BhrSBAxU5WkEAHbTtArsQ
FnoECCgQAQ&usg=AOvVaw1krGb2gM5goBE67FT_uy61

Celestine, Nicole (2019)
What Is Mindful Breathing: Exercises, Scripts, and Videos

https://www.google.com/url?sa=t&source=web&rct=j&opi=8997844
9&url=https://positivepsychology.com/mindful-
breathing/&ved=2ahUKEwiOwci9grSBAxWhSEEAHR5JDOAQFno
ECCgQAQ&usg=AOvVaw11O3g5oOCHNQ0rAUM_e0A3

Cuncin, Arlin (2022)
What Is Active Listening?

https://www.google.com/url?sa=t&source=web&rct=j&opi=8997844
9&url=https://www.verywellmind.com/what-is-active-listening-
3024343&ved=2ahUKEwjv1aGZ_LOBAxWsV0EAHWjTD6YQFn
oECC0QAQ&usg=AOvVaw1d_I2zAHKGLfVWMnoRFgZl

Deupree, Sidney (2023)
CBT for Kids and Teens: How It Works, Examples and Effectiveness

https://www.google.com/url?sa=t&source=web&rct=j&opi=8997844
9&url=https://www.choosingtherapy.com/cbt-kids-
teens/&ved=2ahUKEwim257TgrSBAxWnRkEAHYUSB_YQFnoEC
AwQBQ&usg=AOvVaw1HYfjnFF5htdRJJKmu5Wjn

Forbes Business Council (2019)
Nine Effective Techniques for Encouraging Conversations at Work

https://www.google.com/url?sa=t&source=web&rct=j&opi=8997844
9&url=https://www.forbes.com/sites/forbesbusinesscouncil/2019/10/
30/nine-effective-techniques-for-encouraging-conversations-and-
innovations-at-
work/amp/&ved=2ahUKEwjMhN77_rOBAxX0SkEAHSvvCAgQFn
oECCoQAQ&usg=AOvVaw1N15Y10FRepp2H-Q9SvTlL

Gill, Karen (2019)
How Is Cognitive Behavioral Therapy Different for Kids

https://www.google.com/url?sa=t&source=web&rct=j&opi=8997844
9&url=https://www.healthline.com/health/mental-health/cbt-for-
kids&ved=2ahUKEwim257TgrSBAxWnRkEAHYUSB_YQFnoECC
UQAQ&usg=AOvVaw2Z27VFLrWTfqD8dAcdj42E

Gordon, Sherri (2019)
How to Create an Effective Reward System for Kids

https://www.google.com/url?sa=t&source=web&rct=j&opi=8997844
9&url=https://www.verywellfamily.com/how-to-create-a-reward-
system-for-kids-that-works-1094752&ved=2ahUKEwj_-

OzWhrSBAxV8VkEAHaenCvMQFnoECCgQAQ&usg=AOvVaw0-kyBMjuTqIMtnMy1lLokk

Houston, E (2019)
CBT for Children: A Guide for Helping Kids in Therapy

https://www.google.com/url?sa=t&source=web&rct=j&opi=8997844
9&url=https://positivepsychology.com/cbt-for-children/&ved=2ahUKEwim257TgrSBAxWnRkEAHYUSB_YQFno
ECCYQAQ&usg=AOvVaw0-oYBLcyT8snhwzQ9jrLN

Huddleston, Lauren (2019)
The Power of Positive Communication

https://www.google.com/url?sa=t&source=web&rct=j&opi=8997844
9&url=https://www.edutopia.org/article/power-positive-communication/&ved=2ahUKEwiUs5en-rOBAxUUV0EAHUECA4oQFnoECCsQAQ&usg=AOvVaw2U4T
mhjkfzq9jRMOmF6yYD

Juby, Bethany (2022)
The 4 S's of Secure Attachment and How They Impact Adult Relationships

https://www.google.com/url?sa=t&source=web&rct=j&opi=8997844
9&url=https://psychcentral.com/relationships/the-4-ss-secure-attachment&ved=2ahUKEwjAwdSph7SBAxVFRUEAHZTBDZ8QF
noECCgQAQ&usg=AOvVaw2_pdfFPx6rSEaAJNugxTKp

Kaminskey, Anna (2022)
A Guide to Setting Age-Appropriate Limits for Children

https://www.google.com/url?sa=t&source=web&rct=j&opi=8997844
9&url=https://www.psy-ed.com/wpblog/setting-limits-for-

children/&ved=2ahUKEwiSgK2Xh7SBAxX8S0EAHSZ0ChIQFnoECBsQAQ&usg=AOvVaw3KJhBHPS0DBTaXORF4uJG0

Lehman, James (Retrieved October 2023)
Oppositional Defiant Disorder: The War at Home

https://www.google.com/url?sa=t&source=web&rct=j&opi=89978449&url=https://www.empoweringparents.com/article/oppositional-defiant-disorder-the-war-at-home/&ved=2ahUKEwjz-qfyh7SBAxWZQkEAHd5bDI8QFnoECCkQAQ&usg=AOvVaw232yi00SVLUmjFrC3QUJUW

Majsiak and Young (2022)

7 Ways to Practice Breath Work for Beginners

https://www.google.com/url?sa=t&source=web&rct=j&opi=89978449&url=https://www.everydayhealth.com/alternative-health/living-with/ways-practice-breath-focused-meditation/&ved=2ahUKEwiOwci9grSBAxWhSEEAHR5JDOAQFnoECCcQAQ&usg=AOvVaw2JiXg5wqNs2hvhKcy_uEkb

Mehra, Tanya (2023)
Parenting with Empathy - How to Foster Intelligence in Kids

https://www.google.com/url?sa=t&source=web&rct=j&opi=89978449&url=https://timesofindia.indiatimes.com/blogs/voices/parenting-with-empathy-how-to-foster-intelligence-in-kids/&ved=2ahUKEwiXh7vB-rOBAxVXYEEAHfmjDUoQFnoECCgQAQ&usg=AOvVaw2R0uw7WYJmOa6vLCol7YZk

Moore, Catherine (2019)
Teaching Emotional Intelligence to Children and Teens

https://www.google.com/url?sa=t&source=web&rct=j&opi=8997844
9&url=https://positivepsychology.com/teaching-emotional-
intelligence/&ved=2ahUKEwi9moKsgLSBAxUZXEEAHQUDDYQ
QFnoECCAQAQ&usg=AOvVaw29oSWKb88liiiIf7HWpBVu

Morin, Amy (2021a)
How to Manage Defiant Behavior

https://www.google.com/url?sa=t&source=web&rct=j&opi=8997844
9&url=https://www.verywellfamily.com/ways-deal-childs-defiance-
non-compliance-1094947&ved=2ahUKEwjz-
qfyh7SBAxWZQkEAHd5bDI8QFnoECBEQAQ&usg=AOvVaw19I
mcgwJLfSipzOaYY_YpF

Morin, Amy (2021b)
How to Create Structure in Your Day

https://www.google.com/url?sa=t&source=web&rct=j&opi=8997844
9&url=https://www.verywellfamily.com/how-to-create-structure-in-
your-childs-day-
1094880&ved=2ahUKEwjBlKithrSBAxXDolwKHUFGD-
4QFnoECCcQAQ&usg=AOvVaw3ZyAyoNdCJhsAtXligg1-t

Morin, Amy (2021c)
How to Raise an Emotionally Intelligent Child

https://www.google.com/url?sa=t&source=web&rct=j&opi=8997844
9&url=https://www.verywellfamily.com/tips-for-raising-an-
emotionally-intelligent-child-

4157946&ved=2ahUKEwi9moKsgLSBAxUZXEEAHQUDDYQQF
noECCEQAQ&usg=AOvVaw2Q9a5I1m6xImiDfzY_ra

Morin, Amy (2022a)

11 Anger Management Strategies to Help You Calm Down

https://www.google.com/url?sa=t&source=web&rct=j&opi=8997844
9&url=https://www.verywellmind.com/anger-management-strategies-
4178870&ved=2ahUKEwiUtpSWg7SBAxUqQUEAHWaOAJwQFn
oECCsQAQ&usg=AOvVaw2KgLgIq5ClfH6bkaSCgc8j

Morin, Amy (2022b)

The 4 Types of Parenting Style and How Kids Are Affected

https://www.google.com/url?sa=t&source=web&rct=j&opi=8997844
9&url=https://www.verywellfamily.com/types-of-parenting-styles-
1095045&ved=2ahUKEwiVvq3-
hrSBAxUPQkEAHYvYAD0QFnoECDIQAQ&usg=AOvVaw1sppb6
03uaYo76vKyrbLym

Morin, Amy (2022c)

How to Use Positive Reinforcement to Improve Behavior

https://www.google.com/url?sa=t&source=web&rct=j&opi=8997844
9&url=https://www.verywellfamily.com/positive-reinforcement-child-
behavior-
1094889&ved=2ahUKEwjU6J7BhrSBAxU5WkEAHbTtArsQFnoE
CB4QAQ&usg=AOvVaw3Ks7eSdEBTcW4VDG5q-k8X

Perry, Elizabeth (2021)

How to Carry a Connection - The Art of Making Connections

https://www.google.com/url?sa=t&source=web&rct=j&opi=8997844
9&url=https://www.betterup.com/blog/how-to-carry-a-

conversation%3Fhs_amp%3Dtrue&ved=2ahUKEwjMhN77_rOBAx
X0SkEAHSvvCAgQFnoECCkQAQ&usg=AOvVaw2Lh0E8WoqR2r
gZrb2dcNsE

Seaver, Maggie (2023)
5 Breathing Exercises You Can Do Anywhere, Anytime

https://www.google.com/url?sa=t&source=web&rct=j&opi=8997844
9&url=https://www.realsimple.com/health/mind-mood/breathing-
exercises&ved=2ahUKEwiOwci9grSBAxWhSEEAHR5JDOAQFnoE
CBwQAQ&usg=AOvVaw3UIZvmRKRj6IU4tx0qM16JL

Schenk, Sinead (2020)
6 Ways to Effectively Implement Routines with Your Children

https://www.google.com/url?sa=t&source=web&rct=j&opi=8997844
9&url=https://www.heischools.com/blog/news/implement-routines-
at-
home%3Fhs_amp%3Dtrue&ved=2ahUKEwjBlKithrSBAxXDolwKH
UFGD-
4QFnoECA4QBQ&usg=AOvVaw0ucSk37yYyIzSlM6kZC9um

Souders, Beata (2019)
Positive Reinforcement for Kids: 11+ Examples for Parents

https://www.google.com/url?sa=t&source=web&rct=j&opi=8997844
9&url=https://positivepsychology.com/parenting-positive-
reinforcement/%23:~:text%3DPositive%2520reinforcement%2520ca
n%2520be%2520used,shoes%2520or%2520loading%2520a%2520d
ishwasher.&ved=2ahUKEwjU6J7BhrSBAxU5WkEAHbTtArsQFnoE
CAwQBQ&usg=AOvVaw3Lkup7axKyPg2WC0j2i94

Tominey, Shauna (2017)
Teaching Emotional Intelligence in Early Childhood

https://www.google.com/url?sa=t&source=web&rct=j&opi=8997844
9&url=https://www.naeyc.org/resources/pubs/yc/mar2017/teaching-
emotional-
intelligence&ved=2ahUKEwi9moKsgLSBAxUZXEEAHQUDDYQ
QFnoECB4QAQ&usg=AOvVaw1h1qLf0Maggv0IgZMrjQ1F

Zaino, J (Retrieved October 2023)
Set the Right Expectations for Successful Parent-Teacher Relationships

https://www.google.com/url?sa=t&source=web&rct=j&opi=8997844
9&url=https://www.wgu.edu/heyteach/article/set-the-right-
expectations-for-successful-parent-teacher-
relationships1708.html&ved=2ahUKEwiqmPK0_7OBAxUVVEEAH
bjgDL4QFnoECCkQAQ&usg=AOvVaw2pfzzMuBoOxiNWOhCyh
xtS

(Retrieved October 2023)

https://www.google.com/url?sa=t&source=web&rct=j&opi=8997844
9&url=https://howelldenver.com/the-power-of-positive-
communication/&ved=2ahUKEwiUs5en-
rOBAxUUV0EAHUECA4oQFnoECCUQAQ&usg=AOvVaw2FaU
VQ4sHz5GE7Wp8GB-Rp

(Retrieved October 2023)

https://www.google.com/url?sa=t&source=web&rct=j&opi=8997844
9&url=https://staffsquared.com/blog/the-power-of-positive-
communication/&ved=2ahUKEwiUs5en-

rOBAxUUV0EAHUECA4oQFnoECCgQAQ&usg=AOvVaw0L2EK
Ri2xyphJPNfTrSUd6

(Retrieved October 2023)

https://www.google.com/url?sa=t&source=web&rct=j&opi=8997844
9&url=https://www.lispeech.com/dealing-with-
defiance/&ved=2ahUKEwjz-
qfyh7SBAxWZQkEAHd5bDI8QFnoECA8QAQ&usg=AOvVaw0BS
jKuut_OfUPNOJeqAIWD

(Retrieved October 2023)

https://www.google.com/url?sa=t&source=web&rct=j&opi=8997844
9&url=https://jessup.edu/blog/academic-success/the-psychology-
behind-different-types-of-parenting-styles/&ved=2ahUKEwiVvq3-
hrSBAxUPQkEAHYvYAD0QFnoECBEQAQ&usg=AOvVaw2c1gBe
M-RKUDkYEM_KnmO8

(Retrieved October 2023)

https://www.google.com/url?sa=t&source=web&rct=j&opi=8997844
9&url=https://www.apa.org/act/resources/fact-sheets/parenting-
styles&ved=2ahUKEwiVvq3-
hrSBAxUPQkEAHYvYAD0QFnoECBIQAQ&usg=AOvVaw3v2bxE
kxbvc4oilOonlzVw

(Retrieved October 2023)

https://www.google.com/url?sa=t&source=web&rct=j&opi=8997844
9&url=https://www.bethelccs.com/content/setting-age-appropriate-
limits&ved=2ahUKEwiSgK2Xh7SBAxX8S0EAHSZ0ChIQFnoECCI
QAQ&usg=AOvVaw2JzVsRPEFvv8ThEIT4LbIs

(Retrieved October 2023)

https://www.google.com/url?sa=t&source=web&rct=j&opi=8997844
9&url=https://londongoverness.com/how-to-set-age-appropriate-
boundaries/&ved=2ahUKEwiSgK2Xh7SBAxX8S0EAHSZ0ChIQFno
ECB8QAQ&usg=AOvVaw10lAf2hDtZagPI1tJyNb9d

(Retrieved October 2023)

https://www.google.com/url?sa=t&source=web&rct=j&opi=8997844
9&url=https://education.gov.gy/en/index.php/parents/2286-tips-for-
encouraging-open-communication-in-the-
home&ved=2ahUKEwjMhN77_rOBAxX0SkEAHSvvCAgQFnoECB
sQAQ&usg=AOvVaw33e46vJT_0ZMMxdl39epDZ

(Retrieved October 2023)

https://www.google.com/url?sa=t&source=web&rct=j&opi=8997844
9&url=https://www.familieschange.ca.gov/en/parents/keeping-lines-
communication-
open&ved=2ahUKEwjMhN77_rOBAxX0SkEAHSvvCAgQFnoECB
EQBQ&usg=AOvVaw1_PSJDV26SU1C3wJJjFO5T

(Retrieved October 2023)

https://www.google.com/url?sa=t&source=web&rct=j&opi=8997844
9&url=https://www.helpguide.org/articles/relationships-
communication/nonverbal-
communication.htm&ved=2ahUKEwjIzfaK_7OBAxUPWEEAHWm
oBQAQFnoECCkQAQ&usg=AOvVaw18iu0Pct3hVBlZkO9ivJXS

(Retrieved October 2023)

https://www.google.com/url?sa=t&source=web&rct=j&opi=8997844
9&url=https://wowparenting.com/blog/heres-a-short-guide-for-you-

to-set-realistic-expectations-from-your-
kids/&ved=2ahUKEwiqmPK0_7OBAxUVVEEAHbjgDL4QFnoEC
C4QAQ&usg=AOvVaw37kbra1Zp5cC2l7Pr_y3h

(Retrieved October 2023)

https://www.google.com/url?sa=t&source=web&rct=j&opi=8997844
9&url=https://omgcenter.org/agency-leadership/communicate-clear-
realistic-
expectations/&ved=2ahUKEwj4hNKj_7OBAxVnQkEAHdPSAMsQ
FnoECCoQAQ&usg=AOvVaw29kRkII4n30n9T-vu2_jB

(Retrieved October 2023)

https://www.google.com/url?sa=t&source=web&rct=j&opi=8997844
9&url=https://ggia.berkeley.edu/practice/mindful_breathing&ved=2a
hUKEwiOwci9grSBAxWhSEEAHR5JDOAQFnoECCUQAQ&usg=
AOvVaw1y5qM0nr0BCRjRDyR8QXIf

(Retrieved October 2023)

https://www.google.com/url?sa=t&source=web&rct=j&opi=8997844
9&url=https://www.nature.com/articles/s41467-019-09927-
y&ved=2ahUKEwjooeSEgrSBAxUnQEEAHY3tAzMQFnoECBsQA
Q&usg=AOvVaw3MR3vuXXRwc66PyRN3fEP3

(Retrieved October 2023)

https://www.google.com/url?sa=t&source=web&rct=j&opi=8997844
9&url=https://www.first5la.org/article/empathy-
development/&ved=2ahUKEwjooeSEgrSBAxUnQEEAHY3tAzMQF
noECBgQAQ&usg=AOvVaw3EJss5eVJLVuK-5ENnR9m3

(Retrieved October 2023)

https://www.google.com/url?sa=t&source=web&rct=j&opi=8997844
9&url=https://www.frontiersin.org/articles/10.3389/fpsyg.2020.5729
17&ved=2ahUKEwj36YGYgLSBAxUXXUEAHawfBiIQFnoECCQ
QAQ&usg=AOvVaw0HkES7goljm3zPKmxvv3gi

(Retrieved October 2023)

https://www.google.com/url?sa=t&source=web&rct=j&opi=8997844
9&url=https://education.gov.gy/en/index.php/parents/2286-tips-for-
encouraging-open-communication-in-the-
home&ved=2ahUKEwjMhN77_rOBAxX0SkEAHSvvCAgQFnoECB
sQAQ&usg=AOvVaw33e46vJT_0ZMMxdl39epDZ

(Retrieved October 2023)

https://www.google.com/url?sa=t&source=web&rct=j&opi=8997844
9&url=https://www.familieschange.ca.gov/en/parents/keeping-lines-
communication-
open&ved=2ahUKEwjMhN77_rOBAxX0SkEAHSvvCAgQFnoECB
EQBQ&usg=AOvVaw1_PSJDV26SU1C3wJJjFO5T

(Retrieved October 2023)

https://www.google.com/url?sa=t&source=web&rct=j&opi=8997844
9&url=https://www.helpguide.org/articles/relationships-
communication/nonverbal-
communication.htm&ved=2ahUKEwjIzfaK_7OBAxUPWEEAHWm
oBQAQFnoECCkQAQ&usg=AOvVaw18iu0Pct3hVBlZkO9ivJXS

(Retrieved October 2023)

https://www.google.com/url?sa=t&source=web&rct=j&opi=8997844
9&url=https://wowparenting.com/blog/heres-a-short-guide-for-you-

to-set-realistic-expectations-from-your-kids/&ved=2ahUKEwiqmPK0_7OBAxUVVEEAHbjgDL4QFnoEC
C4QAQ&usg=AOvVaw37kbra1Zp5cC2l7Pr_y3hH

(Retrieved October 2023)

https://www.google.com/url?sa=t&source=web&rct=j&opi=8997844
9&url=https://omgcenter.org/agency-leadership/communicate-clear-realistic-
expectations/&ved=2ahUKEwj4hNKj_7OBAxVnQkEAHdPSAMsQ
FnoECCoQAQ&usg=AOvVaw29kRkII4n30n9T-vu2_jB_

(Retrieved October 2023)

https://www.google.com/url?sa=t&source=web&rct=j&opi=8997844
9&url=https://www.katielear.com/child-therapy-
blog/2020/7/28/explaining-cbt-to-a-
child&ved=2ahUKEwim257TgrSBAxWnRkEAHYUSB_YQFnoEC
CMQAQ&usg=AOvVaw27IAASwEFQMVpy-wmHxVyl

(Retrieved October 2023)

https://www.google.com/url?sa=t&source=web&rct=j&opi=8997844
9&url=https://www.corelifepsychology.com.au/what-is-secure-
attachment/&ved=2ahUKEwjAwdSph7SBAxVFRUEAHZTBDZ8Q
FnoECCwQAQ&usg=AOvVaw1UaZ24ZFZ53l5chqXoukIV

(Retrieved October 2023)

https://www.google.com/url?sa=t&source=web&rct=j&opi=8997844
9&url=https://www.cnbc.com/amp/2021/10/05/child-psychologist-
explains-why-authoritative-parenting-is-the-best-style-for-raising-
smart-confident-kids.html&ved=2ahUKEwiVvq3-

hrSBAxUPQkEAHYvYAD0QFnoECC8QAQ&usg=AOvVaw2nLzz
Wt8aN3qz_S_qR0rT4

(Retrieved October 2023)

https://www.google.com/url?sa=t&source=web&rct=j&opi=8997844
9&url=https://blossomplaytherapy.com/what-is-play-and-creative-
arts-therapy/&ved=2ahUKEwias9_kgrSBAxUuVEEAHfC-
BNsQFnoECCUQAQ&usg=AOvVaw1L1mp9N5_wGJtmklWP-
aGK

(Retrieved October 2023)

https://www.google.com/url?sa=t&source=web&rct=j&opi=8997844
9&url=https://eddinscounseling.com/therapy-child-art-play-
therapy/&ved=2ahUKEwias9_kgrSBAxUuVEEAHfC-
BNsQFnoECB0QAQ&usg=AOvVaw0dJHbU5PCMn1QDI-
IsSCkU

(Retrieved October 2023)

https://www.google.com/url?sa=t&source=web&rct=j&opi=8997844
9&url=https://www.playtherapyhub.com/2318/&ved=2ahUKEwias9
_kgrSBAxUuVEEAHfC-
BNsQFnoECBoQAQ&usg=AOvVaw1ji3Zmjw8wdmwbmKJc75mC

(Retrieved October 2023)

https://www.google.com/url?sa=t&source=web&rct=j&opi=8997844
9&url=https://www.marblewellness.com/post/a-guide-to-creating-an-
emotional-
toolkit&ved=2ahUKEwiXu8OBg7SBAxVtU0EAHZR6B8MQFnoE
CCgQAQ&usg=AOvVaw158a48OExDB4wMyGPp6A4z

(Retrieved October 2023)

https://www.google.com/url?sa=t&source=web&rct=j&opi=8997844
9&url=https://www.twinkl.com.ng/teaching-wiki/emotional-
toolkit&ved=2ahUKEwiXu8OBg7SBAxVtU0EAHZR6B8MQFnoE
CCYQAQ&usg=AOvVaw0QGYa8XV89hqtRzewqvpbx

(Retrieved October 2023)

https://www.google.com/url?sa=t&source=web&rct=j&opi=8997844
9&url=https://www.helpguide.org/articles/mental-health/emotional-
intelligence-
toolkit.htm&ved=2ahUKEwiXu8OBg7SBAxVtU0EAHZR6B8MQF
noECBoQAQ&usg=AOvVaw2irMIJgxEZeJytdUWJtpSp

(Retrieved October 2023)

https://www.google.com/url?sa=t&source=web&rct=j&opi=8997844
9&url=https://www.cdc.gov/parents/essentials/toddlersandpreschooler
s/consequences/rewards.html&ved=2ahUKEwj_-
OzWhrSBAxV8VkEAHaenCvMQFnoECCUQAQ&usg=AOvVaw3
786nsDdnEQWolSX62NT4A

(Retrieved October 2023)

https://www.google.com/url?sa=t&source=web&rct=j&opi=8997844
9&url=https://www.understood.org/en/articles/7-ideas-for-using-
rewards-and-consequences&ved=2ahUKEwj_-
OzWhrSBAxV8VkEAHaenCvMQFnoECBcQAQ&usg=AOvVaw00
G0SwaPIq-X7xycyqTHDu

(Retrieved October 2023)

https://www.google.com/url?sa=t&source=web&rct=j&opi=8997844
9&url=https://www.therapistaid.com/therapy-guide/parenting-

rewards-punishments&ved=2ahUKEwj_-
OzWhrSBAxV8VkEAHaenCvMQFnoECA4QBQ&usg=AOvVaw2
UeXPIfOAzfpaooKx991q7

(Retrieved October 2023)

https://www.google.com/url?sa=t&source=web&rct=j&opi=8997844
9&url=https://thinkkids.org/cps-
overview/&ved=2ahUKEwix_O7rhrSBAxVTQUEAHS3yDj8QFnoE
CBkQAQ&usg=AOvVaw20Z8QmyQwQU5Zdo5RcrfRI

(Retrieved October 2023)

https://www.google.com/url?sa=t&source=web&rct=j&opi=8997844
9&url=https://www.primallyinspired.com/how-to-do-collaborative-
problem-solving-with-
kids/&ved=2ahUKEwix_O7rhrSBAxVTQUEAHS3yDj8QFnoECBo
QAQ&usg=AOvVaw0TZoGLugod16ZWNTec95w3

(Retrieved October 2023)

https://www.google.com/url?sa=t&source=web&rct=j&opi=8997844
9&url=https://www.apa.org/topics/anger/control&ved=2ahUKEwiUt
pSWg7SBAxUqQUEAHWaOAJwQFnoECB4QAQ&usg=AOvVaw
0HU3t7DJmbEUUrrrTdSVYL

(Retrieved October 2023)

https://www.google.com/url?sa=t&source=web&rct=j&opi=8997844
9&url=https://www.organizedmotherhood.com/how-to-establish-
routines-at-home/&ved=2ahUKEwjBlKithrSBAxXDolwKHUFGD-
4QFnoECCYQAQ&usg=AOvVaw3yJLWa_E97TY-poKgLiP8

(Retrieved October 2023)

https://www.google.com/url?sa=t&source=web&rct=j&opi=8997844
9&url=https://www.cdc.gov/parents/essentials/toddlersandpreschooler
s/structure/quicktips.html&ved=2ahUKEwjBlKithrSBAxXDolwKHU
FGD-4QFnoECB4QAQ&usg=AOvVaw3T83ftSAR-
DJEtWuZ7aeDy

(Retrieved October 2023)

https://www.google.com/url?sa=t&source=web&rct=j&opi=8997844
9&url=https://steadfastacademy.com/the-power-of-positive-
reinforcement-for-
children/&ved=2ahUKEwjU6J7BhrSBAxU5WkEAHbTtArsQFnoE
CC4QAQ&usg=AOvVaw33rJGSA53XjAcexKdpLnUb

Made in United States
Orlando, FL
10 September 2024

51351753R00192